GHOSTS of NEW ENGLAND

Another fine haunted publication
from Hans Holzer and Wings Books:

The Lively Ghosts of Ireland

GHOSTS of NEW ENGLAND

True Stories of Encounters with the Phantoms of New England and New York

HANS HOLZER

Previously published in separate volumes as *Yankee Ghosts* and *Ghosts of New England*

WINGS BOOKS
New York

This omnibus edition was previously published in separate volumes:
Yankee Ghosts: Spine-Tingling Encounters with the Phantoms of New York and New England copyright © 1996 by Hans Holzer
Ghosts of New England copyright © 1989 by Hans Holzer

This 1997 edition is published by Wings Books, a division of Random House Value Publishing, Inc., 201 East 50th Street, New York, New York 10022, by arrangement with Hans Holzer.

Wings Books and colophon are trademarks of Random House Value Publishing, Inc.

Random House
New York • Toronto • London • Sydney • Auckland
http://www.randomhouse.com/

Printed and bound in the United States of America

A CIP catalogue record for this book is available from the Library of Congress.

Ghosts of New England / by Hans Holzer / previously published in separate volumes as *Yankee Ghosts* and *Ghosts of New England*

ISBN 0-517-18084-7

8 7 6 5 4 3 2 1

Contents

9   Preface

11   "Ocean-Born" Mary

38   The Ghosts of Barbery Lane

57   The Ghost Clock

63   Hungry Lucy

77   Proper Bostonian Ghosts

86   The Ghost of Gay Street

91   When the Dead Stay On

102   The Ship Chandler's Ghost

108   How the Little Girl Ghost Was Sent Out to Play

122   The Ghost-Servant Problem at Ringwood Manor

134   Return to Clinton Court

147   The Teen-Agers and the Staten Island Ghost

158   The Phantom Admiral

172   The Somerville Ghost

181   Come and Meet My Ghost!

185   Country House Ghosts

193   The Girl Ghost on Riverside Drive

203   The Ghost Who Would Not Leave

230   The Ghost at Port Clyde

252   Haunted Is the Trailer

259   Ghosts around Boston

275   The Possession of Mrs. F.

280   The Ghost at Cap'n Grey's

291   The Strange Case of Mrs. C.'s Late but Lively Husband

297   A Plymouth Ghost

311   A New Hampshire Artist and Her Ghosts

314   John, up in Vermont

318   The Ghosts of Stamford Hill

339   The Haunted Organ at Yale

342   The Terror on the Farm

352   The Old Merchant's House Ghost

369   The Ghosts at the Morris-Jumel Mansion

Preface

In this collection culled from my best and most exciting cases of true ghost stories and hauntings in the New England and New York states, I am once again demonstrating that ghosts know neither time nor place when it comes to reliving their own personal and often painfully emotional traumas.

To people caught between two states of being, which is what ghosts are, the events of their last moments in the physical world have never ceased and the solution continues to escape them.

The people who report these experiences are neither fanciful nor demented but ordinary citizens of a very real world. But so are the ghosts they report: it is just that the two dimensions differ though they coexist.

In this age where so-called Channeling — the alleged ability to speak with the personality of a long-gone master — has become popular, without so much as the need for evidence that these entities ever existed in the real world, it is comforting to know that the spectral communicators of *Ghosts of New England* were all real people with lives in this world when they were still in their physical bodies. Anything less than that kind of reasonable evidence invites uncritical belief in something that cannot really be proven.

If there seem to be, at times, inconsistencies or discrepancies in the transcript of what a medium will say clairvoyantly or in trance, bear in mind that this is a less than perfect means of communication between two very different worlds. In parapsychology we record what is being said *faithfully,* not what reads nicely in a book. We do not editorialize but report what comes through. This is as it should be, if we are to present an accurate picture, not of what the story or case ultimately may be but what our method of research consists of.

We try to verify as many facts, names, and statements made by sensitives as possible; we never succeed in getting them all verified simply because the nature of the transmission is at best, imperfect, and also because the records and documents available to me as a trained professional historian and researcher are far from complete. Just because a statement cannot be verified in a printed source, or a letter, or some other document in the files of a library or other learned institution, does not mean the statement is false; it merely means we have not been able to find that particular verification.

The ghostly encounters I have presented here are all cases I have personally looked into and investigated. I am satisfied that they are true cases of life beyond physical death.

Prof. Hans Holzer, Ph. D.
New York, New York

about the house, but they do leave behind them destruction and litter at times. Needless to say, nobody has ever seen Mary ride in her coach on Halloween. Why should she when she lives there *all year round*?

To explain this last statement, I shall have to take you back to the year 1720, when a group of Scottish and Irish immigrants was approaching the New World aboard a ship called the *Wolf*, from Londonderry, Ireland. The ship's captain, Wilson, had just become the father of a daughter, who was actually born at sea. Within sight of land, the ship was boarded by pirates under the command of a buccaneer named Don Pedro. As the pirates removed all valuables from their prize, Don Pedro went below to the captain's cabin. Instead of gold, he found Mrs. Wilson and her newborn baby girl.

"What's her name?" he demanded.

Unafraid, the mother replied that the child had not yet been baptized, having been recently born.

"If you will name her after my mother, Mary," the pirate said, overcome with an emotion few pirates ever allow into their lives, "I will spare everybody aboard this ship."

Joyously, the mother made the bargain, and "Ocean-Born" Mary received her name. Don Pedro ordered his men to hand back what they had already taken from their prisoners, to set them free, and to leave the captured ship. The vicious-looking crew grumbled and withdrew to their own ship.

Minutes later, however, Don Pedro returned alone. He handed Mrs. Wilson a bundle of silk.

"For Mary's wedding gown," he said simply, and left again.

As soon as the pirate ship was out of sight, the *Wolf* continued her voyage for Boston. Thence Captain and Mrs. Wilson went on to their new home in Londonderry, New Hampshire, where they settled down, and where Mary grew up.

When she was 18, she married a man named Wallace, and over

"Ocean-Born" Mary

Among the ghostly legends of the United States, that of "Ocean-Born" Mary and her fascinating house at Henniker, New Hampshire, is probably one of the best known. To the average literate person who has heard about the colorful tale of Mary Wallace, or the New Englander who knows of it because he lives "Down East," it is, of course, a legend — not to be taken too seriously.

I had a vague idea of its substance when I received a note from a lady named Corinne Russell, who together with her husband, David, had bought the Henniker house and wanted me to know that it was still haunted.

That was in October of 1963. It so happens that Halloween is the traditional date on which the ghost of six-foot Mary Wallace is supposed to "return" to her house in a coach drawn by six horses. On many a Halloween, youngsters from all around Henniker have come and sat around the grounds waiting for Mary to ride in. The local press had done its share of Halloween ghost hunting, so much so that the Russells had come to fear that date as one of the major nuisance days of their year.

After all, Halloween visitors do not pay the usual fee to be shown the years they had four sons. However, shortly after the birth of the fourth son, her husband died and Mary found herself a widow.

Meanwhile, Don Pedro — allegedly an Englishman using the Spanish *nom de pirate* to disguise his noble ancestry — had kept in touch with the Wilsons. Despite the hazards of pirate life, he survived to an old age when thoughts of retirement filled his mind. Somehow he managed to acquire a land grant of 6,000 acres in what is now Henniker, New Hampshire, far away from the sea. On this land, Pedro built himself a stately house. He employed his ship's carpenters, as can be seen in the way the beams are joined. Ship's carpenters have a special way of building, and "Ocean-Born" Mary's house, as it later became known, is an example of this.

The house was barely finished when the aging pirate heard of Mary Wallace's loss of her husband, and he asked Mary and her children to come live with him. She accepted his invitation, and soon became his housekeeper.

The house was then in a rather isolated part of New England, and few callers, if any, came to interrupt the long stillness of the many cold winter nights. Mary took up painting and with her own hands created the eagle that can still be seen gracing the house.

The years went by peacefully, until one night someone attacked Don Pedro and killed him. Whether one of his men had come to challenge the pirate captain for part of the booty, or whether the reputation of a retired pirate had put ideas of treasure in the mind of some local thief, we may never know. All we know is that by the time Mary Wallace got out into the grove at the rear of the house, Don Pedro was dying with a pirate cutlass in his chest. He asked her to bury him under the hearthstone in the kitchen, which is in the rear of the house.

Mary herself inherited the house and what went with it, treasure, buried pirate, and all. She herself passed on in 1814, and ever since then the house had been changing hands.

Unfortunately, we cannot interview the earlier owners of the house, but during the 1930s, it belonged to one Louis Roy, retired and disabled and a permanent guest in what used to be his home. He sold the house to the Russells in the early sixties.

During the great hurricane of 1938, Roy claims that Mary Wallace's ghost saved his life 19 times. Trapped outside the house by falling trees, he somehow was able to get back into the house. His very psychic mother, Mrs. Roy, informed him that she had actually seen the tall, stately figure of "Ocean-Born" Mary moving behind him, as if to help him get through. In the 1950s, *Life* told this story in an illustrated article on famous ghost-haunted houses in America. Mrs. Roy claimed she had seen the ghost of Mary time and again, but since she herself passed on in 1948, I could not get any details from *her*.

Then there were two state troopers who saw the ghost, but again I could not interview them, as they, too, were also on the other side of the veil.

A number of visitors claimed to have felt "special vibrations" when touching the hearthstone, where Don Pedro allegedly was buried. There was, for instance, Mrs. James Nisula of Londonderry, who visited the house several times. She said that she and her "group" of ghost buffs had "felt the vibrations" around the kitchen. Mrs. David Russell, the owner who contacted me, felt nothing.

I promised to look into the "Ocean-Born" Mary haunting the first chance I got. Halloween or about that time would be all right with me, and I wouldn't wait around for any coach!

"There is a lady medium I think you should know," Mrs. Russell said when I spoke of bringing a psychic with me. "She saw Mary the very first time she came here."

My curiosity aroused, I communicated with the lady. She asked that I not use her married name, although she was not so shy several months after our visit to the house, when she gave a two-part interview to a Boston newspaper columnist. (Needless to say, the interview was not authorized by me, since I never allow mediums I work with to talk about their cases for publication. Thus Lorrie shall remain without a family name and anyone wishing to reach this medium will have to do so without my help.)

Lorrie wrote me she would be happy to serve the cause of truth, and I could count on her. There was nothing she wanted in return.

We did not get up to New Hampshire that Halloween. Mr. Russell had to have an operation, the house was unheated in the winter except for Mr. Roy's room, and New England winters are cold enough to freeze any ghost.

Although there was a caretaker at the time to look after the house and Mr. Roy upstairs, the Russells did not stay at the house in the winter, but made their home in nearby Chelmsford, Massachusetts.

I wrote Mrs. Russell postponing the investigation until spring. Mrs. Russell accepted my decision with some disappointment, but she was willing to wait. After all, the ghost at "Ocean-Born" Mary's house is not a malicious type. Mary Wallace just lived there, ever since she died in 1814, and you can't call a lady who likes to hold on to what is hers an intruder.

"We don't want to drive her out," Mrs. Russell repeatedly said to me. "After all, it *is* her house!"

Not many haunted-house owners make statements like that.

But something had happened at the house since our last conversation.

"Our caretaker dropped a space heater all the way down the stairs at the 'Ocean-Born' Mary house, and when it reached the bottom, the kerosene and the flames started to burn the stairs and climb the wall. There was no water in the house, so my husband went out after snow. While I stood there looking at the fire and powerless to do anything about it, the fire went right out all by itself right in front of my eyes; when my husband got back with the snow it was out. It was just as if someone *had smothered it with a blanket*."

This was in December of 1963. I tried to set a new date, as soon as possible, and February 22 seemed possible. This time I would bring Bob Kennedy of WBZ, Boston, and the "Contact" producer Squire Rushnell with me to record my investigation.

Lorrie was willing, asking only that her name not be mentioned.

"I don't want anyone to know about my being different from them," she explained. "When I was young my family used to accuse me of spying because I knew things from the pictures I saw when I touched objects."

Psychometry, I explained, is very common among psychics, and nothing to be ashamed of.

I thought it was time to find out more about Lorrie's experiences at the haunted house.

"I first saw the house in September of 1961," she began. "It was on a misty, humid day, and there was a haze over the fields."

Strange, I thought, I always get my best psychic results when the atmosphere is moist.

Lorrie, who was in her early forties, was Vermont born and raised; she was married and had one daughter, Pauline. She was a tall redhead with sparkling eyes, and, come to think of it, not unlike the accepted picture of the ghostly Mary Wallace. Coincidence?

A friend of Lorrie's had seen the eerie house and suggested she go and see it also. That was all Lorrie knew about it, and she did not really expect anything uncanny to occur. Mr. Roy showed Lorrie and her daughter through the house and nothing startling happened. They left and started to walk down the entrance steps, crossing the garden in front of the house, and had reached the gate when Pauline clutched at her mother's arm and said:

"Mamma, what is that?"

Lorrie turned to look back at the house. In the upstairs window, a woman stood and looked out at them. Lorrie's husband was busy with the family car. Eventually, she called out to him, but as he turned to look, the apparition was gone.

She did not think of it again, and the weeks went by. But the house kept intruding itself into her thoughts more and more. Finally she could not restrain herself any longer, and returned to the house — even though it was 120 miles from her home in Weymouth, Massachusetts.

She confessed her extraordinary experience to the owner, and together they examined the house from top to bottom. She finally returned home.

She promised Roy she would return on All Hallow's Eve to see if the legend of Mary Wallace had any basis of fact. Unfortunately, word of her intentions got out, and when she finally arrived at the house, she had to sneak in the back to avoid the sensation-hungry press outside. During the days between her second visit and Halloween, the urge to go to Henniker kept getting stronger, as if someone were possessing her.

By that time the Russells were negotiating to buy the house, and Lorrie came up with them. Nothing happened to her that Halloween night. Perhaps she was torn between fear and a desire to fight the influence that had brought her out to Henniker to begin with.

Mediums, to be successful, must learn to relax and not allow their own notions to rule them. All through the following winter and summer, Lorrie fought the desire to return to "Ocean-Born" Mary's house. To no avail. She returned time and again, sometimes alone and sometimes with a friend.

Things got out of hand one summer night when she was home alone.

Exhausted from her last visit — the visits always left her an emotional wreck — she went to bed around 9:30 P.M.

"What happened that night?" I interjected. She seemed shaken even now.

"At 11 P.M., Mr. Holzer," Lorrie replied, "I found myself driving on the expressway, wearing my pajamas and robe, with no shoes or slippers, or money, or even a handkerchief. I was ten miles from my home and heading for Henniker. Terrified, I turned around and returned home, only to find my house ablaze with light, the doors open as I had left them, and the garage lights on. I must have left in an awful hurry."

"Have you found out why you are being pulled back to that house?"

She shook her head.

"No idea. But I've been back twice, even after that. I just can't seem to stay away from that house."

I persuaded her that perhaps there was a job to be done in that house, and the ghost wanted her to do it.

We did not go to Henniker in February, because of bad weather. We tried to set a date in May, 1964. The people from WBZ decided Henniker was too far away from Boston and dropped out of the planning.

Summer came around, and I went to Europe instead of Henniker. However, the prospect of a visit in the fall was very much in my mind.

It seemed as if someone were keeping me away from the house very much in the same way someone was pulling Lorrie toward it!

Come October, and we were really on our way, at last. Owen Lake, a public relations man who dabbles in psychic matters, introduced himself as "a friend" of mine and told Lorrie he'd come along, too. I had never met the gentleman, but in the end he could not make it anyway. So just four of us — my wife Catherine and I, Lorrie, and her nice, even-tempered husband, who had volunteered to drive us up to New Hampshire — started out from Boston. It was close to Halloween, all right, only two days before. If Mary Wallace were out haunting the countryside in her coach, we might very well run into her. The coach is out of old Irish folktales; it appears in numerous ghost stories of the Ould Sod. I'm sure that in the telling and retelling of the tale of Mary and her pirate, the coach got added.

The countryside is beautiful in a New England fall. As we rolled toward the New Hampshire state line, I asked Lorrie some more questions.

"When you first saw the ghost of 'Ocean-Born' Mary at the window of the house, Lorrie," I said, "what did she look like?"

"A lovely lady in her thirties, with auburn-colored hair, smiling rather intensely and thoughtfully. She stayed there for maybe three minutes, and then suddenly, *she just wasn't there.*"

"What about her dress?"

"It was a white dress."

Lorrie never saw an apparition of Mary again, but whenever she touched anything in the Henniker house, she received an impression of what the house was like when Mary had it, and she had felt her near the big fireplace several times.

Did she ever get an impression of what it was Mary wanted?

"She was a quick-tempered woman; I sensed that very strongly," Lorrie replied. "I have been to the house maybe twenty times altogether, and still don't know why. She just keeps pulling me there."

Lorrie had always felt the ghost's presence on these visits.

"One day I was walking among the bushes in the back of the house. I was wearing shorts, but I never got a scratch on my legs, because I kept feeling heavy skirts covering my legs. I could feel the brambles pulling at this invisible skirt I had on. I felt enveloped by something, or someone."

Mrs. Roy, the former owner's mother, had told of seeing the apparition many times, Lorrie stated.

"As a matter of fact, I have sensed her ghost in the house, too, but it is not a friendly wraith like Mary is."

Had she ever encountered this other ghost?

"Yes, my arm was grabbed one time by a malevolent entity,"

Lorrie said emphatically. "It was two years ago, and I was standing in what is now the living room, and my arm was taken by the elbow and pulled.

"I snatched my arm back, because I felt she was not friendly."

"What were you doing at the time that she might have objected to?"

"I really don't know."

Did she know of anyone else who had had an uncanny experience at the house?

"A strange thing happened to Mrs. Roy," Lorrie said. "A woman came to the house and said to her, 'What do you mean, the *rest* of the house?' The woman replied, 'Well, I was here yesterday, and a tall woman let me in and only showed me half of the house.' But, of course, there was nobody at the house that day."

What about the two state troopers? Could she elaborate on their experience?

"They met her walking down the road that leads to the house. She was wearing a Colonial-type costume, and they found that odd. Later they realized they had seen a ghost, especially as no one of her description lived in the house at the time."

Rudi D., Lorrie's husband, was a hospital technician. He was with her on two or three occasions when she visited the house. Did he ever feel anything special?

"The only thing unusual I ever felt at the house was that I wanted to get out of there fast," he said.

"The very first time we went up," Lorrie added, "something kept pulling me toward it, but my husband insisted we go back. There was an argument about our continuing the trip, when suddenly the door of the car flew open of its own volition. Somehow we decided to continue on to the house."

An hour later, we drove up a thickly overgrown hill and along a winding road at the end of which the "Ocean-Born" Mary house stood in solitary stateliness, a rectangular building of gray stone and brown trim, very well preserved.

We parked the car and walked across the garden that sets the house well back from the road. There was peace and autumn in the air. We were made welcome by Corinne Russell, her husband David, and two relatives who happened to be with them that day. Entering the main door beneath a magnificent early American eagle, we admired the fine wooden staircase leading to the upstairs — the staircase on which the mysterious fire had taken place — and then entered the room to the left of it, where the family had assembled around an old New England stove.

During the three years the Russells had lived at the house, nothing uncanny had happened to Mrs. Russell, except for the incident with the fire. David Russell, a man almost typical of the shrewd New England Yankee who weighs his every word, was willing to tell me about *his* experiences, however.

"The first night I ever slept in what we call the Lafayette room, upstairs, there was quite a thundershower on, and my dog and I were upstairs. I always keep my dog with me, on account of the boys coming around to do damage to the property.

"Just as I lay down in bed, I heard very heavy footsteps. They sounded to me to be in the two rooms which we had just restored, on the same floor. I was quite annoyed, almost frightened, and I went into the rooms, but there was nobody there or anywhere else in the house."

"Interesting," I said. "Was there more?"

"Now this happened only last summer. A few weeks later, when I was in that same room, I was getting undressed when I suddenly heard somebody pound on my door. I said to myself, "Oh, it's only the house settling," and I got into bed. A few minutes later, the door knob turned back and forth. I jumped out of bed, opened the door, and there was absolutely nobody there. The only other people in the house at the time were the invalid Mr. Roy, locked in his room, and my wife downstairs."

What about visual experiences?

"No, but I went to the cellar not long ago with my dog, about four in the afternoon, or rather tried to — this dog never leaves me, but on this particular occasion, something kept her from going with me into the cellar. Her hair stood up and she would not budge."

The Lafayette room, by the way, is the very room in which the pirate, Don Pedro, is supposed to have lived. The Russells did nothing to change the house structurally, only restored it as it had been and generally cleaned it up.

I now turned to Florence Harmon, an elderly neighbor of the Russells, who had some recollections about the house. Mrs. Harmon recalls the house when she herself was very young, long before the Russells came to live in it.

"Years later, I returned to the house and Mrs. Roy asked me whether I could help her locate 'the treasure' since I was reputed to be psychic."

Was there really a treasure?

"If there was, I think it was found," Mrs. Harmon said. "At the time Mrs. Roy talked to me, she also pointed out that there were two elm trees on the grounds — the only two elm trees around. They looked like some sort of markers to her. But before the Roys had the house, a Mrs. Morrow lived here. I know this from my uncle, who was a stone mason, and who built a vault for her."

I didn't think Mrs. Harmon had added anything material to knowledge of the treasure, so I thanked her and turned my attention to the other large room, on the right hand side of the staircase. Nicely furnished with period pieces, it boasted a fireplace flanked by sofas, and had a rectangular piano in the corner. The high windows were curtained on the sides, and one could see the New England landscape through them.

We seated ourselves around the fireplace and hoped that Mary would honor us with a visit. Earlier I had inspected the entire house, the hearthstone under which Don Pedro allegedly lay buried, and the small bedrooms upstairs where David Russell had heard the footsteps. Each of us had stood at the window in the corridor upstairs and stared out of it, very much the way the ghost must have done when she was observed by Lorrie and her daughter.

And now it was Mary's turn.

"This was her room," Lorrie explained, "and I do feel her presence." But she refused to go into trance, afraid to "let go." Communication would have to be via clairvoyance, with Lorrie as the interpreter. This was not what I had hoped for. Nevertheless we would try to evaluate whatever material we could obtain.

"Sheet and quill," Lorrie said now, and a piece of paper was handed her along with a pencil. Holding it on her lap, Lorrie was poised to write, if Mary wanted to use her hand, so to speak. The pencil suddenly jumped from Lorrie's hand with considerable force.

"Proper quill," the ghost demanded.

I explained about the shape of quills these days, and handed Lorrie my own pencil.

"Look, lady," Lorrie explained to the ghost. "I'll show you it writes. I'll write my name."

And she wrote in her own, smallish, rounded hand, "Lorrie."

There was a moment of silence. Evidently, the ghost was thinking it over. Then Lorrie's hand, seemingly not under her own control, wrote with a great deal of flourish "Mary Wallace." The "M" and "W" had curves and ornamentation typical of eighteenth-century calligraphy. It was not at all like Lorrie's own handwriting.

"Tell her to write some more. The quill is working," I commanded.

Lorrie seemed to be upset by something the ghost told her.

"No," she said. "I can't do that. No."

"What does she want?" I asked.

"She wants me to sleep, but I won't do it."

Trance, I thought — even the ghost demands it. It would have been so interesting to have Mary speak directly to us through Lorrie's entranced lips. You can lead a medium to the ghost, but you can't make her go under if she's scared.

Lorrie instead told the ghost to tell *her,* or to write through her. But no trance, thank you. Evidently, the ghost did not like to be told how to communicate. We waited. Then I suggested that Lorrie be very relaxed and it would be "like sleep" so the ghost could talk to us directly.

"She's very much like me, but not so well trimmed," the ghost said of Lorrie. Had she picked her to carry her message because of physical resemblance, I wondered.

"She's waiting for Young John," Lorrie now said. Not young John. The stress was on young. Perhaps it was one name — Young-john.

"It happened in the north pasture," Mary said through Lorrie now. "He killed Warren Langerford. The Frazier boys found the last bone."

I asked why it concerned her. Was she involved? But there was no reply.

Then the ghost of Mary introduced someone else standing next to her.

"Mrs. Roy is with her, because she killed her daughter," Lorrie said, hesitatingly, and added, on her own, "but I don't believe she did." Later we found out that the ghost was perhaps not lying, but of course nobody had any proof of such a crime — if it were indeed a crime.

"Why do you stay on in this house?" I asked.

"This house is my house, h-o-u-s-e!" "Ocean-Born" Mary reminded me.

"Do you realize you are what is commonly called dead?" I demanded. As so often with ghosts, the question brought on resistance to face reality. Mary seemed insulted and withdrew.

I addressed the ghost openly, offering to help her, and at the same time explaining her present position to her. This was her chance to speak up.

"She's very capricious," Lorrie said. "When you said you'd bring her peace, she started to laugh."

But Mary was gone, for the present anyway.

We waited, and tried again a little later. This time Lorrie said she heard a voice telling her to come back tonight.

"We can't," I decided. "If she wants to be helped, it will have to be now."

Philip Babb, the pirate's real name (as I discovered later), allegedly had built a secret passage under the house. The Russells were still looking for it. There were indeed discrepancies in the thickness of some of the walls, and there were a number of secret holes that didn't lead anywhere. But no passage. Had the pirate taken his secrets to his grave?

I found our experience at Henniker singularly unsatisfactory since no real evidence had been forthcoming from the ghost herself. No doubt another visit would have to be made, but I didn't mind that at all. "Ocean-Born" Mary's place was a place one can easily visit time and again. The rural charm of the place and the timeless atmosphere of the old house made it a first-rate tourist attraction. Thousands of people came to the house every year.

We returned to New York and I thought no more about it until I received a letter from James Caron, who had heard me discuss the house on the "Contact" program in Boston. He had been to the house in quest of pirate lore and found it very much haunted.

James Caron was in the garage business at Bridgewater, Massachusetts. He had a high school and trade school education, and was married, with two children. Searching for stories of buried treasure and pirates was a hobby of his, and he sometimes lectured on it. He had met Gus Roy about six years before. Roy complained that his deceased mother was trying to contact him for some reason. Her picture kept falling off the wall where it was hung, and he constantly felt "a presence." Would Mr. Caron know of a good medium?

In August of 1959, James Caron brought a spiritualist named Paul Amsdent to the "Ocean-Born" Mary house. Present at the ensuing séance were Harold Peters, a furniture salesman; Hugh Blanchard, a lawyer; Ernest Walbourne, a fireman, and brother-in-law of Caron; Gus Roy; and Mr. Caron himself. Tape recording the séance, Caron had trouble with his equipment. Strange sounds kept intruding. Unfortunately, there was among those present someone with hostility toward psychic work, and Gus Roy's mother did not manifest. However, something else did happen.

"There appear to be people buried somewhere around or in the house," the medium Amsdent said, "enclosed by a stone wall of some sort."

I thought of the hearthstone and of Mrs. Harmon's vault. Coincidence?

Mr. Caron used metal detectors all over the place to satisfy Gus Roy that there was no "pirate treasure" buried in or near the house.

A little later, James Caron visited the house again. This time he was accompanied by Mrs. Caron and Mr. and Mrs. Walbourne. Both ladies were frightened by the sound of a heavy door opening and closing with no one around and no air current in the house.

Mrs. Caron had a strong urge to go to the attic, but Mr. Caron stopped her. Ernest Walbourne, a skeptic, was alone in the so-called "death" room upstairs, looking at some pictures stacked in a corner. Suddenly, he clearly heard a female voice telling him to get out of the house. He looked around, but there was nobody upstairs. Frightened, he left the house at once and later required medication for a nervous condition!

"There, you see," June Havoc said. The ghost had greeted us in style.

I stepped forward at once.

"What do you want?" I demanded.

Immediately, the noise stopped.

While we waited for the other participants in the investigation to arrive, June Havoc pointed to the rear wall.

"It has been furred out," she explained. "That is to say, there was another wall against the wall, which made the room smaller. Why, no one knows."

Soon *New York Post* columnist Earl Wilson and Mrs. Wilson, Gail Benedict, and Robert Winter-Berger, also a publicist, arrived, along with a woman from *Life* magazine, notebook in hand. A little later Sybil Leek swept into the room. There was a bit of casual conversation, in which nothing whatever was said about the ghost, and then we seated ourselves in the rear portion of the apartment. Sybil took the chair next to the spot where the noises always originated. June Havoc sat on her right, and I on her left. The lights were very bright since we were filming the entire scene for Miss Havoc's television show.

Soon enough, Sybil began to "go under."

"Hungry," Sybil mumbled faintly.

"Why are you hungry?" I asked.

"No food," the voice said.

The usually calm voice of Sybil Leek was panting in desperation now.

"I want some food, some food!" she cried.

I promised to help her and asked for her name.

"Don't cry. I will help you," I promised.

"Food . . . I want some food . . ." the voice continued to sob.

"Who are you?"

"Lucy Ryan."

"Do you live in this house?"

Again, things quieted down as far as "Ocean-Born" Mary was concerned, until I saw a lengthy story — two parts, in fact — in the *Boston Record-American*, in which my erstwhile medium Lorrie had let her hair down to columnist Harold Banks.

It seemed that Lorrie could not forget Henniker, after all. With publicist Owen Lake, she returned to the house in November, 1964, bringing with her some oil of wintergreen, which she claimed Mary Wallace asked her to bring along.

Two weeks later, the report went on, Lorrie felt Mary Wallace in her home in Weymouth near Boston. Lorrie was afraid that Mary Wallace might "get into my body and use it for whatever purpose she wants to. I might wake up some day and *be* Mary Wallace."

That's the danger of being a medium without proper safeguards. They tend to identify with a personality that has come through them. Especially when they read all there is in print about them.

I decided to take someone to the house who knew nothing about it, someone who was not likely to succumb to the wiles of amateur "ESP experts," inquisitive columnists and such, someone who would do exactly what I required of her: Sybil Leek, famed British psychic.

It was a glorious day late in spring when we arrived at "Ocean-Born" Mary's house in a Volkswagen station wagon driven by two alert young students from Goddard College in Vermont: Jerry Weener and Jay Lawrence. They had come to Boston to fetch us and take us all the way up to their campus, where I was to address the students and faculty. I proposed that they drive us by way of Henniker, and the two young students of parapsychology agreed enthusiastically. It was their first experience with an actual séance and they brought with them a lively dose of curiosity.

Sybil Leek brought with her something else: "Mr. Sasha," a healthy four-foot boa constrictor someone had given her for a pet. At first I thought she was kidding when she spoke with tender care of her snake, coiled peacefully in his little basket. But practical Sybil, author of some nine books, saw still another possibility in "Life with Sasha" and for that reason kept the snake on with her. On the way to Henniker, the car had a flat tire and we took this opportunity to get acquainted with Sasha, as Sybil gave him a run around the New Hampshire countryside.

Although I have always had a deep-seated dislike for anything reptilian, snakes, serpents, and other slitherers, terrestrial or maritime, I must confess that I found this critter less repulsive than I had thought he would be. At any rate, "Mr. Sasha" was collected once more and carefully replaced in his basket and the journey continued to Henniker, where the Russells were expecting us with great anticipation.

After a delightful buffet luncheon — "Mr. Sasha" had his the week before, as snakes are slow digesters — we proceeded to the large room upstairs to the right of the entrance door, commonly called the Lafayette room, and Sybil took the chair near the fireplace. The rest of us — the Russells, a minister friend of theirs, two neighbors, my wife Catherine and I, and our two student friends — gathered around her in a circle.

It was early afternoon. The sun was bright and clear. It didn't seem like it would be a good day for ghosts. Still, we had come to have a talk with the elusive Mary Wallace in her own domain, and if I knew Sybil, she would not disappoint us. Sybil is a very powerful medium, and something *always* happens.

Sybil knew nothing about the house since I had told our hosts not to discuss it with her before the trance session. I asked her if she had any clairvoyant impressions about the house.

"My main impressions were outside," Sybil replied, "near where the irises are. I was drawn to that spot and felt very strange. There is something outside this house which means more than things inside!"

"What about inside the house? What do you feel here?"

"The most impressive room I think is the loom room," Sybil said, and I thought, that's where Ernest Walbourne heard the voice telling him to get out, in the area that's also called the "death" room.

"They don't want us here . . . there is a conflict between two people . . . somebody wants something he can't have . . ."

Presently, Sybil was in trance. There was a moment of silence as I waited anxiously for the ghost of Mary Wallace to manifest itself through Sybil. The first words coming from the lips of the entranced medium were almost unintelligible.

Gradually, the voice became clearer and I had her repeat the words until I could be sure of them.

"Say-mon go to the lion's head," she said now. "To the lion's head. Be careful."

"Why should I be careful?"

"In case he catches you."

"Who are you?"

"Mary Degan."

"What are you doing here?"

"Waiting. Someone fetch me."

She said *"Witing"* with a strong cockney accent, and suddenly I realized that the *"say-mon"* was probably a seaman.

"Whose house is this?" I inquired.

"Daniel Burn's." (Perhaps it was "Birch.")

"What year is this?"

"1798."

"Who built this house?"

"Burn . . ."

"How did you get here?"

"All the time, come and go . . . to hide . . . I have to wait. He wants the money. Burn. Daniel Burn."

I began to wonder what had happened to Mary Wallace. Who was this new member of the ghostly cast? Sybil knew nothing whatever of a pirate or a pirate treasure connected by legend to this house. Yet her very first trance words concerned *a seaman and money*.

Did Mary Degan have someone else with her, I hinted. Maybe this was only the first act and the lady of the house was being coy in time for a second act appearance.

But the ghost insisted that she was Mary Degan and that she lived here, "with the old idiot."

"Who was the old idiot?" I demanded.

"Mary," the Degan girl replied.

"What is Mary's family name?"

"Birch," she replied without hesitation.

I looked at Mrs. Russell, who shook her head. Nobody knew of Mary Wallace by any other name. Had she had another husband we did not know about?

Was there anyone else with her, I asked.

"Mary Birch, Daniel, and Jonathan," she replied.

"Who is Jonathan?"

"Jonathan Harrison Flood," the ghostly girl said.

A week or so later, I checked with my good friend Robert Nesmith, expert in pirate lore. Was there a pirate by that name? There had been, but his date is given as 1610, far too early for our man. But then Flood was a very common name. Also, this Flood might have used another name as his *nom de pirate* and Flood might have been his real, civilian name.

"What are they doing in this house?" I demanded.

"They come to look for their money," Sybil in trance replied. "The old idiot took it."

"What sort of money was it?"

"Dutch money," came the reply. "Very long ago."

"Who brought the money to this house?"

"Mary. Not me."

"Whose money was it?"

"Johnny's."

"How did he get it?"

"Very funny . . . he helped himself . . . so we did."

"What profession did he have?"

"Went down to the sea. Had a lot of funny business. Then he got caught, you know. So they did him in."

"Who did him in?"

"The runners. In the bay."

"What year was that?"

"Ninety-nine."

"What happened to the money after that?"

"She hid it. Outside. Near the lion's head."

"Where is the lion's head?"

"You go down past the little rocks, in the middle of the rocks, a little bit like a lion's head."

"If I left this house by the front entrance, which way would I turn?"

"The right, down past the little rock on the right. Through the trees, down the little . . . "

"How far from the house?"

"Three minutes."

"Is it under the rock?"

"Lion's head."

"How far below?"

"As big as a boy."

"What will I find there?"

"The gold. Dutch gold."

"Anything else?"

"No, unless she put it there."

"Why did she put it there?"

"Because he came back for it."

"What did she do?"

"She said it was hers. Then he went away. Then they caught him, and good thing, too. He never came back and she went off, too."

"When did she leave here?"

"Eighteen three."

"What was she like? Describe her."

"Round, not as big as me, dumpy thing, she thought she owned everything."

"How was Jonathan related to Daniel?"

"Daniel stayed here when Johnny went away and then they would divide the money, but they didn't because of Mary. She took it."

"Did you see the money?"

"I got some money. Gold. It says 1747."

"Is anyone buried in this ground?"

"Sometimes they brought them back here when they got killed down by the river."

"Who is buried in the house?"

"I think Johnny."

I now told Mary Degan to fetch me the other Mary, the lady of the house. But the girl demurred. The other Mary did not like to talk to strangers.

"What do *you* look like?" I asked. I still was not sure if Mary Wallace was not masquerading as her own servant girl to fool us.

"Skinny and tall."

"What do you wear?"

"A gray dress."

"What is your favorite spot in this house?"

"The little loom room. Peaceful."

"Do you always stay there?"

"No." The voice was proud now. "I go where I want."

"Whose house is this?" Perhaps I could trap her if she was indeed Mary Wallace.

"Mary Birch."

"Has she got a husband?"

"They come and go. There's always company here — that's why I go to the loom room."

I tried to send her away, but she wouldn't go.

"Nobody speaks to me," she complained. "Johnny . . . she won't let him speak to me. Nobody is going to send me away."

"Is there a sea captain in this house?" I asked.

She almost shouted the reply.

"*Johnny!*"

"Where is he from?"

"Johnny is from the island."

She then explained that the trouble with Johnny and Mary was about the sea. Especially about the money the captain had.

"Will the money be found?" I asked.

"Not until I let it."

I asked Mary Degan to find me Mary Wallace. No dice. The lady wanted to be coaxed. Did she want some presents, I asked. That hit a happier note.

"Brandy . . . some clothes," she said. "She needs some hair . . . hasn't got much hair."

"Ask her if she could do with some oil of wintergreen," I said, sending up a trial balloon.

"She's got a bad back," the ghost said, and I could tell from the surprised expression on Mrs. Russell's face that Mary Wallace had indeed had a bad back.

"She makes it . . . people bring her things . . . rub her back . . . back's bad . . . she won't let you get the money . . . not yet . . . may want to build another house, in the garden . . . in case she needs it . . . sell it . . . she knows she is not what she used to be because her back's bad . . . she'll never go. Not now."

I assured her that the Russells wanted her to stay as long as she liked. After all, it was her house, too.

"Where is Johnny's body buried?" I now asked.

"Johnny's body," she murmured, "is under the fireplace."

Nobody had told Sybil about the persistent rumors that the old pirate lay under the hearthstone.

"Don't tell anyone," she whispered.

"How deep?"

"Had to be deep."

"Who put him there?"

"I shan't tell you."

"Did you bury anything with him?"

"I shan't tell. He is no trouble now. Poor Johnny."

"How did Johnny meet Mary?"

"I think they met on a ship."

"Ocean-Born" Mary, I thought. Sybil did not even know the name of the house, much less the story of how it got that name.

"All right," I said. "Did Mary have any children?"

"Four . . . in the garden. You can never tell with her."

"Did anyone kill anyone in this house at any time?"

"Johnny was killed, you know. Near the money. The runners chased him and he was very sick, we thought he was dead, and then he came here. I think she pushed him when he hurt his leg. We both brought him back here and put him under the fireplace. I didn't think he was dead."

"But you buried him anyway?" I said.

"She did," the ghost servant replied. "Better gone, she said. He's only come back for the money."

"Then Mary and Johnny weren't exactly friendly?"

"They were once."

"What changed things?"

"The money. She took his money. The money he fought for. Fighting money."

Suddenly, the tone of voice of the servant girl changed.

"I want to go outside," she begged. "She watches me. I can go out because her back is bad today. Can't get up, you see. So I can go out."

I promised to help her.

Suspiciously, she asked, "What do you want?"

"Go outside. You are free to go," I intoned.

"Sit on the rocks," the voice said. "If she calls out? She can get very angry."

"I will protect you," I promised.

"She says there are other places under the floor . . ." the girl ghost added, suddenly.

"Any secret passages?" I asked.

"Yes. Near the old nursery. First floor. Up the stairs, the loom room, the right hand wall. You can get out in the smoke room!"

Mr. Russell had told me of his suspicions that on structural evidence alone there was a hidden passage behind the smoke room. How would Sybil know this? Nobody had discussed it with her or showed her the spot.

I waited for more. But she did not know of any other passages, except one leading to the rear of the house.

"What about the well?"

"She did not like that either, because she thought *he* put his money there."

"Did he?"

"Perhaps he did. She used to put money in one place, he into another, and I think he put some money into the smoke room. He was always around there. Always watching each other. Watch me, too. Back of the house used to be where he could hide. People always looking for Johnny. Runners."

"Who was Mr. Birch?"

"Johnny had a lot to do with his house, but he was away a lot and so there was always some man here while he was away."

"Who paid for the house originally?"

"I think Johnny."

"Why did he want this house?"

"When he got enough money, he would come here and stay forever. He could not stay long ever, went back to the sea, and she came."

I tried another tack.

"Who was Don Pedro?" That was the name given the pirate in the popular tale.

She had heard the name, but could not place it.

"What about Mary Wallace?"

"Mary Wallace was Mary *Birch,*" the ghost said, as if correcting me. "She had several names."

"Why?"

"Because she had several husbands."

Logical enough, if true.

"Wallace lived here a little while, I think," she added.

"Who was first, Wallace or Birch?"

"Birch. Mary Wallace, Mary Birch, is good enough."

Did the name Philip Babb mean anything to her? That allegedly was the pirate's real name.

"She had a little boy named Philip," the ghost said, and I thought, why not? After all, they had named Mary for the pirate's mother, why not reciprocate and name *her* son for the old man? Especially with all that loot around.

"If I don't go now, she'll wake up," the girl said. "Philip Babb, Philip Babb, he was somewhere in the back room. That was his room. I remember him."

How did Philip get on with Johnny? I wanted to know if they were one and the same person or not.

"Not so good," the ghost said. "Johnny did not like men here, you know."

I promised to watch out for Mary, and sent the girl on her way.

I then brought Sybil out of trance.

A few moments later, we decided to start our treasure hunt in the garden, following the instructions given us by Mary Degan, girl ghost.

Sybil was told nothing more than to go outside and let her intuition lead her toward any spot she thought important. The rest of us followed her like spectators at the National Open Golf Tournament.

We did not have to walk far. About twenty yards from the house, near some beautiful iris in bloom, we located the three stones. The one in the middle looked indeed somewhat like a lion's head, when viewed at a distance. I asked the others in the group to look at it. There was no doubt about it. If there was a lion's head on the grounds, this was it. What lay underneath? What indeed was underneath the hearthstone in the house itself?

The Russells promised to get a mine detector to examine the areas involved. If there was metal in the ground, the instrument would show it. Meanwhile, the lore about "Ocean-Born" Mary had been enriched by the presence in the nether world of Mary Degan, servant girl, and the intriguing picture of two pirates — Johnny and Philip Babb. Much of this is very difficult to trace. But the fact is that Sybil Leek, who came to Henniker a total stranger, was able, in trance, to tell about a man at sea, a Mary, a pirate treasure, hidden passages, a child named Philip, four children of Mary, and the presence of a ghost in the loom room upstairs. All of this had been checked.

Why should not the rest be true also? Including, perhaps, the elusive treasure?

Only time will tell.

The Ghosts of Barbery Lane

"**I** know a house in Rye, New York, with a ghost," painter Mary Melikian said to me, and there was pleasure in her voice at being the harbinger of good news. Mary knew how eager I was to find a haunted house, preferably one that was still haunted.

"A ghost," Mary repeated and added, tantalizingly, "a ghost that *likes to slam doors.*"

I pumped Mary for details. One of her friends was the celebrated portrait painter Molly Guion, known in Rye as Mrs. John Smythe. Molly and her husband, an architect, lived in a sprawling mid-nineteenth-century house atop a bluff overlooking the old New Haven Railroad bed, surrounded by houses built in later years. The Smythes' house was the first one on the tract, the original Manor House, built there around 1860 by one Jared B. Peck.

I arranged with Mrs. Smythe to visit the house the following week, in August of 1963. My wife Catherine and I were met at the train by Mrs. Smythe, whose husband also came along to welcome us. The drive to the house (originally called "The Cedars" but now only known as a number on Barbery Lane) took less than five minutes, yet you might well have entered another world — so serene and rural was the atmosphere that greeted us that moonlit evening, when the station wagon pulled up to the gleaming-white 100-year-old house the Smythes had called home since the summer of 1957.

Rising to four floors, the structure reminded me of the stylized paintings of Victorian houses associated with another world. A wide porch went around it at the ground level, and shady trees protected it from view and intrusion.

The huge living room was tastefully furnished with fine antiques and all over the house we encountered the marvelously alive portraits painted by Molly Guion, which blended naturally into the decor of the house. This was a stately mansion, only an hour from New York but as quiet and removed from the city of subways as if it stood in the Deep South or Down East. We seated ourselves comfortably. Then I came right to the point.

"This ghost," I began. "What exactly does it do and when did you first notice anything unusual in the house?"

This is my standard opener. Molly Guion was more than happy to tell us everything. Her husband left for a while to tend to some chores.

"We arrived in this house on a hot summer day in 1957 — in July," she recalled. "About a week later — I remember it was a particularly hot night — we heard a door slam. Both my husband and I heard it."

"Well?"

"But there was absolutely nobody in the house at the time except us," Molly said, significantly. "We heard it many times after that. Maybe six or seven separate instances. Once around ten o'clock at night I heard the front door open and close again with a characteristic squeak. Mother was living with us then and I was not feeling well, so that a nurse was staying with me. I called out 'Mother,' thinking she had come home a bit early, but there was no reply. Since then I've heard the front door open many times, but there is never anyone there."

"Is it the front door then?"

"No, not always. Sometimes it is the front door and sometimes it is this door on the second floor. Come, I'll show you."

Molly led us up the winding stairs to a second floor containing many small rooms, all exquisitely furnished with the solid furniture of the Victorian period. There was a tiny room on one side of the corridor leading to the rear of the house, and across from it, the door that was heard to slam. It was a heavy wooden door, leading to a narrow winding staircase which in turn led up another flight of stairs to the third floor. Here Molly Guion had built herself a magnificent studio, taking up most of the floor space.

"One day in January of 1962," she volunteered, "I was downstairs in the kitchen talking to an exterminator, when I heard a door slam hard — it seemed to me. Yet, there was no one in the house at the time, only we two downstairs."

"Outside of yourself and your husband, has anyone else heard these uncanny noises?"

Molly nodded quickly.

"There was this colored man that worked for me. He said, 'Mrs. Smythe, every time I'm alone in the house, I hear a door slam!'"

"Anyone else?"

"A Scottish cleaning woman, name of Roberta Gillan. She lives in Harrison, New York. She once came to me and said, 'Did you just slam a door?' Of course, I hadn't."

We were now seated in a small room off the second-floor corridor. The light was moody and the air dank. There was a quietness around the house so heavy I almost *wished* I could hear a door slam. Molly had more to reveal.

"Once, a little girl named Andree, age eleven, came to visit us and within seconds exclaimed — 'Mamma, there is a ghost in this house!'"

Our hostess admitted to being somewhat psychic, with sometimes comical results. Years ago, when a boyfriend had failed to keep their date, she saw him clearly in a dream-vision with a certain blonde girl. He later explained his absence in a casual way, but she nailed him with a description of his blonde — and he confessed the truth.

Two years after she moved into the house, Molly developed a case of asthma, the kind very old people sometimes suffer from. Strangely, it bothered her only in certain rooms and not at all in others. It started like a kind of allergy, and gradually worsened until it became a fully grown asthmatic condition. Although two rooms were side by side, sleeping in one would aggravate the condition, but sleeping in the other made her completely free of it!

"Did you hear any other noises — I mean, outside of the door slamming?" I asked.

"Yes. Not so long ago we had a dinner party here, and among the guests was a John Gardner, a vice president of the Bankers Trust Company."

Suddenly she had heard someone rap at the window of the big room downstairs. They tried to ignore the noise, but Gardner heard it too.

"Is someone rapping at your window?" he inquired.

He was assured it was nothing. Later he took Molly aside and remonstrated with her. "I distinctly heard the raps," he said. Molly just smiled.

Finally the Smythes called on the American Society for Psychic Research to find an explanation for all these goings-on. But the Society was in no hurry to do anything about the case. They suggested Molly write them a letter, which she did, but they still took no action.

I thoroughly inspected the premises — walked up the narrow staircase into Molly Guion's studio where some of the best portrait oils hung. Her paintings of famous Britons had just toured as an exhibition and the house was full of those she owned (the greater part of her work was commissioned and scattered in collections, museums, and private homes).

There was a tiny bedroom next to the landing in back of the studio, evidently a servant's room, since the entire floor had originally been servants' quarters. The house had sixteen rooms in all.

By now Mr. Smythe had joined us and I explained my mission. Had he ever noticed anything unusual about the house?

"Oh yes," he volunteered, speaking slowly and deliberately. "There are all sorts of noises in this house and they're not ordinary noises — I mean, the kind you can *explain.*"

"For instance?"

"I was sleeping up here one night in the little bedroom here," he said, pointing to the servant's room in back of the landing, "when I heard footsteps. They were the steps of an older person."

But there was no one about, he asserted.

Jared Peck, who built the house in 1860, died in 1895, and the house passed into the hands of his estate to be rented to various tenants. In 1910, Stuyvesant Wainwright bought the property. In the following year, his ex-wife, now Mrs. Catlin, bought it from him and lived in it until her death in the 1920s.

The former Mrs. Wainwright turned out to be a colorful person. Born wealthy, she had a very short temper and the servants never stayed long in her house.

"She certainly liked to slam doors," Mr. Smythe observed. "I mean she was the kind of person who would do that sort of thing."

"One day she became very ill and everybody thought she would die," Molly related. "There she was stretched out on this very couch and the doctor felt free to talk about her condition. 'She won't last much longer,' he said, and shrugged. Mrs. Wainwright sat up with a angry jolt and barked, 'I intend to!' And she did, for many more years of hot-tempered shenanigans."

In her later years Mrs. Wainwright moved to the former servants' quarters on the second floor — whether out of economy or for reasons of privacy no one knows for sure. The *slamming door* was right in the heart of her rooms and no doubt she traveled up those narrow stairs to the floor above many times.

The plumber, painter, and carpenter who worked for Mrs. Wainwright were still living in Rye and they all remembered her as a willful and headstrong woman who liked to have her own way. Her granddaughter, Mrs. Condit, recalled her vividly. The Smythes were pretty sure that Mrs. Wainwright slept up there on the second floor — they found a screen marked "My bedroom window" that fit no other window in any of the rooms.

The Smythes acquired the handsome house from the next owner, one Arthur Flemming, who used Mrs. Wainwright's old room. But he didn't experience anything unusual, or at any rate said nothing about it.

There was a big theft once in the house and Mrs. Wainwright may have been worried about it. Strongly attached to worldly possessions, she kept valuables in various trunks on the third floor, and ran up to look at them from time to time to make sure everything was still there.

Could the slamming of the door be a re-enactment of these frequent nervous expeditions up the stairs? Could the opening and closing of the entrance door be a fearful examination of the door to see if the lock was secure, or if there was anyone strange lurking about outside?

The very day after our visit to this haunted house, a young painter friend of Molly's named Helen Charleton, of Bronxville, New York, was alone in the studio that Molly let her use occasionally to do some painting of her own. She was quite alone in the big house when she clearly heard the front door open. Calling out, she received no answer. Thinking that the gardener might have a key, and that she might be in danger, she took hold of what heavy objects she could put her hands on and waited anxiously for the steps that were sure to resound any moment. No steps came. An hour later, the doorbell rang and she finally dashed down to the entrance door. *The door was tightly shut,* and no one was about. Yet she *had* heard the characteristic noise of the opening of the old-fashioned door!

The mailman's truck was just pulling away, so she assumed it was he who had rung the bell. Just then Molly returned.

"I've heard the door slam many times," Helen Charleton said to me, "and it always sounds so far away. I think it's on the first floor, but I can't be sure."

Was Mrs. Wainwright still walking the Victorian corridors of "The Cedars," guarding her treasures upstairs?

When Catherine and I returned from Europe in the fall of 1964, Molly Guion had news for us. All was far from quiet in Rye. In the upstairs room where Molly's invalid mother was bedridden, a knob had flown off a table while Mrs. Guion stood next to it. In the presence of a nurse, the bathroom lights had gone on and off by themselves. More sinister, a heavy ashtray had taken off on its own to sail clear across the room. A door had opened by itself, and footsteps had been heard again.

A new nurse had come, and the number of witnesses who had heard or seen uncanny goings-on was now eight.

I decided it was time for a séance, and on January 6, 1965, medium Ethel Meyers, Mary Melikian, Catherine and I took a New Haven train for Rye, where John Smythe picked us up in his station wagon.

While Ethel Meyers waited in the large sitting room downstairs, I checked on the house and got the latest word on the hauntings. Molly Guion took me to the kitchen to show me the spot where one of the most frightening incidents had taken place.

"Last Christmas, my mother, my husband, and I were here in the kitchen having lunch, and right near us on a small table next to the wall was a great big bread knife. Suddenly, to our amazement, *the knife took off into the air,* performed an arc in the air and landed about a yard away from the table. This was about noon, in good light."

"Was that the only time something like this happened?"

"The other day the same thing happened. We were down in the kitchen again at nighttime. My husband and I heard a terrific crash upstairs. It was in the area of the servants' quarters on the second floor, which is in the area where that door keeps slamming. I went up to investigate and found a heavy ashtray lying on the floor about a yard away from the table in my husband's den."

"And there was no one upstairs — flesh-and-blood, that is?"

"No. The object could not have just slipped off the table. It landed some distance away."

"Amazing," I conceded. "Was there more?"

"Last week I was standing in the upstairs sitting room with one of the nurses, when a piece of a chair that was lying in the center of a table took off and landed in the middle of the floor."

"Before your eyes?"

"Before our eyes."

"What would you say is the most frequent phenomenon here?" I asked.

"The opening of the front door downstairs. We and others have heard this characteristic noise any number of times, and there is never anyone there."

I turned to Mrs. Witty, the nurse currently on duty with Molly Guion's mother.

"How long have you been in this house?"

"Since October, 1964."

"Have you noticed anything unusual in these four months?"

"Well, Mrs. Smythe and I were in the patient's bedroom upstairs, when we heard the front door downstairs open. I remarked to Mrs. Smythe that she had a visitor, and went down to the front door, and looked. *The heavy chain was swinging loose, and the front door was slightly ajar!*"

"Did you see any visitor?"

"No. I opened the door, looked all around, but there was no one there."

"Anything else?"

"A couple of weeks later, the same thing happened. I was alone in the house with the patient, and the door was locked securely. An hour after I had myself locked it, I heard the door shut tightly, but the chain was again swinging by itself."

I next turned to Mr. Smythe to check up on his own experiences since we had last talked. Mr. Smythe was a naval architect and very cautious in his appraisal of the uncanny. He was still hearing the "measured steps" in the attic room where he sometimes slept, even when he was all alone in the house.

I returned to Ethel Meyers, the medium, who had seated herself in a large chair in the front sitting room downstairs.

"Anything happening?" I asked, for I noticed a peculiar expression on Ethel's face, as if she were observing something or someone.

"I picture a woman clairvoyantly," Ethel said. "She looks at me with a great deal of defiance."

"Why are you pointing across the room at that sofa?" I asked my wife.

"I saw a light from the corner of my eye and I thought it was a car, but no car has passed by," Catherine said.

If a car *had* passed by, no reflection could have been seen at that spot, since no window faced in that direction.

While Ethel prepared for the trance sitting, I went outside the room to talk to Georgia Anne Warren, a young dancer who had modeled for some of Molly Guion's paintings. Her full-length nude study graced the studio upstairs, and there amid the Churchill portraits and faces of the famous or near-famous, it was like a shining beacon of beauty. But Miss Warren wasn't only posing for a painter, we discovered — she was also modeling for a ghost.

"I heard a thumping noise, as if someone were going upstairs. I was in the kitchen. The steps sounded as if they were coming from the dining room. There was no one coming in. The only people in the house at the time were Molly Guion and myself. No doubt about it."

I thanked the redheaded model and followed Ethel Meyers up the stairs, to which she seemed propelled by a sudden impulse. There, on the winding Victorian steps, Ethel made her first contact with the ghost.

"Make the body very cold. Don't put it in the ground when it's warm. Let it get very cold!" she mumbled, as if not quite herself.

"Let her speak through you," I suggested.

"She is," Ethel replied, and continued in a somewhat strange voice. "Ring around the rosies, a pocketful of posies . . . "

I turned toward the stairwell and asked the ghost to communicate with us, tell her tale, and find help through us. There was no further answer.

I led Mrs. Meyers back to her chair, and asked Molly Guion to dim the lights a little so we could all relax. Meanwhile, other witnesses had arrived. They included *New York Times* reporter N. Berkowitz, Benton & Bowles vice-president Gordon Webber, publicist Bill Ryan, and book critic John K. Hutchins. We formed a long oval around Ethel Meyers and waited for the ghost to make her appearance.

We did not have to wait long. With a sudden shriek, Ethel, deep in trance, leapt to her feet, and in the awkward posture of an old crone, walked toward the front door. Nothing I could do would hold her back. I followed her quickly, as the medium, now possessed by the ghost, made her way through the long room to the door.

As if a strong wind had swept into the sitting room, the rest of the guests were thrown back by the sheer drive of Ethel's advance. She flung herself against the heavy wooden door and started to alternately gnaw at it and pound against it in an unmistakable desire to open it and go through. Then she seized the brass chain — the one Mrs. Witty had twice seen swinging by itself — and pulled it with astonishing force. I had all I could do to keep the medium from falling as she threw her body against the door.

In one hand I held a microphone, which I pressed close to her lips to catch as much of the dialogue as possible. I kept the other hand ready to prevent Ethel's fall to the floor.

"Rotten," the entranced medium now mumbled, still clutching the chain.

I tried to coax her back to the chair, but the ghost evidently would have none of it.

"It stinks . . . Where is it?"

"Is this your house?" I asked.

Heavy breathing.

"Yes. Get out!"

"I've come to help you. What is your name?"

"Get out!" the microphone picked up.

"What is it that you want?" I asked.

"My body."

"You've passed on, don't you understand?"

"No . . . I want my body. Where is it?"

I explained again that this was no longer her house, but she kept calling for the return of "her body" in such anger and despair that I began to wonder if it had not been buried on the premises.

"They took it, my body. I saw them, I saw them!"

"You must let go of this house. It is no longer yours," I said.

"No, my house, my house. They took it. My body. I have nothing. Get it. I feel I have one."

I explained that we had lent her a body to speak through for the moment.

"Who are you?" *It* sounded quieter.

"A friend," I replied, "come to help you."

Instead of replying, the entranced medium grabbed the door again.

"Why do you want to open the door?" I asked. It took a moment for the answer to come through trembling lips.

"Go out," she finally said. "I don't know you. Let me go, let me go."

I continued to question the ghost.

"Who are you? Did you live in this house?"

"My house. They took it out. My body is out there!"

I explained about the passage of time.

"You were not well. You've died."

"No, no . . . I wasn't cold."

"You are free to go from this door. Your loved ones, your family, await you outside."

"They hate me."

"No, they have made up with you. Why should they hate you?"

"They took me out the door."

Then, suddenly the medium's expression changed. Had someone come to fetch her?

"Oh, Baba, darling . . . Oh, he loved me."

There was hysterical crying now.

"He's gone . . . My beloved . . . "

"What is his name?"

"*Wain* . . . Where is he . . . Let me go!"

The crying was now almost uncontrollable, so I sent the ghost on her way. At the same time I asked that Albert, Ethel's control on the etheric side of the veil, take over her physical body for the moment to speak to us.

It took a moment or two until Albert was in command. The medium's body visibly straightened out and all traces of a bent old crone vanished. Albert's crisp voice was heard.

"She's a former tenant here, who has not been too well beloved. She also seems to have been carried out before complete death. This has brought her back to try and rectify it and make contact with the physical body. But here is always unhappiness. I believe there was no love toward her as she was older."

"Can you get a name?" I asked.

"If she refuses, I cannot."

"How long ago was this?"

"During the Nineties. Between 1890 and 1900."

"Is this a woman?"

"Yes."

"Anything peculiar about her appearance?"

"Large eyes, and almost a harelip."

"Why is she concerned about her body?"

"There was no great funeral for her. She was put in a box and a few words were said over her grave. That is part of her problem, that she was thus rejected and neglected."

"Why does she run up to the attic?"

"This was her house, and it was denied to her later in life."

"By whom?"

"By those living here. Relatives to her."

"Her heirs?"

"Those who took it over when she could no longer function. She was still alive."

"Anything else we should know?"

"There is a great deal of hate for anyone in this house. Her last days were full of hate. Should she return, if she is spoken to kindly, she will leave. We will help her."

"Why is she so full of hate?"

"Her grief, her oppressions. She never left her tongue quiet when she was disrupted in her desire to go from her quarters to the rest of the house."

"What was her character?"

"As a young person she was indeed a lady. Later in life, a strong personality, going slightly toward dual personality. She was an autocrat. At the very end, not beloved."

"And her relationship with the servants?"

"Not too friendly. Tyrannical."

"What troubled her about her servants?"

"They knew too much."

"Of what?"

"Her downfall. Her pride was hurt."

"Before that, how was she?"

"A suspicious woman. She could not help but take things from others which she believed were hers by right."

"What did she think her servants were doing?"

"They pried on her secret life. She trusted no one toward the end of life."

"Before she was prevented, as you say, from freely going about the house — did she have any belongings in the attic?"

"Yes, hidden. She trusted no one."

I then suggested that the "instrument" be brought back to herself. A very surprised Ethel Meyers awakened to find herself leaning against the entrance door.

"What's the matter with my lip?" she asked when she was able to speak. After a moment, Ethel Meyers was her old self, and the excursion into Mrs. Wainwright's world had come to an end.

The following morning Molly Smythe called me on the phone. "Remember about Albert's remarks that Mrs. Wainwright was restrained within her own rooms?"

Of course I remembered.

"Well," Molly continued, "we've just made a thorough investigation of all the doors upstairs in the servants' quarters where she spent her last years. They all show evidence of locks having been on them, later removed. *Someone was locked up there for sure.*"

Ironically, death had not released Mrs. Wainwright from confinement. To her, freedom still lay beyond the heavy wooden door with its brass chain.

Now that her spirit self had been taken in hand, perhaps she would find her way out of the maze of her delusions to rejoin her first husband, for whom she had called.

The next time Molly Smythe hears the front door opening, it'll be just her husband coming home from the office. *Or so I thought.*

But the last week of April, 1965, Molly called me again. Footsteps had been heard *upstairs* this time, and the sound of a door somewhere being opened and closed, and of course, on inspection, there was no one *visible* about.

Before I could make arrangements to come out to Rye once again, something else happened. Mr. Smythe was in the bathtub, when a large tube of toothpaste, safely resting well back on a shelf, flew off the shelf by its own volition. No vibration or other *natural* cause could account for it. Also, a hypodermic needle belonging to one of the nurses attending Molly's invalid mother had somehow disappeared.

I promised to bring Sybil Leek to the house. The British medium knew nothing whatever of the earlier history of the case, and I was curious to see if she would make contact with the same or different conditions, as sometimes happens when two mediums are used in the same house. It's like tuning in on different radio wavelengths.

It was a cool, wet day in May when we seated ourselves in a circle upstairs in the "haunted room." Present in addition to the hosts, Sybil Leek, and myself, were Mrs. Betty Salter (Molly's sister); David Ellingson, a reporter from the Port Chester, N.Y., *Item*; Mr. and Mrs. Robert Bendick, neighbors and friends of the Smythes; and Mary Melikian. Mr. Bendick was a television producer specializing in news programs.

Sybil went into hypnotic trance. It took several minutes before anything audible could be recorded.

"Who are you?" I asked.

A feeble voice answered:

"Marion . . . Marion Gernt . . ."

Before going into trance, Sybil had volunteered the information that the name "Grant," or something like it, had been on her mind ever since she set foot into the house.

"What year is this?" I asked.

"1706."

"Who built the house?"

"My father . . . Walden."

She then complained that people in the house were disturbing *her*, and that therefore she was *pulling it down*.

"My face is swollen," she added. "I'm sick . . . Blood."

Suddenly, something went wrong with my reliable tape recorder. In all my previous investigations it had worked perfectly. Now it wouldn't, and some parts of the conversation were not recorded. The wheels would turn and then stop, and then start again, as if someone were sticking their fingers into them at will!

I tried my camera, and to my amazement, I couldn't take any pictures. All of a sudden, the mechanism wouldn't function properly, and the shutter could not be un-cocked. I did not get any photographs. Bob Bendick, after the séance, took a good look at the camera. In a moment it was working fine again. After the séance, too, we tried to make the tape recorder work. It started and then stopped completely.

"The batteries have run out," I explained, confident that there was nothing more than that to it. So we put the machine on house current. Nothing happened. It wasn't the batteries. It was something else.

After we left the "haunted room" and went downstairs, I put the tape recorder into my traveling case. About ten minutes later, I heard a ghostly voice coming from my case. *My* voice. The tape recorder

that I had left in a secure turn-off position had started up by itself
. . . or . . . so it seemed.

But one can't be sure in haunted houses. *Item* reporter David
Ellingson and Mary Melikian were standing next to me when it
happened. John Smythe was wondering if someone had turned on
the radio or TV. So much for the instruments that didn't work —
temporarily.

But, let us get back to Sybil and the ghost speaking through her.
She claimed to have been burned all over in a fire. John Smythe
confirmed later that there were traces of a fire in the house that have
never been satisfactorily explained.

The ghost seemed confused about it. She was burned, on this
spot, in what was then a little house. The place was called Rocher.
Her named was spelled M-a-r-i-o-n G-e-r-n-t. She was born at
Rodey, eight miles distant. She was not sure about her age. At first
she said 29, then it was 57. The house was built by one Dion, of
Rocher.

I then tried to explain, as I always do, that the house belonged to
someone else and that she must not stay.

"Go away," the ghost mumbled, not at all pleased with the idea
of moving. But I insisted. I told her of her husband who wanted her
to join him "over there."

"I hate him!" she volunteered, then added — "I start moving
things . . . I break things up . . . I want my chair."

"You must not stay here," I pleaded. "You're not wanted here."

"*He* said that," she replied in a sullen voice. "Alfred did. My
husband."

"You must join him and your children."

"I'll stay."

I repeated the incantation for her to leave.

"I can't go. I'm burned. I can't move," she countered.

I explained that these were only memories.

Finally she relented, and said — "I'll need a lot of rags . . . to cover myself."

Gently now, she started to fade.

"I need my chair," she pleaded, and I told her she could have it.

Then she was gone.

Sybil came back now. Still in trance, she responded quickly to my questions about what she saw and felt on the other side of the veil. This is a technique I find particularly effective when used prior to bringing the medium out of trance or from under hypnosis.

"An old lady," Sybil said. "She is quite small. I think she is Dutch. Shriveled. She is very difficult. Can't move. Very unpleasant. Throws things because she can't walk. This is her house. She lived here about three hundred years ago. She wants everything *as it was*. She has marks on her face. She was in a fire."

"Did she die in it?" I asked.

"No. She died near here. Doesn't communicate well."

"There is a box with two hearts, two shields," Sybil said. "It means something to this woman."

"Were there any others around?" I asked.

"Lots, like shadows," Sybil explained, "but this little woman was the one causing the commotion."

"She likes to throw things," Sybil added, and I couldn't help thinking that she had never been briefed on all the objects the ghost had been throwing.

"She doesn't know where any doors are, so she just goes on. The door worries her a lot, because she doesn't know where it is. The front and rear have been changed around."

Sybil, of course, knew nothing of the noises centering around the main door, nor the fact that the rear of the house was once the front.

I told Sybil to send her away, and in a quiet voice, Sybil did so.

The séance was over, at least for the time being.

A little later, we went up to the top floor, where both Molly and

Sybil suddenly sensed a strong odor of perfume. I joined them, and I smelled it, too. It was as if *someone were following us about the house!*

But it was time to return to New York. Our hosts offered to drive us to the city.

"Too bad," I said in parting, "that nobody has *seen* an apparition here. Only sounds seem to have been noticed."

Betty Salter, Mrs. Smythe's perky sister, shook her head.

"Not true," she said. "I was here not so long ago when I saw a black figure downstairs in the dining room. I thought it was Molly, but on checking found that I was quite alone downstairs . . . That is, except for *her.*"

Mrs. Wainwright, of course, was of Dutch ancestry, and the description of the character, appearance, and general impression of the ghost Sybil gave did rather fit Mrs. Wainwright.

Was the 1706 lady an ancestor or just someone who happened to be on the spot when only a small farm house occupied the site?

The Smythes really didn't care whether they have two ghosts or one ghost. They preferred to have none.

The Ghost Clock

New England is full of ghosts. A young woman with the improbable first name of Dixie-Lee, and the acquired-by-marriage second name of Danforth, lived in the small town of Milford, just over the border in New Hampshire. She chanced to hear me on a Boston radio program, and presto, there was a note in the mail about something pretty eerie that had happened to her.

In 1954, when Dixie-Lee was 17, she took on a two-week job as companion to an elderly lady by the name of Mrs. William Collar. Mrs. Collar, then 82 years old, had been a fine artist, and had lived a happy life all over the world. Dixie-Lee found being a companion an easy way to make some extra money. Mrs. Collar's housekeeper went home nights, and the elderly lady wanted someone with her in the large, rambling house, at least until she could find a full-time housekeeper who would sleep in.

The Collars had met in France, both studying there, and though they married against the wishes of their parents, they had a wonderful and happy life together. When Mr. William Collar died, things were never the same. They had occupied a large double room on the second floor, with a bed on either side, and a wash basin for each. They truly lived close together.

After her husband's death, Mrs. Collar moved out of the room, and never slept in it again. She left everything as it was, including a big grandfather clock, which was never wound again after Mr. Collar's passing. Finally, in 1958, she joined her Bill. She may have been able to prepare herself for it, for she was often heard talking to "her Bill" when no one else could be seen in the room.

There was a fight over the will. The Collars had had no children, and a niece inherited the house.

But let me get back to Dixie-Lee and 1954. The young girl had moved into Mrs. Collar's imposing white house at New Ipswich, as the section was called, and given a room on the second floor next to the large bedroom once occupied by Mr. and Mrs. Collar. She had barely enough time to admire the expensive antique furniture around the house, when it was time to retire for the night.

Mrs. Dixie-Lee Danforth had come to Boston to meet me, and I questioned her about what happened then.

"I went to bed," she said, "and in the wee hours of the morning I awoke to the faint sound of footsteps and ticking of a clock. The sound of both kept getting louder — louder — till it seemed to beat against my brain."

At first she thought she was dreaming, but, biting her own hand, she realized she was fully awake. Cold sweat stood on her forehead when she realized that Mrs. Collar was an invalid *who could not walk*. What was more, the big clock had not worked for years. Suddenly, just as suddenly as it had come, it ceased. Dixie-Lee lay still for a while in sheer terror, then she turned on the light. Her bedroom door was firmly closed, just as she had left it before going to bed. She checked the door leading to what was once the Collars' big bedroom. It was shut tight, too. She ventured out onto the narrow landing of the staircase leading to the lower floor. It was shut off from the downstairs part of the house by a hall door. That, too, was shut. She retraced her steps and suddenly noticed a rope and pulley. She pulled it and another door appeared.

"I opened it, heart in my mouth," Dixie-Lee said, "and was

relieved to find a pretty, light bedroom behind it. It was furnished with modern furniture, and seemed to me much gayer and more peaceful than the rest of the house. The room was empty."

"What did you do then?" I wondered.

"First, I checked the big clock in my room. It was not going. Just as dead as it had been all those years. I looked around the house for other clocks. The only one in going condition was downstairs in the room occupied by Mrs. Collar, and I'd have to have had super-hearing to hear that one tick all the way up to the second floor through three sets of closed doors and a heavy wooden floor!"

I readily agreed that was not very likely, and wondered if she had told anyone of her frightening experience that night.

"I told the daytime housekeeper, with whom I was friendly, and she laughed. But I refused to stay another moment unless someone else stayed with me. She and her young daughter moved in with me upstairs, and stayed the full two weeks. I never heard the footsteps or the ticking of the clock again while they were with me. But after I left, housekeepers came and went. Nobody seemed to stay very long at the big white house in New Ipswich. Possibly they, too, heard the uncanny noises."

I nodded and asked about Mrs. Collar. Could she have gotten out of bed somehow?

"Not a chance," Dixie-Lee replied. "She was a total invalid. I checked on her in the morning. She had never left her bed. She couldn't have. Besides, the footsteps I heard weren't those of a frail old woman. *They were a man's heavy footfalls.* I never told Mrs. Collar about my experience though. Why frighten her to death?"

"Quite so," I agreed, and we talked about Dixie-Lee now. Was she psychic to any degree?

Dixie-Lee came from a most unusual family. Her great-grand-mother knew how 'to work the table.' Her grandfather saw the ghost of his sister, and Dixie-Lee herself had felt her late grandfather in his house whenever she visited, and she had numerous premonitions of impending danger.

On at least one such occasion she had a feeling she should not go on a certain trip, and insisted on stopping the car. On investigation, she found the wheels damaged. She might have been killed had she not heeded the warning!

We parted. Mrs. Danforth returned to her somewhat-more-than skeptical husband in Milford, and I took the next plane back to New York.

But the haunted house in New Ipswich never left my mind. I was due back in New England around Halloween, 1963, and decided to join Mrs. Danforth in a little trip up to the New Hampshire border country. A friend of hers, their children, a Boston-teacher friend of ours named Carol Bowman, and my wife and I completed the party that drove up to New Ipswich on that warm fall day. We weren't exactly expected, since I did not know the name of the present owner of the house. But Mrs. Danforth had sent word of our coming ahead. It turned out the word was never received, and we actually were lucky to find anyone in, luckier yet to be as cordially welcomed as we were by the lady of the house, whom we shall call Mrs. F.

Mrs. Jeanette F. was a sophisticated, well-educated lady whose husband was a psychiatrist, who was once also interested in parapsychology. She asked that I not use her full name here. A strange "feeling" of expecting us made her bid us a cordial welcome. I wasn't surprised to hear this — in this business, nothing surprises me anymore.

The F.'s had only had the house for a year when we visited them. They had not intended to buy the house, although they were on the lookout for a home in New England. But they passed it in their car, and fell in love with it . . . or rather were somehow made to buy the place. They discovered it was built in 1789. That wasn't all they discovered after they moved in.

"I always had the feeling," Mrs. F. said, "that we were only *allowed* to live here . . . but never really alone. Mrs. Collar's bedroom, for instance. I had the distinct feeling something was buried there under the floorboards. My sister-in-law slept upstairs. The next morning she told me she had 'heard things.' Right after we moved in, I heard footsteps upstairs."

"You too?" marveled Dixie-Lee, shooting a triumphant side glance at me, as if I had doubted her story.

"Last winter at dusk one day, I heard a woman scream. Both of us heard it, but we thought — or rather, *liked* to think — that it was a bobcat. Soon thereafter, we heard it again, only now it sounded more like a *child crying*. We heard it on several occasions and it gave us the willies."

On another occasion, there had been five people in the house when they heard the scream, followed by a growl. They went out to look for a bobcat . . . but there were absolutely no traces in the fresh snow, of either animal or human. There had also been all sorts of noises in the basement.

"Something strange about this child crying," Mrs. F. continued. "When we moved in, a neighbor came to see us and said when they saw we had a child, 'You've brought life back to the Collar house.'"

Dixie-Lee broke in.

"I seem to recall there was something about a child. I mean that they had a child."

"And it died?" I asked.

"I don't know," Mrs. F. said. "But there were diaries — they were almost lost, but one of Bill Collar's best friends, Archie Eaton, saved them. Here they are."

Mrs. F. showed us the remarkable books, all written in longhand. On cursory examination I did not uncover the secret of the child.

There is a hollow area in the basement. We went down to get "impressions," and Dixie-Lee felt very uneasy all of a sudden, and didn't feel like joining us downstairs, even though moments before she had been the spirit of adventure personified.

We returned to the ground floor and had some coffee.

I decided to return with a medium, and hold a séance next to the chimney down in the basement, underneath the room where Mrs. F. felt the floorboards held a secret.

But somehow we were thwarted in this effort.

In December of 1963, we were told that our visit would have to be postponed, and Mrs. F. asked us to come later in the winter. Too many living relatives in the house were making it difficult to listen for the dead.

"Something happened yesterday," she added, "that will interest you. My housekeeper is a very bright and trusted woman. She has never mentioned anything strange about the house. Yesterday I was telling her about our plans to sell the house. As I spoke, she was looking in the room next to me — I was standing in the kitchen. She was looking into the dining room, when she turned pale and interrupted me. She had seen a short, old woman in a long gray dress walk through the dining room. Now I questioned her about anything she might have seen in the past. She admitted she had seen figures on several occasions, but was afraid to be ridiculed. Strangely enough, she wants to buy the house despite these experiences. She calls it 'the house that watches,' because she always feels she is being observed while she cares for the children, even when she has them in the garden."

In February, 1964, we tried to fix a new date to visit the house. My letters remained unanswered. Had the house changed hands again?

But no matter who actually *lived* there. It seemed the *real* owner was still Mrs. Collar.

Hungry Lucy

"**J**une Havoc's got a ghost in her townhouse," Gail Benedict said gaily on the telephone. Gail was in public relations, and a devoted ghost-finder ever since I had been able to rid her sister's apartment of a poltergeist the year before.

The house in question was 104 years old, stashed away in what New Yorkers called "Hell's Kitchen," the old area in the 40s between Ninth and Tenth Avenues, close to the theater district. Built on the corner of Forty-fourth Street and Ninth Avenue, it had been in the possession of the Rodenberg family until a Mr. Payne bought it. He remodeled it carefully, with a great deal of respect for the old plans. He did nothing to change its quaint Victorian appearance, inside or out.

About three years later, glamorous stage and television star June Havoc bought the house, and rented the upper floors to various tenants. She herself moved into the downstairs apartment, simply because no one else wanted it. It didn't strike her as strange at the time that no tenant had ever renewed the lease on that floor-through downstairs apartment, but now she knows why. It was all because of *Hungry Lucy*.

The morning after Gail's call, June Havoc telephoned me, and a séance was arranged for Friday of that week. I immediately reached British medium Sybil Leek, but I gave no details. I merely invited her to help me get rid of a noisy ghost. Noise was what June Havoc complained about.

"It seems to be a series of *insistent* sounds," she said. "First, they were rather soft. I didn't really notice them three years ago. Then I had the architect who built that balcony in the back come in and asked him to investigate these sounds. He said there was nothing whatever the matter with the house. Then I had the plumber up, because I thought it was the steam pipes. He said it was not that either. Then I had the carpenter in, for it is a very old house, but he couldn't find any structural defects whatever."

"When do you hear these tapping noises?"

"At all times. Lately, they seem to be more insistent. More demanding. We refer to it as 'tap dancing,' for that is exactly what it sounds like."

The wooden floors were in such excellent state that Miss Havoc didn't cover them with carpets. The yellow pine used for the floorboards cannot be replaced today.

June Havoc's maid had heard loud tapping in Miss Havoc's absence, and many of her actor friends had remarked on it.

"It is always in this area," June Havoc pointed out, "and seems to come from underneath the kitchen floor. It has become impossible to sleep a full night's sleep in this room."

The kitchen leads directly into the rear section of the floor-through apartment, to a room used as a bedroom. Consequently, any noise disturbed her sleep.

Underneath Miss Havoc's apartment, there was another floor-through, but the tenants had never reported anything unusual there, nor had the ones on the upper floors. Only Miss Havoc's place was noisy.

We now walked from the front of the apartment into the back half. Suddenly there was a loud tapping sound from underneath the floor, as if someone had shot off a machine gun. Catherine and I had arrived earlier than the rest, and there were just the three of us.

"No house here."

"How long have you been here?"

"A long time."

"What year is this?"

"Seventeen ninety-two."

"What do you do in this house?"

"No house . . . people . . . fields . . . "

"Why then are you here? What is there here for you?"

The ghost snorted.

"Hm . . . men."

"Who brought you here?"

"Came . . . people sent us away . . . soldiers . . . follow them . . . sent me away . . . ."

"What army? Which regiment?"

"Napier."

"How old are you?"

"Twenty."

"Where were you born?"

"Hawthorne . . . not very far away from here."

I was not sure whether she said "Hawthorne" or "Hawgton," or some similar name.

"What is your father's name?"

Silence.

"Your mother's name?"

Silence.

"Were you baptized?"

"Baptized?"

She didn't remember that either.

I explained that she had passed on. It did not matter.

"Stay here . . . until I get some food . . . meat . . . meat and corn . . . "

"Have you tried to communicate with anyone in this house?"

"Nobody listens."

"How are you trying to make them listen?"

"I make a noise because I want food."

"Why do you stay in one area? Why don't you move around freely?"

"Can't. Can't go away. Too many people. Soldiers."

"Where are your parents?"

"Dead."

"What is your mother's name?"

"Mae."

"Her maiden name?"

"Don't know."

"Your father's first name?"

"Terry."

"Were any of your family in the army?"

Ironical laughter punctuated her next words.

"Only . . . me."

"Tell me the names of some of the officers in the army you knew."

"Alfred . . . Wait."

"Any rank?"

"No rank."

"What regiment did you follow?"

"Just this . . . Alfred."

"And he left you?"

"Yes. I went with some other man, then I was hungry and I came here."

"Why here?"

"I was sent here."

"By whom?"

"They made me come. Picked me up. Man brought me here. Put me down on the ground."

"Did you die in this spot?"

"Die, die? I'm not dead. *I'm hungry*."

I then asked her to join her parents, those who loved her, and to leave this spot. She refused. She wanted to walk by the river, she said. I suggested that she was not receiving food and could leave freely. After a while, the ghost seemed to slip away peacefully and Sybil Leek returned to her own body, temporarily vacated so that Lucy could speak through it. As usual, Sybil remembered absolutely nothing of what went on when she was in deep trance. She was crying, but thought her mascara was the cause of it.

Suddenly, the ghost was back. The floorboards were reverberating with the staccato sound of an angry tap, loud, strong, and demanding.

"What do you want?" I asked again, although I knew now what she wanted.

Sybil also extended a helping hand. But the sound stopped as abruptly as it had begun.

A while later, we sat down again. Sybil reported feeling two presences.

"One is a girl, the other is a man. A man with a stick. Or a gun. The girl is stronger. She wants something."

Suddenly, Sybil pointed to the kitchen area.

"What happened in the corner?"

Nobody had told Sybil of the area in which the disturbances had always taken place.

"I feel her behind me now. A youngish girl, not very well dressed, Georgian period. I don't get the man too well."

At this point, we brought into the room a small Victorian wooden table, a gift from Gail Benedict.

Within seconds after Sybil, June Havoc, and I had lightly placed our hands upon it, it started to move, seemingly of its own volition!

Rapidly, it began to tap out a word, using a kind of Morse code. While Earl Wilson was taking notes, we allowed the table to jump hither and yon, tapping out a message.

None of us touched the table top except lightly. There was no question of manipulating the table. The light was very bright, and our hands almost touched, so that any pressure by one of us would have been instantly noticed by the other two. This type of communication is slow, since the table runs through the entire alphabet until it reaches the desired letter, then the next letter, until an entire word has been spelled out.

"L-e-a-v-e," the communicator said, not exactly in a friendly mood.

Evidently she wanted the place to herself and thought *we* were the intruders.

I tried to get some more information about her. But instead of tapping out another word in an orderly fashion, the table became very excited — if that is the word for emotional tables — and practically leapt from beneath our hands. We were required to follow it to keep up the contact, as it careened wildly through the room. When I was speaking, it moved toward me and practically crept onto my lap. When I wasn't speaking, it ran to someone else in the room. Eventually, it became so wild, at times entirely off the floor, that it slipped from our light touch and, as the power was broken, instantly rolled into a corner — just another table with no life of its own.

We repaired to the garden, a few steps down an iron staircase, in the rear of the house.

"Sybil, what do you feel down here?" I asked.

"I had a tremendous urge to come out here. I didn't know there was a garden. Underneath my feet almost is the cause of the disturbance."

We were standing at a spot adjacent to the basement wall and close to the center of the tapping disturbance we had heard.

"Someone may be buried here," Sybil remarked, pointing to a mound of earth underneath our feet. "It's a girl."

"Do you see the wire covering the area behind you?" June Havoc said. "I tried to plant seeds there, and the wire was to protect them — but somehow nothing, nothing will grow there."

"Plant something on this mound," Sybil suggested. "It may well pacify *her*."

We returned to the upstairs apartment, and soon after broke up the "ghost hunting party," as columnist Sheila Graham called it later.

The next morning, I called June Havoc to see how things were. I knew from experience that the ghost would either be totally gone, or totally mad, but not the same as before.

Lucy, I was told, was rather mad. Twice as noisy, she still demanded her pound of flesh. I promised June Havoc that we'd return until the ghost was completely gone.

A few days passed. Things became a little quieter, as if Lucy were hesitating. Then something odd happened the next night. Instead of tapping from her accustomed corner area, Lucy moved away from it and tapped away from above June's bed. She had never been heard from that spot before.

I decided it was time to have a chat with Lucy again. Meanwhile, corroboration of the information we had obtained had come to us quickly. The morning after our first séance, Bob Winter-Berger called. He had been to the New York Public Library and checked on Napier, the officer named by the medium as the man in charge of the soldier's regiment.

The *Dictionary of National Biography* contained the answer. Colonel George Napier, a British officer, had served on the staff of Governor Sir Henry Clinton. How exciting, I thought. The Clinton mansion once occupied the very ground we were having the séance on. In fact, I had reported on a ghost at Clinton Court, two short blocks to the north, in *Ghost Hunter* and again in *Ghosts I've Met*. As far as I knew, the place was still not entirely free of the uncanny, for reports continued to reach me of strange steps and doors opening by themselves.

Although the mansion itself no longer stands, the carriage house in the rear was now part of Clinton Court, a reconstructed apartment house on West Forty-sixth Street. How could Sybil Leek, only recently arrived from England, have known of these things?

Napier was indeed the man who had charge of a regiment on this very spot, and the years 1781-1782 are given as the time when Napier's family contracted the dreaded yellow fever and died. Sir Henry Clinton forbade his aide to be in touch with them, and the Colonel was shipped off to England, half-dead himself, while his wife and family passed away on the spot that later became Potter's Field.

Many Irish immigrants came to the New World in those years. Perhaps the Ryan girl was one of them, or her parents were. Unfortunately, history does not keep much of a record of camp followers.

On January 15, 1965, precisely at midnight, I placed Sybil Leek into deep trance in my apartment on Riverside Drive. In the past we had succeeded in contacting *former* ghosts once they had been pried loose in an initial séance in the haunted house itself. I had high hopes that Lucy would communicate and I wasn't disappointed.

"Tick, tock, tickety-tock, June's clock stops, June's clock stops," the entranced medium murmured, barely audibly.

"Tickety-tock, June's clock stops, tickety-tock . . . "

"Who are you?" I asked.

"Lucy."

"Lucy, what does this mean?"

"June's clock stops, June's clock stops, frightened June, frightened June," she repeated like a child reciting a poem.

"Why do you want to frighten June?"

"Go away."

"Why do you want her to go away?"

"People there . . . too much house . . . too much June . . . too many clocks . . . she sings, she dances, she makes a lot of noise . . . I'm hungry, I'm always hungry. You don't do a thing about it . . . "

"Will you go away if I get you some food? Can we come to an agreement?"

"Why?"

"Because I want to help you, help June."

"Ah, same old story."

"You're not happy. Would you like to see Alfred again?"

"Yes . . . he's gone."

"Not very far. I'll get you together with Alfred if you will leave the house."

"Where would I go?"

"Alfred has a house of his own for you."

"Where?"

"Not very far."

"Frightened to go . . . don't know where to go . . . nobody likes me. She makes noises, I make noises. I don't like that clock."

"Where were you born, Lucy?"

"Larches by the Sea . . . Larchmont . . . by the Sea . . . people disturb me."

Again I asked her to go to join her Alfred, to find happiness again. I suggested she call for him by name, which she did, hesitatingly at first, more desperately later.

"No . . . I can't go from here. He said he would come. He said *wait*. Wait . . . here. Wait. Alfred, why don't you come? Too many clocks. Time, time, time . . . noisy creature. Time, time . . . three o'clock."

"What happened at three o'clock?" I demanded.

"He said he'd come," the ghost replied. "I waited for him."

"Why at three o'clock in the middle of the night?"

"Why do you think? Couldn't get out. Locked in. Not allowed out at night. I'll wait. He'll come."

"Did you meet any of his friends?"

"Not many . . . what would *I* say?"

"What was Alfred's name?"

"Bailey . . . Alfred said 'Wait, wait . . . I'll go away,' he said. 'They'll never find me.'"

"Go to him with my love," I said, calmly repeating over and over the formula used in rescue circle operations to send the earthbound ghost across the threshold.

As I spoke, Lucy slipped away from us, not violently as she had come, but more or less resignedly.

I telephoned June Havoc to see what had happened that night between midnight and 12:30. She had heard Lucy's tapping precisely then, but nothing more as the night passed — a quiet night for a change.

Was Lucy on her way to her Alfred?

We would know soon enough.

In the weeks that followed, I made periodic inquiries of June Havoc. Was the ghost still in evidence? Miss Havoc did not stay at her townhouse all the time, prefering the quiet charm of her Connecticut estate. But on the nights when she did sleep in the house on Forty-fourth Street, she was able to observe that Lucy Ryan had changed considerably in personality — the ghost had been freed, yes, but had not yet been driven from the house. In fact, the terrible noise was now all over the house, although less frequent and less vehement — *as if she were thinking things over.*

I decided we had to finish the job as well as we could and another séance was arranged for late March, 1965. Present were — in addition to our hostess and chief sufferer — my wife Catherine and myself; Emory Lewis, editor of *Cue* magazine; Barry Farber, WOR commentator; and two friends of June Havoc. We grouped ourselves around a table in the *front room* this time. This soon proved to be a mistake. No Lucy Ryan. No ghost. We repaired to the other room where the original manifestations had taken place, with more luck this time.

Sybil, in trance, told us that the girl had gone, but that Alfred had no intention of leaving. He was waiting for *her* now. I asked for the name of his commanding officer and was told it was Napier. This we knew already. But who was the next in rank?

"Lieutenant William Watkins."

"What about the commanding general?"

He did not know.

He had been born in Hawthorne, just like Lucy, he told Sybil. I had been able to trace this Hawthorne to a place not far away in Westchester County.

There were people all over, Sybil said in trance, and they were falling down. They were ill.

"Send Alfred to join his Lucy," I commanded, and Sybil in a low voice told the stubborn ghost to go.

After an interlude of table tipping, in which several characters from the nether world made their auditory appearance, she returned to trance. Sybil in trance was near the river again, among the sick.

But no Lucy Ryan. Lucy's gone, she said.

"The smell makes me sick," Sybil said, and you could see stark horror in her sensitive face.

"Dirty people, rags, people in uniform too, with dirty trousers. There is a big house across the river."

"Whose house is it?"

"Mr. Dawson's. Doctor Dawson. Dr. James Dawson . . . Lee Point. Must go there. Feel sick. Rocks and trees, just the house across the river."

"What year is this?"

"Ninety-two."

She then described Dr. Dawson's house as having three windows on the left, two on the right, and five above, and said that it was called Lee Point — Hawthorne. It sounded a little like Hawgton to me, but I can't be sure.

Over the river, she said. She described a "round thing on a post" in front of the house, like a shell. For messages, she thought.

"What is the name of the country we're in?" I asked.

"Vinelands. Vinelands."

I decided to change the subject back to Hungry Lucy. How did she get sick?

"She didn't get any food, and then she got cold, by the river.

". . . Nobody helped them here. Let them die. Buried them in a pit."

"What is the name of the river?"

"Mo . . . Mo-something."

"Do you see anyone else still around?"

"Lots of people with black faces, black shapes."

The plague, I thought, and how little the doctors could do in those days to stem it.

I asked about the man in charge and she said "Napier" and I wondered who would be left in command after Napier left, and the answer this time was, "Clinton . . . old fool. Georgie."

There were a Henry Clinton and a George Clinton, fairly contemporary with each other.

"What happened after that?"

"Napier died."

"Any other officers around?"

"Little Boy Richardson . . . Lieutenant."

"What regiment?"

"Burgoyne."

Sybil, entranced, started to hiss and whistle. "Signals," she murmured. "As the men go away, they whistle."

I decided the time had come to bring Sybil out of trance. She felt none the worse for it, and asked for something to drink. *Hungry*, like Lucy, she wasn't.

We began to evaluate the information just obtained. Dr. James

Dawson may very well have lived. The A.M.A. membership directories aren't that old. I found the mention of Lee Point and Hawthorne interesting, inasmuch as the two locations are quite close. Lee, of course, would be Fort Lee, and there is a "point" or promontory in the river at that spot.

The town of Vinelands does exist in New Jersey, but the river beginning with "Mo-" may be the Mohawk. That Burgoyne was a general in the British army during the Revolution is well known.

So there you have it. Sybil Leek knows very little, if anything, about the New Jersey and Westchester countryside, having only recently come to America. Even I, then a New York resident for 27 years, had never heard of Hawthorne before. Yet there it is on the way to Pleasantville, New York.

The proof of the ghostly pudding, however, was not the regimental roster, but the state of affairs at June Havoc's house.

A later report had it that Lucy, Alfred, or whoever was responsible, had quieted down considerably.

They were down, but not out.

I tactfully explained to June Havoc that feeling sorry for a hungry ghost makes things tough for a parapsychologist. The emotional pull of a genuine attachment, no matter how unconscious it may be, can provide the energies necessary to prolong the stay of the ghost.

Gradually, as June Havoc — wanting a peaceful house, especially at 3 A.M. — allowed practical sense to outweigh sentimentality, the shades of Hungry Lucy and her soldier-boy faded into the distant past, whence they came.

Proper Bostonian Ghosts

The proper Bostonian ghosts here are not the political skeletons rattling in many a Back Bay closet. In Boston, a ghost is a ghost. But make no mistake, something of their English forebears has rubbed off on many a Bostonian. They take their specters with grim pride and a matter of nature — it is part of the regional scenery, so to speak, and really all terribly chic, but the Bostonian prefers to pretend it's nothing much. Far from it. New England ghosts can be pretty exciting stuff.

Sometimes New Englanders take the memories of their ghosts with them even when they move to other states. A Mrs. C. E. Foster once wrote me from Indianapolis about her grandmother, who seems to have been buried alive. At the time her grandmother, Louisa Wallace, was lowered into her grave in Revere, Massachusetts, Mrs. Foster had a vision of her in the casket . . . and heard her cough. The dead don't do that, and Mrs. Foster thinks her grandmother tried to tell her that she wasn't quite ready yet. Unfortunately, nothing was done about it at the time, so she went, ready or not.

. . . .

Many of my contacts have been made through a Boston radio program called "Contact," with Bob Kennedy, on Station WBZ. I appeared on it many times and always found it most rewarding. After one of my radio stints in the fall of 1963, I was approached by a young lady with the appealing name of Aimee Violante, a nurse who had a most interesting and rather touching experience she wanted to tell me about.

"In 1957, my boyfriend took me to Lake Quannapowette outside of Boston. We rented a rowboat and rowed to the other side of the lake to go swimming, as swimming was prohibited there.

"In the boat, I sat facing the opposite shore. We were heading for a strip of beach with a few benches on it. There were three benches. It was nearing dusk. Sitting on these benches were elderly people all dressed in white. The ladies were dressed in silky dresses, wearing big picture hats and gloves. The men wore white suits. They were just sitting watching us. They weren't frightening, so I didn't pay too much attention to them, but I was angry that my boyfriend was pulling in there, as I thought they would say something about us going swimming. He didn't see them, as his back was toward them, and when we pulled up, they were gone.

"When we rowed back, I was wondering where they all went to, so I asked him. When I told him about the people I saw, he got frightened and hurried me back to the car. There he told me that on the side we were on was a cemetery, and there was no way any people could get to the benches once the gates were closed."

....

The Peter Hofmann family consisted of husband, wife Pennie, and baby — then about three or four years old. The parents were articulate, well-educated people making their home in Harvard. Not Harvard University, but Harvard near Ayer, Massachusetts, about an hour's ride from the university.

An automobile accident in 1956 had left Mrs. Hofmann partially paralyzed, but her keen gift of observation was not impaired. She had always had a peculiar liking for graveyards, and her first psychic experience, in 1951, consisted of a vision of a horse-drawn hearse that had passed near a cemetery. One could argue that lots of such hearses used to pull into cemeteries, but the fact remains that Mrs. Hofmann's was not a real one.

Their house stands next to a house built by Mrs. Hofmann's father, a well-known physician, and it seemed that both houses were haunted. The larger house, owned by Mrs. Hofmann's father, was built in 1721 "on the bounty received from an Indian scalp."

From the first moment she saw it, Pennie Hofmann had odd sensations about it. In 1960 or 1961, she and her husband were spending the night there, when at about two in the morning they both woke up for no apparent reason.

"I spoke to what I thought was Pete," she said, "as I could see someone by the front window, but it turned out that Pete was *behind* me. Needless to say, we left right away."

Peter Hofmann nodded and added: "I myself have been in the house at night a few times alone, and I've always had the feeling I was being watched."

Then in late October, 1963, Pennie Hofmann phoned me in New York. Could I please come to Boston and tell her if she was *seeing things?*

What sort of things, I asked.

"Well," she replied, somewhat upset, "we'd been staying over in my father's house again a week ago. I saw a soldier in the bedroom. He was dark and had a noose around the neck; the rope was cut and his face seemed almost luminous. I swear I saw him."

I hurried to Boston and they met me at radio station WBZ.

What about the ghostly soldier? Any clues?

Both Hofmanns nodded.

"We've checked in Nourse's *History of the Town of Harvard*," Mrs. Hoffman said gravely, "and there was a Colonial drummer named Hill who was hanged in this area . . . for some misdeeds."

I remembered her telling me of a ghost in their own house on Poor Farm Road, and Mrs. Hofmann filled me in on this far gentler wraith.

"During the summer months, " she explained, "there is what appears to be a Quaker lady that walks across our front lawn, usually during the afternoon. This person often appears many times a day."

Her husband added that she had given him many details of the ghost's dress, which he checked for authenticity. He found that they were indeed worn by the Quaker women of the eighteenth century.

Why a member of so gentle a persuasion as the Quakers would turn into a ghost we may never know, but perhaps someday the Quaker lady will walk again for me.

．．．．．．．．．．．．．．．．．．．．．．．．．．

There is said to be the ghost of a pirate near the water's edge in old Boston, where so many secret passages existed in the days when Massachusetts was British. The *Black Lady of Warren Island,* out in the bay, has been seen by a number of people. She was executed during the Civil War for helping her husband, a Yankee prisoner, break out of prison.

Boston's emotional climate is fine for special activities. There may not be any medieval castles, but Beacon Hill can look pretty forbidding, too — especially on a chilly November night when the fog drifts in from the sea.

In September of 1963 I appeared on WBZ-TV on Mike Douglas's television show, discussing my ever-present interest in haunted houses. As a consequence, there was an avalanche of letters, many of which contained leads to new cases.

One came from a Mrs. Anne Valukis, of South Natick, near Boston, Massachusetts. She wrote me of an old house she lived in where the stairs creaked unaccountably at odd times, as if someone were walking up and down them; of the strange behavior her little boy showed whenever he was in a certain room of the house; and of an overall atmosphere of the uncanny prevailing throughout the house, as if an unseen force were always present.

I wrote for additional data about herself and the background of the house. Meanwhile, the public television station in Boston, Channel 2, took an interest in my work, and the station and I decided to join forces for an expedition to the haunted house in South Natick. Fred Barzyk, the director, undertook the preliminary task of additional research. My visit was scheduled for the last week of October. Mrs. Valukis wasn't long in answering me.

"The stairs haven't creaked for over a week, but my four year old woke Saturday night four times, and was really scared, so much so he would not go back upstairs to his room . . . Years ago this house was kind of a speakeasy, connected to a dance hall that was on the Charles River. Probably anything could have happened here. Who knows?"

Not because of the spooky stairs, but for other reasons, the Valukis family decided to move to Anne's parents' house. This made our visit problematical, until Fred Barzyk discovered that the house belonging to Mrs. Valukis' parents was even more haunted than Anne Valukis' place.

Mrs. Rose Josselyn, Anne's mother, was a Canadian Indian, and, like many of her people, had had psychic experiences all her life.

About 39 years before I met her, Mrs. Josselyn was living in Annapolis Royal, Canada, in what was purported to be a haunted house. Frequently she awoke in the middle of the night and found it difficult to breathe. Her arms seemed to be pinned down by an unseen force and she was unable to move even so much as a finger!

"It felt as if someone were choking me," she said to me later. "I tried to scream, but could not move my lips."

This had gone on for about a year. Finally Rose told her mother,

who was mediumistic herself, and Rose was forbidden ever to sleep
again in "that room." Twenty years later, Mrs. Josselyn still remembered the stark terror of those nights in Canada, but nothing like it
had happened to her since — nothing, that is, until she moved into
this house.

The house itself was a gray-white, medium-sized early American
house, built in the stately manner of early Georgian architecture and
very well preserved. It was set back from the road a bit, framed by
tall, shady trees, and one had the feeling of being far from the bustle
of the big city. Built about 150 years before, the house had an upper
story and a total of eight rooms. Bordering on the lawn of the house
was a cemetery, separated from the Josselyn house by an iron gate
and fence.

When the Josselyns moved in with their family, Mrs. Josselyn had
no thoughts of anything psychic or uncanny. She soon learned
differently.

Upstairs, there were two bedrooms separated only by a thin wall.
The larger one belonged to Mrs. Josselyn; the smaller one, to the rear
of the house, to her husband Roy. It was in her bedroom that Mrs.
Josselyn had another attack of the terrible feeling she had experienced in her Canadian youth. Pinned down on her bed, it was as if
someone were upon her, holding her.

"Whose bedroom was this before you took it?" I inquired.

"Well, my daughter-in-law slept here for awhile," Mrs. Josselyn
confided, "that is, before she died."

I asked further questions about this girl. At the age of 21, she had
fallen ill and suffered her last agonies in this very room, before being
taken off to a hospital, never to return. Her only child, to whom she
was naturally very attached, was reared by Mrs. Josselyn and Mrs.
Valukis.

I walked across the floor to a small room belonging to David
Josselyn, 17, the brother of Mrs. Valukis. Here I was shown a hand-

made wooden chair that was said to creak at odd moments, as if someone were sitting in it. David himself had been awakened many times by this unearthly behavior of his chair, and Anne had also observed the noise. I tried the chair. It was sturdy enough, and only strong efforts on my part produced any kind of noise. It could not have creaked by itself.

"Who gave you this chair?" I asked.

"The same man who made our clock downstairs," David said. I recalled seeing a beautiful wooden grandfather clock in the corner of the downstairs room. The odd thing about that clock was it sometimes ticked and the hands moved, even though it no longer had any works or pendulum!

The clock, chair, and a desk in David's room were the work of a skilled craftsman named Thomas Council, who was a well-liked house guest of the Josselyns and gave them these things to show his gratitude for their hospitality. He was a lonely bachelor and the Josselyns were his only close friends. David in particular was the apple of his eye. Thomas Council's body rested comfortably, it is hoped, across the way in the cemetery, and the Josselyns made sure there were always fresh flowers on his grave.

I decided to return to Mrs. Josselyn's room.

"Outside of your nightmarish experiences here and in Canada," I said, "have you had any other psychic incidents?"

Mrs. Josselyn, a serious, quiet woman of about 59, thought for a moment.

"Yes, frequently. Whenever my children are in some sort of trouble, I just know it. No matter how trifling. You might say we have telepathic contact."

"Did you also hear those stairs creak at your daughter's house across the road?"

"Yes, many times."

"Was that after or before your daughter-in-law passed away?"

"After."

"I clearly heard those steps upstairs, and there wasn't anyone but me and the baby in the house," added Anne Valukis for corroboration.

They all had been visited, it seemed to me, except the father, Roy Josselyn. It was time I turned my attention in his direction.

Mr. Josselyn sat on the bed in his room, quietly smoking a pipe. I had been warned by Fred Barzyk that the man of the house was no particular believer in the supernatural. To my relief, I discovered Mr. Josselyn at least had an open mind. I also discovered that a great-aunt of his in Vermont had been a spiritualistic medium.

I asked if he had seen or heard anything unusual.

"Well," he said, "about a year ago I started to hear some moans and groans around here . . . " he pointed toward the wall adjoining the bedroom occupied by his wife. "At first I thought it was my wife, but there was no one in her room at the time. I looked."

"This moaning . . . was it a human voice?"

"Oh yes, very human. Couldn't sleep a wink while it lasted."

"When did you last hear it?"

"Yesterday," he said laconically.

"How did you and your daughter-in-law get along?" I suddenly felt compelled to ask.

"Very well," he said. "As a matter of fact, she took more to me than to anyone else. You know how women are — a bit jealous. She was a little on the possessive side as far as her baby was concerned. I mean, she was very much worried about the child."

"But she wasn't jealous of you?"

"No, not of me. We were very close."

I thought of the 21-year-old girl taken by death without being ready for it, and the thoughts of fear for her child that must have gone through her mind those dreadful last hours when her moaning filled the air of the room next to Roy Josselyn's.

I also thought about Mrs. Roy Josselyn's background — the fact that she was Princess of the Micmac Indian Tribe. I remembered how frequent psychic experiences were among Indians, who are so much closer to nature than we city-dwellers.

Perhaps the restless spirit of the 21-year-old girl wanted some attention. Perhaps her final moments had only impressed themselves on the atmosphere of the upstairs room and were relived by the psychically sensitive members of the family. Perhaps, too, Thomas Council, the family friend, roamed the house now and then to make sure everything was all right with his favorite family.

When we drove back to Boston late that night, I felt sure I had met a haunted family, for better or worse.

The Ghost of Gay Street

Frank Paris and T. E. Lewis were puppeteers. Children came to admire the little theater the two puppeteers had set up in the high-ceilinged basement of their old house in Greenwich Village, that old section of New York going back to the 1700s. The house at number 12 Gay Street was a typical old townhouse, smallish, the kind New Yorkers built around 1800 when "the village" meant *far uptown*.

In 1924, a second section was added to the house, covering the garden that used to grace the back of the house. This architectural graft created a kind of duplex, one apartment on top of another, with small rooms at the sides in the rear.

The ownership of the house in the early days is hazy. At one time a sculptor owned number 12, possibly before the 1930s. Evidently he was fond of bootleg liquor, for he built a trap door in the ground floor of the newer section of the house, probably over his hidden liquor cabinet. Before that, Mayor Jimmy Walker owned the house, and used it *well*, although not *wisely*. One of his many loves is said to have been the tenant there. By a strange set of circumstances, the records of the house vanished like a ghost from the files of the Hall of Records around that time.

Later, real-estate broker Mary Ellen Strunsky lived in the house. In 1956, she sold it to the puppeteer team of Paris and Lewis, who had been there ever since, living in the upstairs apartment and using the lower portion as a workroom and studio for their little theater.

None of this, incidentally, was known to me until after the visit I paid the house in the company of my medium for the evening, Betty Ritter.

It all started when a reporter from the *New York World-Telegram*, Cindy Hughes, came to interview me, and casually dropped a hint that she knew of a haunted house. Faster than you can say *Journal-American*, I had her promise to lead me to this house. On a particularly warm night in May of 1963, I followed Miss Hughes down to Gay Street. Betty Ritter knew nothing at all about the case; she didn't even know the address where we were going.

We were greeted warmly by Frank Paris, who led us up the stairs into the upper apartment. The sight of the elaborately furnished, huge living room was surprising. Oriental figurines, heavy drapes, paintings, statuary, and antiques filled the room.

In two comfortable chairs we found awaiting us two friends of the owners: an intense looking man in his thirties, Richard X., who, I later discovered, was an editor by profession, and Alice May Hall, a charming lady of undetermined age.

I managed to get Betty out of earshot, so I could question these people without her getting impressions from our conversation.

"What is this about the house being haunted?" I asked Frank Paris.

He nodded gravely.

"I was working downstairs with some lacquer. It was late, around 3 A.M. Suddenly, I began to smell a strong odor of violets. My black spaniel here also smelled it, for he started to sniff rather strangely. And yet, Ted, my partner, in the same room with me, did not get the strange scent at all. But there is more. People waltz up and down the stairs at night, time and again."

"What do you mean, *waltz?*"

"I mean they go up and down, up and down, as if they had business here," Frank explained, and I thought, perhaps they had, perhaps they had.

"A weekend visitor also had a most peculiar experience here," Frank Paris continued. "He knew nothing about our haunted reputation, of course. We were away on a short trip, and when we got back, he greeted us with — 'Say, who are all these people going up and down the stairs?' He had thought that the house next door was somehow connected to ours, and that what he heard were people from next door. But of course, there is no connection whatever."

"And did you ever investigate these mysterious footsteps?" I asked.

"Many times," Frank and Ted nodded simultaneously, "but there was never anyone there — anyone of flesh-and-blood, that is."

I thanked them, and wondered aloud if they weren't psychic, since they had experienced what can only be called psychic phenomena.

Frank Paris hesitated, then admitted that he thought both of them were to some extent.

"We had a little dog which we had to have put away one day. We loved the dog very much, but it was one of those things that had to be done. For over a year after the dog's death, both of us felt him poking us in the leg — a habit he had in life. This happened on many occasions to both of us."

I walked over to where Miss Hall, the gray-haired little lady, sat.

"Oh, there is a ghost here all right," she volunteered. "It was in February of 1963, and I happened to be in the house, since the boys and I are good friends. I was sitting here in this very spot, relaxing and casually looking toward the entrance door through which you just came — the one that leads to the hallway and the stairs. There was a man there, wearing evening clothes, and an Inverness Cape —

I saw him quite plainly. He had dark hair. It was dusk, and there was still some light outside."

"What did you do?"

"I turned my head to tell Frank Paris about the stranger, and that instant he was gone like a puff of smoke."

Paris broke in.

"I questioned her about this, since I didn't really believe it. But a week later, at dawn this time, I saw the ghost myself, exactly as Alice had described him — wearing evening clothes, a cape, hat, and his face somewhat obscured by the shadows of the hallway. Both Alice and I are sure he was a youngish man, and had sparkling eyes. What's more, our dog also saw the intruder. He went up to the ghost, friendly-like, as if to greet him."

Those were the facts of the case. A ghost in evening clothes, an old house where heaven knows what might have happened at one time or another, and a handful of psychic people.

I returned to Betty Ritter, and asked her to gather psychic impressions while walking about the house.

"A crime was committed here," the medium said, and described a terrible argument upstairs between an Oriental and a woman. She described a gambling den, opium smokers, and a language she could not understand. The man's name was Ming, she said. Ming is a very common Chinese word meaning, I believe, Sun.

Betty also told Frank Paris that someone close to him by the name of John had passed on and that he had something wrong with his right eye, which Paris acknowledged was correct. She told Ted Lewis that a Bernard L. was around him, not knowing, of course, that Lewis' father was named Bernham Lewis. She told Richard X. that he worked with books, and it was not until after the séance that I learned he was an editor by profession. I don't know about the Chinese and the opium den, but they are possibilities in an area so far removed from the bright lights of the city as the Village once was.

We went downstairs and, in the almost total darkness, formed a circle. Betty fell into trance, her neck suddenly falling back as if she were being possessed by a woman whose neck had been hurt.

"Emil," she mumbled, and added the woman had been decapitated, and her bones were still about. She then came out of trance and we walked back up the stairs to the oldest part of the house. Still "seeing" clairvoyantly, Betty Ritter again mumbled "Emil," and said she saw documents with government seals on them. She also felt someone named Mary Ellen had lived here and earlier some "well-known government official named Wilkins or Wilkinson."

Betty, of course, knew nothing about real-estate broker Mary Ellen Strunsky or Jimmy Walker, the former New York Mayor, who had been in this house for so long.

It now remained for us to find those bones Betty had talked about. We returned to the downstairs portion of the house, but Betty refused to go farther. Her impression of tragedy was so strong she urged us to desist.

Thus it was that the Ghost of Gay Street, whoever he may be, would have to wait just a little longer until the bones could be properly sorted out. It wasn't half bad, considering that Frank Paris and Ted Lewis put on a pretty nice puppet show every so often, down there in the murky basement theater at number 12 Gay Street.

When the Dead Stay On

Nothing is so exasperating as a dead person in a living household. I mean a ghost has a way of disturbing things far beyond the powers held by the wraith while still among the quick. Very few people realize that a ghost is not someone out to pester you for the sake of being an annoyance, or to attract attention for the sake of being difficult. Far from it. We know by now that ghosts are unhappy beings caught between two states and unable to adjust to either one.

Most people "pass over" without difficulty and are rarely heard from again, except when a spiritualist insists on raising them, or when an emergency occurs among the family that makes intervention by the departed a desired, or even necessary, matter.

They do their bit, and then go again, looking back at their handiwork with justified pride. *The dead are always among us,* make no mistake about that. They obey their own set of laws that forbids them to approach us or let us know their presence except when conditions require it. But they can do other things to let us feel them near, and these little things can mean a great deal when they are recognized as sure signs of a loved one's nearness.

Tragedies create ghosts through shock conditions, and nothing can send them out of the place where they found a sad end except the realization of their own emotional entanglement. This can be accomplished by allowing them to communicate through trance. But there are also cases in which the tragedy is not sudden, but gradual, and the unnatural attachment to physical life creates the ghost syndrome. The person who refuses to accept peacefully the transition called death, and holds on to material surroundings, becomes a ghost when these feelings of resistance and attachment become psychotic.

Such persons will then regard the houses they lived and died in as still theirs, and will look on later owners or tenants as merely unwanted intruders who must be forced out of the place by any means available. The natural way to accomplish this is to show themselves to the living as often as possible, to assert their continued ownership. If that won't do it, move objects, throw things, make noises — let them know whose house this is!

The reports of such happenings are many. Every week brings new cases from reliable and verified witnesses, and the pattern begins to emerge pretty clearly.

A lady from Ridgewood, New York, wrote to me about a certain house on Division Avenue in Brooklyn, where she had lived as a child. A young grandmother, Mrs. Petre had a good education and an equally good memory. She remembered the name of her landlord while she was still a youngster, and even the names of *all* her teachers at Public School 19. The house her family had rented consisted of a basement, parlor floor, and a top floor where the bedrooms were located.

On a certain warm October day, she found herself in the basement, while her mother was upstairs. She knew there was no one else in the house. When she glanced at the glass door shutting off the stairs, with the glass pane acting almost like a mirror, she saw to her amazement a man peeking around the doorway. Moments before she had heard heavy footsteps coming down the stairs, and wondered if someone had gotten into the house while she and her mother had been out shopping. She screamed and ran out of the house, but did not tell her family about the stranger.

Sometime after, she sat facing the same stairs in the company of her brother and sister-in-law, when she heard the footsteps again and the stranger appeared. Only this time she got a good look at him and was able to describe his thin, very pale face, his black hair, and the black suit and fedora hat he wore.

Nobody believed the girl, of course, and even the landlady accused her of imagining all this. But after a year, her father became alarmed at his daughter's nervousness and decided to move. Finally, the landlady asked for details of the apparition, and listened as the girl described the ghost she had seen.

"My God," the landlady, a Mrs. Grimshaw, finally said. "I knew that man — he hanged himself on the top floor!"

....

Sometimes the dead will only stay on until things have been straightened out to their taste. Anna Arrington was a lady with the gift of mediumship who lived in New York State. In 1944, her mother-in-law, a woman of some wealth, passed on in Wilmington, North Carolina, and was buried there. There was some question about her will. Three days after her death, Mrs. Arrington was awakened from heavy sleep at 3 A.M. by a hand touching hers.

Her first thought was that one of her two children wanted something. On awakening, however, she saw her mother-in-law in a flowing white gown standing at the foot of her bed. While her husband continued to snore, the ghost put a finger to Mrs. Arrington's lips and asked her not to awaken her son, but to remember that the missing will was in the dining room of her house on top of the dish closet under a sugar bowl. Mrs. Arrington was roundly laughed at by her husband the next morning, but several days later his sister returned from Wilmington (the Arringtons lived in New York City at the time) and confirmed that the will had indeed been found where the ghost had indicated.

....

Back in the 1960s, I was approached by a gentleman named Paul Herring, who was born in Germany, and who lived in a small apartment on Manhattan's Eastside as well as in a country house in Westchester County, New York. He was in the restaurant business and not given to dreaming or speculation. He struck me as a simple, solid citizen. His aged mother, also German-born, lived with him, and a large German shepherd dog completed the household.

Mr. Herring was not married, and his mother was a widow. What caused them to reach me was the peculiar way in which steps were heard around the Westchester house when nobody was walking. On three separate occasions, Mrs. Herring saw an apparition in her living room.

"It was sort of blackish," she said, "but I recognized it instantly. It was my late husband."

The "black outline" of a man also appeared near light fixtures, and there were noises in the house that had no natural origins.

"The doors are forever opening and closing by themselves," the son added. "We're going crazy trying to keep up with that spook."

Their bedspreads were being pulled off at night. They were touched on the face by an unseen hand, especially after dark.

The September before, Mrs. Herring was approaching the swinging doors of the living room, when the door moved out by itself and met her! A table in the kitchen moved by its own volition in plain daylight.

Her other son, Max, who lived in Norfolk, Virginia, always left the house in a hurry because "he can't breathe" in it. Her dog, Noxy, was forever disturbed when they were out in the Westchester house.

"How long has this been going on, Mrs. Herring?" I asked.

"About four years at least," the spunky lady replied, "but my husband died ten years ago."

It then developed that he had divorced her and married another woman, and there were no surviving children from that union. Still, the "other woman" had kept all of Mr. Herring Sr.'s money — no valid will was ever found. Was the ghost protesting this injustice to his companion of so many years? Was he regretting his hasty step divorcing her and marrying another?

The Herrings weren't the only ones to hear the footsteps. A prospective tenant who came to rent the country house fled after hearing someone walk *through a closed door.*

. . . .

Mrs. E. F. Newbold seems to have been followed by ghosts since childhood — as if she were carrying a lamp aloft to let the denizens of the nether world know she had the sixth sense.

"I'm haunted," she said. "I've been followed by a 'what's it' since I was quite young. It simply pulls the back of my skirt. No more than that, but when you're alone in the middle of a room, this can be awfully disconcerting."

I thought of Grandma Thurston's ghost, and how she had pulled my elbow a couple of years before while I was investigating an empty room in a pre-Colonial house in Connecticut, and I couldn't agree more. Mrs. Newbold's family had psychic experiences also. Her little girl had felt a hand on her shoulder. It ran in the family.

"My husband's aunt died in Florida, while I was in New Jersey. We had been very close, and I said good-bye to her body here at the funeral at 10 A.M. At 9 P.M. I went into my kitchen and though I could not see her, I *knew* she was sitting at the table, staring at my back, and pleading with me."

"What about this skirt pulling?"

"It has followed me through a house, an apartment, a succession of rented rooms, two new houses, and two old houses. I've had a feeling of not being alone, and of sadness. I've also felt a hand on my shoulder, and heard pacing footsteps, always overhead.

"The next house we lived in was about 35 years old, had had only one owner, still alive, and no one had died there. It looked like a haunted house, but it was only from neglect. We modernized it, and *then* it started! Pulling at my skirt went on fairly often. One night when I was alone, that is, my husband was out of town and our three children were sound asleep — I checked them just before and just after — I was watching TV in the living room, when I heard the outside cellar door open. I looked out the window to see if someone was breaking in, since I had locked the door shortly before. While I was watching, I *heard* it close firmly. The door didn't move, however. This door had a distinctive sound so I couldn't have mistaken it.

"I went back to my seat and picked up my scissors, wishing for a gun. I was sure I heard a prowler. Now I heard slow footsteps come up from the cellar, through the laundry room, kitchen, into the living room, right past me, and up the stairs to the second floor. They stopped at the top of the stairs, and I never heard it again. Nor do I want to. Those steps went past me, no more than five feet away, and the room was empty. Unfortunately, I have no corroboration, but I *was* wide awake and perfectly sober!"

So much for the lady from Harrington Park, New Jersey.

....

Miss Margaret C. and her family lived in what surely was a haunted house, so that I won't give her full name. But here is her report.

"In December of 1955, just two days before Christmas, I traveled to Pennsylvania to spend the holidays with my sister and her husband. They lived on the second floor (the apartment I am now renting) of a spacious mid-Victorian-style home built around a hundred years ago.

"Due to the death of my sister's mother-in-law, who had resided on the first floor of the house, the occasion was not an entirely joyous one, but we came for the sake of my brother-in-law.

"Having come all the way from Schenectady, New York, we retired between ten-thirty and eleven o'clock. The room I slept in was closest to the passage leading to the downstairs, and the two were separated only by a door.

"Once in bed, I found it rather difficult to sleep. As I lay there, I heard a piano playing. It sounded like a very old piano and it played church music. I thought it quite strange that my brother-in-law's father would be listening to his radio at that hour, but felt more annoyed than curious.

"The next morning, as we were having coffee, I mentioned this to my sister. She assured me that her father-in-law would *not* be listening to the radio at that hour and I assured *her* that I *had* heard piano music. It was then she mentioned the old piano her husband's mother had owned for many years and which sat in the downstairs front room.

"We decided to go and have a look at it. The dust that had settled on the keyboard was quite thick, and as definite as they could possibly be were the imprints of someone's fingers. Not normal fingers, but apparently quite thin and bony fingers. My sister's mother-in-law had been terribly thin and she loved to play her piano, especially church music. There was positively no one else in the house who even knew how to play the piano, except my mother, who lived with my sister and her husband."

....

Another New Jersey lady named Louise B., whose full name and address I have in my files, told me of an experience she will never forget.

"I cannot explain why I am sending this on to you, merely that I feel compelled to do so, and after many years of following my compulsions, as I call them, must do so.

"My mother had a bachelor cousin who died and was buried around Valentine's Day, 1932. He had lived with two maiden aunts in Ridgewood, New Jersey, for most of his lifetime. He was a well-known architect in this area. He designed local monuments, one of which is standing in the Park in Ridgewood today. He was short of stature, with piercing eyes and a bushy gray full beard, and he smoked too many cigars. I was not quite 14 years old when he passed away.

"My parents decided to spare me the burial detail, and they left me at home on the way to the cemetery with instructions to stay at home until they returned. They planned on attending the burial, going back to the house with my great-aunts and then coming home before dinner, which in our house was 6 P.M.

"I have no recollection of what I did with my time in the afternoon, but remember that just before dusk I had gone indoors and at the time I was in our dining room, probably setting the table for dinner, as this was one of my chores.

"We had three rooms downstairs: the living room faced north and ran the full length of the house, while the kitchen and dining room faced southeast and southwest respectively, and a T-shaped partition divided the rooms. There was a large archway separating the dining and living rooms.

"I don't recall when I became aware of a 'presence.' I didn't see anything with my eyes, rather I *felt* what I 'saw,' or somehow sensed it and my sense 'saw.' This is not a good explanation, but about the closest I can come to what I felt.

"This presence was not in any one spot in the room, but something that was gradually surrounding me, like the air that I was breathing, and it was frightening and menacing and very evil and stronger, and somehow the word *denser* seemed to apply and I knew that it was 'Uncle' Oscar. I could feel him coming at me from every direction (like music that gets louder and louder), and my senses 'saw' him as he had been dressed in the casket, with a red ribbon draped across his chest, only he was alive and I was aware of some terrible determination on his part and suddenly I knew that somehow he was trying to 'get inside me' and I began to back away. I don't recall speaking, nor his speaking to me. I just knew what his intention was and who he was. I last remember screaming helplessly and uselessly at him to go away. I do not know how long this lasted. I only know that suddenly he was gone, and my parents came into the room. I was hysterical, they tell me, and it took some doing to quiet me."

Many years later Mrs. B. discovered that "Uncle" Oscar had died a raving maniac to the last.

....

Grace Rivers was a secretary by profession, a lady of good background, and not given to hallucinations or emotional outbursts. I had spoken with her several times and always found her most reluctant to discuss what to her seemed incredible.

It seemed that on weekends, Miss Rivers and another secretary, by the name of Juliet, were the house guests of their employer, John Bergner, in Westbrook, Connecticut. Miss Rivers was also a good friend of this furniture manufacturer, a man in his middle fifties. She had joined the Bergner firm in 1948, six years after John Bergner had become the owner of a country house built in 1865.

Bergner liked to spend his weekends among his favorite employees, and sometimes asked some of the office boys as well as his two secretaries to come up to Connecticut with him. All was most idyllic until the early 1950s, when John Bergner met an advertising man by the name of Philip Mervin. This business relationship soon broadened into a social friendship, and before long Mr. Mervin was a steady and often self-invited house guest in Westbrook.

At first, this did not disturb anyone very much, but when Mervin noticed the deep and growing friendship between Bergner and his right-hand girl, something akin to jealousy prompted him to interfere with this relationship at every turn. What made this triangle even more difficult for Mervin to bear was the apparent innocence with which Bergner treated Mervin's approaches. Naturally, a feeling of dislike grew into hatred between Miss Rivers and the intruder, but before it came to any open argument, the advertising man suddenly died of a heart attack at age 51.

But that did not seem to be the end of it by a long shot.

Soon after his demise, the Connecticut weekends were again interrupted, this time by strange noises no natural cause could account for. Most of the uncanny experiences were witnessed by both girls as well as by some of the office boys, who seemed frightened by it all. With the detachment of a good executive secretary, Miss Rivers lists the phenomena:

Objects moving in space.

Stones hurled at us inside and outside the house.

Clanging of tools in the garage at night (when nobody was there).

Washing machine starting up at 1 A.M., *by itself.*

Heavy footsteps, banging of doors, in the middle of the night.

Television sets turning themselves on and off at will.

A spoon constantly leaping out of a cutlery tray.

The feeling of a cold wind being swept over one.

And there was more, much more.

When a priest was brought to the house to exorcise the ghost, things only got worse. Evidently the deceased had little regard for holy men.

Juliet, the other secretary, brought her husband along. One night in 1962, when Juliet's husband slept in what was once the advertising man's favorite guest room, he heard clearly a series of knocks, as if someone were hitting the top of the bureau. Needless to say, her husband had been alone in the room, and he did not do the knocking.

It became so bad that Grace Rivers no longer looked forward to those weekend invitations at her employer's country home. She feared them. It was then that she remembered, with terrifying suddenness, a remark the late Mr. Mervin had made to her fellow-workers.

"If anything ever happens to me and I die, I'm going to walk after those two girls the rest of their lives!" he had said.

Miss Rivers realized that he was keeping his word.

Her only hope was that the ghost of Mr. Mervin would someday be distracted by an earlier specter that was sharing the house with him. On several occasions, an old woman in black had been seen emerging from a side door of the house. A local man, sitting in front of the house during the weekdays when it was unoccupied — Bergner came up only on weekends — was wondering aloud to Miss Rivers about the "old lady who claimed she occupied the back part of the house." He had encountered her on many occasions, always seeing her disappear into the house by that same, seldom-used, side door. One of the office boys invited by John Bergner also saw her around 1:30 A.M. on a Sunday morning, when he stood outside the house, unable to go to sleep. When she saw him she said hello, and mentioned something about money, then disappeared into a field.

Grace Rivers looked into the background of the house and discovered that it had previously belonged to a very aged man who lived there with his mother. When she died, he found money buried in the house, but he claimed his mother had hidden more money that he had never been able to locate. Evidently the ghost of his mother felt the same way about it, and was still searching. For that's how it is with ghosts sometimes — they become forgetful about material things.

The Ship
Chandler's Ghost

It is a well-known fact among ghost hunting experts that structural changes in a house can have dire effects. Take out a wall, and you've got a *poltergeist* mad as a wet hen. I proved that in the case of the Leighton Buzzard ghost in *Ghosts I've Met*. Take down the building, like the studio building at New York's 51 West Tenth Street, and put up a modern apartment house, and you've got no ghost at all. Just a lot of curious tenants. If the ghost is inside the house before the changes are realized, he may bump into walls and doors that weren't there before — not the way he remembered things at all.

But move a whole house several yards away from the shore where it belongs, and you're asking for trouble. Big trouble. And big trouble is what the historical society in Cohasset, Massachusetts, got when they moved the old Ship's Chandlery in Cohasset. With my good friend Bob Kennedy of WBZ, Boston, I set out for the quaint old town south of Boston on a chilly evening in the fall of 1964.

When we arrived at the wooden structure on a corner of the Post Road — it had a nautical look, its two stories squarely set down as if to withstand any gale — we found several people already assembled. Among them were Mrs. E. Stoddard Marsh, the lively curator of the museum, which was what the Ship's Chandlery became, and her associate, lean, quiet Robert Fraser. The others were friends and neighbors who had heard of the coming of a parapsychologist, and didn't want to miss anything. We entered the building and walked around the downstairs portion of it, admiring its displays of nautical supplies, ranging from fishing tackle and scrimshaw made from walrus teeth to heavy anchors, hoists, and rudders — all the instruments and wares of a ship chandler's business.

Built in the late eighteenth century by Samuel Bates, the building was owned by the Bates family; notably by one John Bates, second of the family to have the place, who had died 78 years before our visit. Something of a local character, John Bates had cut a swath around the area as a dashing gentleman. He could well afford the role, for he owned a fishing fleet of 24 vessels, and business was good in those far-off days when the New England coast was dotted with major ports for fishing and shipping. A handwritten record of his daily catch can be seen next to a mysterious closet full of ladies' clothes. Mr. Bates led a full life.

After the arrival of Dorothy Damon, a reporter from the *Boston Traveler*, we started to question the curator about uncanny happenings in the building.

"The building used to be right on the waterfront, at Cohasset Cove, and it had its own pier," Mrs. Marsh began, "and in 1957 we moved it to its present site."

"Was there any report of uncanny happenings before that date?"

"Nothing I know of, but the building was in a bad state of disrepair."

"After the building was brought to its present site, then," I said, "what was the first unusual thing you heard?"

"Two years ago we were having a lecture here. There were about forty people listening to Francis Hagerty talk about old sailing boats. I was sitting over here to the left — on this ground floor — with Robert Fraser, when all of a sudden we heard heavy footsteps upstairs and things being moved and dragged — so I said to Mr. Fraser, 'Someone is up there; will you please tell him to be quiet?' I thought it was kids."

"Did you know whether there was in fact anyone upstairs at the time?"

"We did not know. Mr. Fraser went upstairs and after a moment he came down looking most peculiar and said, 'There is no one there.'"

"Now, there is no other way to get down from upstairs, only this one stairway. Nobody had come down it. We were interrupted three times on that evening."

I asked Robert Fraser what he had seen upstairs.

"There was enough light from the little office that is upstairs, and I could see pretty well upstairs, and I looked all over, but there was nobody upstairs."

"And the other times?"

"Same thing. Windows all closed, too. Nobody could have come down or gotten out. But I'm sure those were footsteps."

I returned to Mrs. Marsh and questioned her further about anything that might have occurred after that eventful evening of footsteps.

"We were kept so busy fixing up the museum that we paid scant attention to anything like that, but this summer something happened that brought it all back to us."

"What happened?" I asked, and the lady reporter perked up her ears.

"It was on one of the few rainy Sundays we had last July," Mrs. Marsh began. "You see, this place is not open on Sundays. I was bringing over some things from the other two buildings, and had my arms full. I opened the front door, when I heard those heavy footsteps upstairs."

"What did you do — drop everything?"

"I thought it was one of our committee or one of the other curators, so I called out, 'Hello — who's up there?' But I got no answer, and I thought, well, someone sure is pretty stuffy, not answering me back, so I was a little peeved and I called again."

"Did you get a reply?"

"No, but *the steps hesitated* when I called. But then they continued again, and I yelled, 'For Heaven's sake, why don't you answer?' — and I went up the stairs, but just as I got to the top of the stairs, they stopped."

There was a man who had helped them with the work at the museum who had lately stayed away for reasons unknown. Could he have heard the footsteps too and decided that caution was the better part of valor?

"The other day, just recently, four of us went into the room this gentleman occupies when he is here, and *the door closed on us*, by itself. It has never done that before."

I soon established that Fraser did not hear the steps when he was *alone* in the building, but that Mrs. Marsh did. I asked her about anything psychic in her background.

"My family has been interested in psychic matters since I was ten years old," she said in a matter-of-fact tone. "I could have become a medium, but I didn't care to. I saw an apparition of my mother immediately after she passed away. My brother also appeared to me six months after his death, to let me know he was all right, I guess."

"Since last July has there been any other manifestation?"

"I haven't been here much," Mrs. Marsh replied. "I had a lot of work with our costume collection in the main building. So I really don't know."

We decided to go upstairs now, and see if Mr. Bates — or whoever the ghost might be — felt like walking for us. We quietly waited in the semi-darkness upstairs, near the area where the footsteps had been heard, but nothing happened.

"The steps went back and forth," Mrs. Marsh reiterated. "Heavy, masculine steps, the kind a big man would make."

She showed us how it sounded, allowing of course for the fact she was wearing high heels. It sounded hollow enough for ten ghosts.

I pointed at a small office in the middle of the upstairs floor.

"This was John Bates' office," Mrs. Marsh explained, "and here is an Indian doll that falls down from a secure shelf now and then as if someone were throwing it."

I examined the doll. It was one of those early nineteenth-century dolls that Indians in New England used to make and sell.

"The people at the lecture also heard the noises," Mrs. Marsh said, "but they just laughed and nobody bothered thinking about it."

I turned to one of the local ladies, a Mrs. Hudley, who had come up with us. Did she feel anything peculiar up here, since she had the reputation of being psychic?

"I feel disturbed. Sort of a strange sensation," she began, haltingly, "as though there was a 'presence' who was in a disturbed frame of mind. It's a man."

Another lady, by the name of McCarthy, also had a strange feeling as we stood around waiting for the ghost to make himself known. Of course, suggestion and atmosphere made me discount most of what those who were around us that night might say, but I still wanted to hear it.

"I felt I had to get to a window and get some air," Mrs. McCarthy said. "The atmosphere seemed disturbed somehow."

I asked them all to be quiet for a moment and addressed myself to the unseen ghost.

"John Bates," I began, "if this is you, may I, as a stranger come to this house in order to help you find peace, ask that you manifest in some form so I know you can hear me?"

Only the sound of a distant car horn answered me.

I repeated my invitation to the ghost to come forward and be counted. Either I addressed myself to the wrong ghost or perhaps John Bates disliked the intrusion of so many people — only silence greeted us.

"Mr. Bates," I said in my most dulcet tones, "please forgive these people for moving your beautiful house inland. They did not do so out of irreverence for your person or work. They did this so that many more people could come and admire your house and come away with a sense of respect and admiration for the great man that you were."

It was so quiet when I spoke, you could have heard a mouse breathe.

Quietly, we tiptoed down the haunted stairs, and out into the cool evening air. Cowboy star Rex Trailer and his wife, who had come with us from Boston, wondered about the future — would the footsteps ever come back? Or was John Bates reconciled with the fact that the sea breezes no longer caressed his ghostly brow as they did when his house was down by the shore?

Then, too, what was the reason he was still around to begin with? Had someone given him his quietus in that little office upstairs? There are rumors of violence in the famous bachelor's life, and the number of women whose affections he had trifled with was legion. Someone might very well have met him one night and ended the highly successful career of the ship chandlery's owner.

A year went by, and I heard nothing further from the curator. Evidently, all was quiet at John Bates' old house. Maybe old John finally joined up with one of the crews that sail the ghost ships on the other side of the curtain of life.

How the Little Girl Ghost Was Sent Out to Play

Ed Harvey ran a pretty good talk show called "Talk of Philadelphia" on WCAU radio. It was the sort of program people listened to in their homes and cars. They listened in large numbers. I know, for the telephone calls came in fast and furious in the show's final half hour, when calls from the public were answered on the air.

One day in April, 1965, Ed and his charming wife, Marion, went to a cocktail party at a friend's house. There he got to talking to Jack Buffington, who was a regional director of a world-wide relief organization and a pretty down-to-earth fellow, as Ed soon found out. Somehow the talk turned to ghosts, and Buffington had a few things to say on that subject since he lived in a haunted house. At that point, Ed Harvey asked permission for Sybil Leek and myself to come down and have a go at the house.

We arrived at Buffington's house on Lansdowne Avenue, in Lansdowne, a Philadelphia suburb, around 10 o'clock. It was a little hard to find in the dark, and when we got there it did not look ghostly at all, just a nice old Victorian house, big and sprawling. Jack Buffington welcomed us at the door.

As I always do on such occasions, I asked Sybil to wait in another room where she could not hear any of the conversation, while I talked to those who had had experiences in the house.

After Sybil had graciously left, we seated ourselves and took inventory. What I saw was a tastefully furnished Victorian house with several wooden staircases and banisters, and lots of fine small antiques. Our host was joined by his dark-haired Italian-born wife, and two friends from his office. My wife Catherine immediately made friends with Mrs. Buffington, and then we started to find out what this was all about.

The Buffingtons, who had a four-year-old daughter named Allegra, had come to the house just nine months before. A lot had happened to them in those nine months.

"We came home from a trip to Scranton," Jack Buffington began, "and when we got back and I inserted the key in the front door, the hall light went on by itself. It has two switches, one on the upstairs level, so I raced upstairs to see who was in the house, but there was no one there. Periodically this happens, and I thought it was faulty wiring at first, but it has been checked and there is nothing wrong with it. The cellar light and the light in the third floor bathroom also go on and off by themselves. I've seen it, and so have my wife and our little girl."

"Anything else happening here?" I asked casually.

"There are many things that go bump in the night here. The first noise that happened recurrently was the sound of an old treadle sewing machine, which is heard on the average of once every month. This happens in a small room on the second floor, which we now use as a dressing room, but which may well have been a sewing room at one time."

I walked up the narrow stairs and looked at the little room. It had all the marks of a Victorian sewing room where tired servants or a worried mother worked at the clothes for her child.

"It's always around three in the morning, and it awakens us," Mr. Buffington continued, "and then there are footsteps and often they sound like children's footsteps."

"Children's footsteps?"

"Yes, and it is rather startling," Mr. Buffington added, "since we do have a small child in the house and inevitably go and check that it isn't she who is doing it. It never is."

"Is it downstairs?"

"All over the place. There are two stories, or three flights, including the basement. And there are a front and back stairway. There is never any pattern about these things. There may be a lot of happenings at the same time, then there is nothing for weeks, and then it starts again."

"Outside of the child's footsteps, did you ever have any indication of a grown-up presence?" I asked.

"Well, I saw the figure of a woman in the doorway of the dining room, walking down this hall, and through these curtains here, and I heard footsteps in conjunction with it. I thought it was my wife, and I called to her. I was hanging a picture in the dining room at the time. No answer. I was getting annoyed and called her several times over, but there was no response. Finally she answered from the second floor — she had not been downstairs at all."

"What happened to the other woman in the meantime?"

"I walked in here — the hall — and there was no one here."

"How was she dressed?"

"She had on a long skirt, looking like a turn-of-the-century skirt, and she did have her hair on top of her head, and she was tall and slender."

Mrs. Buffington is not very tall, but she does wear dark clothes.

"It was a perfectly solid figure I saw — nothing nebulous or transparent," our host added. "The spring lock at the entrance door was locked securely."

"Did anyone else see an apparition here?"

"My brother met a woman on the stairway — that is, the stairway leading to the third floor. He was spending the night with us, around Thanksgiving time. There was a party that evening and he mistook her for a guest who had somehow remained behind after all the other guests had gone home. She passed him going *up* while he was coming *down*, and she walked into his room, which he thought odd, so he went back to ask if he could help her, but there wasn't anybody there!"

Jack Buffington gave a rather nervous laugh.

I took a good look at the upstairs. Nobody could have gotten out of the house quickly. The stairs were narrow and difficult to negotiate, and the back stairs, in the servants' half of the house, were even more difficult. Anyone descending them rapidly was likely to slip and fall. The two brothers hadn't talked much about all this, I was told, since that time.

"Our little girl must be seeing her, too, for she frequently says she is going up to play with her lady friend," Jack Buffington said.

I started to wander around the house to get the feeling of it. The house was built in 1876 to the specifications of George Penn, a well-known local builder. Although it was now a duplex, it was originally a townhouse for just one family.

The upper stories contained several small, high-ceilinged rooms, and there was about them the forbidding atmosphere of a mid-Victorian house in a small town. The Buffingtons had furnished their house with taste, and the Italian background of the lady of the house was evident in the works of art and antiques strewn about the house.

As I soon discovered, tragedy had befallen the house on Lansdowne Avenue at least twice as far as it was known. The original builder had a sister who suffered from mental illness and was hospitalized many times. She also spent many years in this house. Then a family named Hopkins came to live in it, and it was at that time that the house was divided into two parts. Incidentally, no manifestations had been reported from the other half of the house. About six years before — the exact time was none too clear, and it may be further back — a family named Johnson rented the half now occupied by the Buffingtons. They had a retarded child, a girl, *who was kept locked up in a room on the third floor*. She died in her early teens, they say, in a hospital not far away. Then the house stood empty, looking out onto quiet Lansdowne Avenue with an air of tragedy and secret passion.

Three years went by before the Buffingtons, returning from Italy, took over the house.

"Have there been any unusual manifestations on the third floor?" I asked Mr. Buffington.

"Just one. Something carries on in the trunk up on the third floor. The trunk is empty and there is no reason for those frightful noises. We have both heard it. It is above where the child sleeps."

Mr. Buffington added that a book he read at night in bed often disappeared and showed up in the most peculiar spots around the house — spots that their little four year old couldn't possibly reach. On one occasion, he found it in a bathroom; at least once it traveled from his room upstairs to the top bookshelf downstairs, all by itself.

"My impression of this ghost," Mr. Buffington said, "is that it means no harm. Rather, it has the mischievousness of a child."

I now turned my attention to petite Mrs. Buffington, who had been waiting to tell me of her own most unusual experiences in the house.

"On one occasion I was on the second floor with the child," she began. "It was about eleven in the morning, and I was taking some clothes out of a cabinet. The back staircase is very close to this particular cabinet. Suddenly, I very distinctly heard a voice calling 'Mamma,' a voice of a person standing close to the cabinet, and it was a girl's voice, a child's voice and quite distinct — in fact, my daughter, Allegra, also heard it, for she turned to me and asked 'Mammi, who is it?'"

"What did you do?"

"I pretended to be nonchalant about it, looked all over, went up the stairs, opened cabinets — but, of course, there was no one there."

"And your daughter?"

"When we did not find anyone, she said, 'Oh, it must be our lady upstairs.'"

"Any other experiences you can recall?"

"Yes, tonight, in fact," Mrs. Buffington replied. "I was in the kitchen feeding the child, and I was putting something into the garbage container, when I heard a child's voice saying 'It's lower down' — just that, nothing more."

"Amazing," I conceded.

"It was a young girl's voice," Mrs. Buffington added. "I looked at Allegra, but it was obvious to me that the voice had come from the opposite direction. At any rate, Allegra was busy eating. I've been very nervous the past few days and about a week ago, when my husband was away in Washington, I spent the night alone, and having had some strong coffee, could not find sleep right away. I had moved the child in with me, so I did not have to stay by myself. I switched the light off, and the door to the landing of the second floor staircase was open. Just on that spot I suddenly heard those crashing noises as if somebody were rolling down. I was terrified. As soon as I switched the light back on, it stopped. There was nothing on the stairs. I sat on the bed for a moment, then decided it was my nerves, and turned the light off again. Immediately, the same noise returned, even louder. There was no mistaking the origin of the noises this time. They came from the stairs in front of the room. I switched the light on again and they stopped, and I left the lights burning the rest of the night. I finally fell asleep from sheer exhaustion."

"One more thing," Jack Buffington broke in. "On the back staircase, there is an area about four feet long which is a terribly frigid area sporadically. My little girl wouldn't walk up that staircase if she could possibly help it. Both my wife and I felt the cold spot."

"Is this in the area of the room where the little child was kept?" I asked.

"It is one floor below it, but it is the area, yes," Mrs. Buffington admitted.

I had heard enough by now to call in Sybil Leek, who had been outside waiting patiently for the call to lend her considerable psychic talents to the case.

After she had seated herself in one of the comfortable leather chairs, and we had grouped ourselves around her in the usual fashion, I quickly placed her into trance. Within a few minutes, her lips started to quiver gently, and then a voice broke through.

"Can't play," a plaintive child's voice said.

"Why not?" I asked immediately, bringing the microphone close to Sybil's entranced lips to catch every word.

"No one to play with. I want to play."

"Who do you want to play with?"

"Anyone. I don't like being alone."

"What is your name?"

"Elizabeth."

"What is your family name?"

"Streiber."

"How old are you?"

"Nine."

"What is your father's name?"

"Joseph Streiber."

Now Sybil had no knowledge that a child's ghost had been heard in the house. Nor had she overheard our conversation about it. Yet, the very first to manifest when trance had set in was a little girl!

I continued to question her.

"Your mother's name?"

"Mammi."

"What is her first name?"

The child thought for a moment, as if searching, then repeated: "Mammi."

With sudden impact, I thought of the ghostly voice calling for "Mamma" heard on the steps by Mrs. Buffington and her little daughter.

"Do you go to school?"

The answer was almost angry.

"No! I play."

"Where do you live in this house?"

"Funny house . . . I get lost . . . too big."

"Where is your room?"

"On the stairs."

"Who else lives in the house?"

"Mammi."

"Anyone else?"

"No one."

"Where were you born?"

"Here."

"What is your birthday?"

"Eight . . . Eighteen . . . Twenty-One."

"What month?"

"March."

Did she mean that she was born in 1821? The house was built in 1876 and before that time, only a field existed on the site. Or was she trying to say: March 8th, 1921? Dates always confuse a ghost, I have found.

"Are you feeling well?"

A plaintive "no" was the answer. What was wrong with her, I wanted to know.

"I slip on the stairs," the ghost said. "I slipped down the stairs. I like to do that."

"Did you get hurt?"

"Yes."

"What happened then?"

"So I sit on the stairs," the little girl ghost said, "and sometimes I run down one staircase. Not the other. Then I have fun."

"Is there anyone else with you?"

"Mammi."

Again I thought of the apparition in the Victorian dress Jack Buffington had seen in the hall.

"Do you see her now?" I asked.

An emphatic "no" was the answer.

"When have you seen her last?"

She thought that one over for a moment.

"Two days."

"Is she living?"

"Yes . . . she goes away, and then I'm lost."

"Does she come back?"

"Yes."

"What about your father?"

"Don't like my father. Not very nice time with my father. He shouts."

"What floor is your room on?"

"At the top."

I recalled that the retarded little girl had been kept in a locked room on the top floor.

"Do you ever go downstairs?"

"Of course I go downstairs. I play on the stairs. And I'm going to sit on the stairs all the time until somebody plays with me!"

"Isn't there any other little girl or boy around?" I asked.

"I don't get at him . . . they take him away and hide him."

"Who does?"

"People here."

"Do you see people?"

"Yes."

"Do people see *you*?"

"They think they do . . . they're not very nice, really."

"Do you talk to them?" She seemed to nod. "What do you tell them?"

"I want to play."

"Do you call out for anyone?" I asked.

"Mammi."

"Is there anyone else in this house you can see? Any children?"

"Yes, but they won't play."

"What sort of children are there in this house?"

"They won't play."

How do you explain to a child that she is a ghost?

"Would you like to meet some other children like yourself who do want to play?" I asked. She liked that very much. I told her to imagine such children at play and to think of nothing else. But she wanted to play in this house.

"I live here."

I persisted in telling her that there were children outside, in a beautiful meadow, just waiting for her to join them.

"My father tells me not to."

"But he is not here."

"Sometimes I see him."

"Come outside now."

"I don't go outside in the daytime."

"What do you do in the daytime then?"

"I get up early and play on the stairs."

She was afraid to go outside, she said, but preferred to wait for "them" in the house, so she would not miss them. I explained things to her ever so gently. She listened. Eventually, she was willing to go, wondering only — "When do I come back?"

"You won't want to come back, Elizabeth," I replied, and asked if she understood these things now.

She thought for a moment, then said:

"Funny man . . ."

"You see, something happened to you, and you are not quite the same as before," I tried to explain. "People in this house are not like you and that's why you can't play with them. But outside in the meadow there are many like you. Children to play with all your life!"

And then I sent her away.

There was a strange, rapping noise on the staircase now, as if someone were saying good-bye in a hurry. Abruptly, the noise ceased and I recalled Sybil, still entranced, to her own body.

I asked her to describe what she saw on her side of the veil.

"The child is difficult," she said. "Doesn't want to leave the house. She's frightened of her father. She's about ten. Died here, fell."

I instructed the medium to help the child out of the house and across the border. This she did.

"There is also a woman here," Sybil said. "I think she followed the child. She is tied to this house because the child would not go."

"What does she look like?"

"Medium fair, full face, not thin — she wears a green dress in one piece, dark dress — she comes and goes — she worries about the child — I think *she left the child.*"

Guilt, I thought, so often the cause of a haunting!

"When she came back, something had happened," Sybil continued. "The child had been injured and now she keeps coming back to find the child. But the child only wants to play and sit on the stairs."

"Can you contact the woman for us?" I asked.

"The woman is not a good person," Sybil replied slowly. "She is sorry. She listens now."

"Tell her we've sent the child away."

"She knows."

"Tell her she need no longer haunt this house; her guilt feelings are a matter of the past."

"She wants to follow the child. She wants to go now."

"She should think of the child with love, and she will join her."

"She doesn't love the child."

"She will have to desire to see her family again, then, to cross over. Instruct her."

In a quiet voice, Sybil suggested to the ghost that she must go from the house and never return here.

"She won't upset the house, now that the child is gone," Sybil assured us. "The search for the child was the cause of it all."

"Was the child ill?" I asked.

"The child was difficult and lonely, and she fell."

Again I heard rapping noises for a moment.

"Was there anything wrong with this child?"

"I'm not so sure. I think she was a little *fou*. She was florid, you know, nobody to look after her, looking for things all the time and frightened to go out."

"Did she die in this house or was she taken somewhere?"

"She died here."

Sometimes the ghost reattaches himself to the last refuge he had on the earth plane, even though the body may expire elsewhere, and instantly returns to that place, never to leave it again, until freed by someone like myself.

"The woman is gone now," Sybil mumbled. "The child went a long way, and the woman is gone now, too."

I thanked Sybil and led her back to consciousness, step by step, until she woke up in the present, fully relaxed as if after a good night's rest, and, of course, not remembering a thing that had come through her entranced lips the past hour.

Mr. Buffington got up, since the spell of the foregoing had been broken, and motioned me to follow him to the next room.

"There is something I just remembered," he said. "My daughter, Allegra, took a fall on the staircase on the spot where those chills have been felt. She wore one of her mother's high heels and the likelihood of a spill was plausible — still, it was on *that* very spot."

The next morning, I called a number of people who knew Lansdowne history and past residents well enough to be called experts. I spoke to the librarian at the Chester County Historical Society and the librarian at Media, and to a long-time resident Mrs. Susan Worell, but none of them knew of a Joseph Streiber with a little girl named Elizabeth. The records back into the twenties or even earlier are pretty scanty in this area and research was almost hopeless. Quite conceivably, the Streibers were among the tenants who had the house in a transitory way during the years of which Jack Buffington had no records — but then again, there are certain parallels between fact and trance results that cannot be dismissed lightly.

Jack Buffington thought the description of the woman he saw and that given by the medium do not fully correspond, but then he did not see the specter long enough to be really sure.

The retarded child Sybil Leek brought through had an amazing similarity to the actual retarded girl of about ten who had lived in the house and died in a nearby hospital, and the word "Mamma" that Mrs. Buffington had heard so clearly was also close to what the ghost girl said she kept calling her mother.

There was some mystery about the dates — and even the long-time residents of the area I interviewed could not help me pin down the facts. Was there a man by that name with a little girl?

Records were not well kept in this respect and people in America could come and go far more easily than in European countries, for instance, where there was an official duty to report one's moves to either the police or some other government office.

A day or two after our visit, Jack Buffington reported that the noises were worse than ever! It was as if our contact with the wraiths had unleashed their fury; having been told the truth about their status, they would naturally have a feeling of frustration and resentment, or at least the woman would. This resentment often occurs after an investigation in which trance contact is made. But eventually things quiet down and I had the feeling that the woman's guilt feelings would also cease. That the little girl ghost had been sent out to play, I have no doubt. Perhaps that aftermath was the mother's fury at having her no longer in her sight. But then I never said that ghosts are the easiest people to live with.

The Ghost-Servant Problem at Ringwood Manor

Ringwood, in the south of England, has an American counterpart in New Jersey. I had never heard of Ringwood Manor in New Jersey until Mrs. Edward Tholl, a resident of nearby Saddle River, brought it to my attention. An avid history buff and a talented geographer and map maker, Mrs. Tholl had been to the Manor House and on several occasions felt "a presence." The mountain people who still inhabited the Ramapo Mountains of the region wouldn't go near the Manor House at night.

"Robert Erskine, geographer to Washington's army, is buried on the grounds," Mrs. Tholl told me.

The Manor House land was purchased by the Ogden family of Newark in 1740, and an iron-smelting furnace was built on it two years later. The area abounds in mine deposits and was at one time a center of iron mining and smelting. In 1762, when a second furnace was built, a small house was also built. This house still stands and now forms part of the haphazard arrangement that constitutes the Manor House today. One Peter Hasenclever bought the house and iron works in 1764. He ran the enterprise with such ostentation that he was known as "The Baron." But Hasenclever did not produce enough iron to suit his backers, and was soon replaced by Robert Erskine. When the War of Independence broke out, the iron works were forced to close. Erskine himself died "of exposure" in 1780.

By 1807, the iron business was going full blast again, this time under the aegis of Martin Ryerson, who tore down the ramshackle old house and rebuilt it completely. After the iron business failed in the 1830s, the property passed into the hands of famed Peter Cooper in 1853. His son-in-law Abram S. Hewitt, one-time Mayor of New York, lived in the Manor House.

Mrs. Hewitt, Cooper's daughter, turned the drab house into an impressive mansion of 51 rooms, very much as it appears today. Various older buildings already on the grounds were uprooted and added to the house, giving it a checkered character without a real center. The Hewitt family continued to live at Ringwood until Erskine Hewitt deeded the estate to the State of New Jersey in 1936, and the mansion became a museum through which visitors were shown daily for a small fee.

During troubled times, tragedies may well have occurred in and around the house. There was a holdup in 1778, and in the graveyard nearby, many French soldiers were buried who died there during an epidemic. There is also on record an incident, in later years, when a cook was threatened by a butler with a knife, and there were disasters that took many lives in the nearby iron mines.

One of the Hewitt girls, Sally, had been particularly given to mischief. If anyone were to haunt the place, she'd be a prime candidate for the job. I thanked Claire Tholl for her help, and called on Ethel Johnson Meyers to accompany me to New Jersey. Of course, I didn't give her any details. We arranged to get to the house around dusk, after all the tourists had gone.

My wife Catherine and I, with Ethel Meyers as passenger, drove out to the house on a humid afternoon in May, 1965. Jim Byrne joined us at the house with *Saturday Review* writer Haskell Frankel in tow.

We were about an hour late, but it was still light, and the peaceful setting of the park with the Manor House in its center reminded one indeed of similar houses gracing the English countryside.

We stood around battling New Jersey mosquitoes for a while, then I asked Catherine to take Ethel away from the house for a moment, so I could talk to Mrs. Tholl and others who had witnessed ghostly goings-on in the house.

"I've had a feeling in certain parts of the house that I was not alone," Mrs. Tholl said, "but other than that I cannot honestly say I have had uncanny experiences here."

Alexander Waldron had been the superintendent of Ringwood Manor for many years, until a year before, in fact. He consented to join us for the occasion. A jovial, gray-haired man, he seemed rather deliberate in his report, giving me only what to him were actual facts.

"I was superintendent here for eighteen years," Mr. Waldron began. "I was sitting at my desk one day, in the late afternoon, like today, and the door to the next room was closed. My office is on the ground floor. I heard two people come walking toward me at a fast pace. That did not seem unusual, for we do have workmen here frequently. When the steps reached my door, nothing happened. Without thinking too much, I opened the door for them. But there was no one there. I called out, but there was no answer. Shortly after, two workmen did come in from outside, and together we searched the whole building, but found no one who could have made the sound."

"Could anyone have walked away without being seen by you?"

"Impossible. There was good light."

"Did anything else happen after that?"

"Over the years we've had a few things we could not explain. For instance, doors we had shut at night, we found open the next morning. Some years ago, when I had my boys living here with me, they decided to build a so-called monster down in the basement. One boy was of high-school age, the other in grammar school — sixteen and thirteen. One of them came in by himself one night, when he heard footsteps overhead, on the ground floor. He thought it was his brother who had come over from the house.

"He thought his brother was just trying to scare him, so he continued to work downstairs. But the footsteps continued and finally he got fed up with it and came upstairs. All was dark, and nobody was around. He ran back to the house, where he found his brother, who had never been to the Manor at all."

Bradley Waldron probably never worked on his "monster" again after that.

There are stories among the local hill folk of Robert Erskine's ghost walking with a lantern, or sitting on his grave half a mile down the road from the Manor House, or racing up the staircase in the house itself.

Wayne Daniels, who had accompanied Mrs. Tholl to the House, spoke up now. Mr. Daniels had lived in the region all his life, and was a professional restorer of early American structures.

"I have felt strange in one corner of the old dining room, and in two rooms upstairs," he volunteered. "I feel hostility in those areas, somehow."

It was time to begin our search in the house itself.

I asked Ethel Meyers to join us, and we entered the Manor House, making our way slowly along the now-deserted corridors and passages of the ground floor, following Ethel as she began to get her psychic bearings.

Suddenly, Ethel remarked that she felt a man outside the windows, but could not pin down her impression.

"Someone died under a curse around here," she mumbled, then

added as if it were an afterthought, "Jackson White . . . what does that mean?"

I had never heard the name before, but Claire Tholl explained that "Jackson White" was a peculiar local name for people of mixed blood, who live in the Ramapo hills. Ethel added that someone had been in slavery at one time.

Ethel was taken aback by the explanation of "Jackson White." She had taken it for granted that it was an individual name. Jackson Whites, I gathered, are partly American Indian and partly black, but not white.

We now entered a large bedroom elegantly furnished in the manner of the early nineteenth century, with a large bed against one wall and a table against the other. Ethel looked around the room uncertainly, as if looking for something she did not yet see.

"Someone with a bad conscience died in this room," she said. "A man and a woman lived here, who were miles apart somehow."

It was Mrs. Erskine's bedroom we were in. We went through a small door into another room that lay directly behind the rather large bedroom; it must have been a servant's room at one time. Nevertheless, it was elegant, with a marble fireplace and a heavy oak table, around which a number of chairs had been placed. We sat down but before I had time to adjust my tape recorder and camera, Ethel Meyers fell into deep trance. From her lips came the well-modulated voice of Albert, her control. He explained that several layers of consciousness covered the room, that there were blacks brought here by one Jackson, who came in the eighteenth century. One of them seemed present in the room, he felt.

"One met death at the entrance . . . a woman named Lucy Bell, she says. She was a servant here."

Suddenly, Albert was gone. In his stead, there was a shrill, desperate female voice, crying out to all who would listen.

"No . . . I didn't . . . before my God I didn't . . . I show you where . . . I didn't touch it . . . never . . . "

She seemed to be speaking to an unseen tormentor now, for Ethel, possessed by the ghost, pulled back from the table and cried:

"No . . . don't . . . don't!" Was she being beaten or tortured?

"He didn't either!" the ghost added.

I tried to calm her.

"I didn't touch . . . I didn't touch . . ." she kept repeating.

I asked for her name.

"Lucy," she said in a tormented, high-pitched voice completely different from Ethel Meyers' normal tones.

"I believe you," I said, and told the ghost who we were and why we had come. The uncontrollable crying subsided for the moment.

"He's innocent too," she finally said. "I can't walk," she added. Ethel pointed to her side. Had she been hurt?

"I didn't take it," she reiterated. "It's right there."

What didn't she take? I coaxed her gently to tell me all about it.

"I've come as a *friend,*" I said, and the word finally hit home. She got very excited and wanted to know where I was since she could not see me.

"A friend, Jeremiah, do you hear?" she intoned.

"Who is Jeremiah?"

"He didn't do it either," she replied. Jeremiah, I gathered, lived here, too, but she did not know any family name — just Jeremiah. Then Ethel Meyers grabbed my hand, mumbling "friend," and almost crushed my fingers. I managed to pull it away. Ethel ordinarily has a very feminine, soft grip — a great contrast to the desperately fierce clasp of the ghost possessing the medium!

"Don't go!"

I promised to stay if she would talk.

"I have never stolen," she said. "It's dark . . . I can't see now . . . where do I go to see always?"

"I will show you the way," I promised.

"Marie . . . Marie . . . where are you?" she intoned pleadingly.

"What is Jeremiah doing?"

"He is begging for his honor."

"Where is he now?"

"Here with me."

"Who is the person you worked for?" I asked.

"Old lady . . . I don't want her . . . "

"If she did you wrong, should we punish her? What is her name?"

"I never wished evil on anyone . . . I would forgive her . . . if she forgives me. She is here . . . I saw her, and she hates me . . . "

The voice became shrill and emotional again. I started to send her away, and in a few moments, she slipped out. Suddenly, there was an entirely different person occupying Ethel's body. Proudly sitting up, she seemed to eye us, with closed eyes, of course, as if we were riff-raff invading her precincts.

"What is your name?" I demanded.

"I am in no court of justice," was the stiff reply in a proper upper-middle-class accent. "I cannot speak to you. I have no desire. It is futile for you to give me any advice."

"What about this servant girl?" I asked.

"You may take yourself away," the lady replied, haughtily. "Depart!"

"What did the girl take?" I asked, ignoring her outburst of cold fury.

"I am not divulging anything to you."

"Is she innocent then?"

This gave her some thought, and the next words were a little more communicative.

"How come you are in my house?" she demanded.

"Is it your house?"

"I will call the servants and have you taken out by the scruff of your neck," she threatened.

"Will the servants know who you are?" I countered.

"I am lady in my own."

"What is your name?"

"I refuse to reveal myself or talk to you!"

I explained about the passage of time. It made no impression.

"I will call her . . . Old Jeremiah is under his own disgrace. You are friend to him?"

I explained about Ethel Meyers and how she, the ghost, was able to communicate with us.

She hit the table hard with Ethel's fist.

"The man is mad," the ghost said. "Take him away!"

I didn't intend to be taken away by ghostly men-in-white. I continued to plead with "the lady" to come to her senses and listen. She kept calling for her servants, but evidently nobody answered her calls.

"Jeremiah, if you want to preserve yourself in my estimation and not stand by this girl, take this . . . "

Somehow the medium's eyes opened for a moment, and the ghost could "see." Then they closed again. It came as a shock, for "the lady" suddenly stopped her angry denunciation and instead "looked" at me in panic.

"What is this? Doctor . . . where is he . . . Laura! Laura! I am ill. Very ill. I can't see. I can't see. I hear something talking to me, but I can't see it. Laura, call a doctor. I'm going to die!"

"As a matter of fact," I said calmly, "you have died already."

"It was my mother's." The ghost sobbed hysterically. "Don't let her keep it. Don't let it go to the scum! I must have it. Don't let me die like this. Oh, oh . . . "

I called on Albert, the control, to take the unhappy ghost away and lead her to the other side of the veil, if possible. The sobbing slowly subsided as the ghost's essence drifted away out of our reach in that chilly Georgian room at Ringwood.

It wasn't Albert's crisp, precise voice that answered me. Another stranger, obviously male, now made his coughing entry and spoke in a lower-class accent.

"What's the matter?"

"Who is this?" I asked.

The voice sounded strangely muffled, as if coming from far away.

"Jeremiah . . . What's the matter with everybody?" The voice had distinct black overtones.

"I'm so sleepy," the voice said.

"Who owns this house?"

"Ho, ho, I do," the ghost said. "I have a funny dream, what's the matter with everybody?" Then the voice cleared up a little, as he became more aware of the strange surroundings into which he had entered.

"Are you one of these white trashes?" he demanded.

"What is the old lady's name?" I asked.

"She's a Bob," he replied, enigmatically, and added, "real bumby, with many knots in it, many knots in the brain."

"Who else is here?"

"I don't like you. I don't know you and I don't like who I don't know," the servant's ghost said.

"You're white trash," he continued. "I seed you!" The stress was on *white*.

"How long have you been living here?"

"My father . . . Luke."

Again, I explained about death and consequences, but the reception was even less friendly than I had received from "the lady."

Jeremiah wanted no truck with death.

"What will the old squaw say? What will she say?" he wondered. "She needs me."

"Not really," I replied. "After all, she's dead, too." He could hardly believe the news. Evidently, the formidable "squaw" was immune to such events as death in his mind.

"What do you have against my mother?" he demanded now. Things were getting confusing. Was the "old lady" his mother?

"Lucy white trash too," he commented.

"Was she your wife?"

"Call it that."

"Can you see her?"

"She's here."

"Then you know you have died and must go from this house?" I asked.

"'dominable treek, man, 'dominable treek," he said, furiously.

"This house is no longer yours."

"It never was," he shot back. "The squaw is here. We're not dead, great white spirit — laugh at you."

"What do you want in this house?"

"Squaw very good," he said. "I tell you, my mother, squaw very good. Lucy Bell, white trash, but good. Like Great White Spirit. Work my fingers down to the bone. I am told! I am thief, too. Just yesterday. Look at my back! Look at my squaw! Red Fox, look at her. Look at my back, look at it!"

He seemed to have spent his anger. The voice became softer now.

"I am so sleepy," he said. "So sleepy . . . my Lucy will never walk again . . . angel spirit . . . my people suffer . . . her skin should be like mine . . . help me, help my Lucy. . ."

I promised to help and to send him to his father, Luke, who was awaiting him.

"I should have listened to my father," the ghost mumbled.

Then he recognized his father, evidently come to guide him out of the house, and wondered what he was doing here.

I explained what I thought was the reason for his father's presence. There was some crying, and then they all went away.

"Albert," I said. "Please take over the instrument."

In a moment, the control's cool voice was heard, and Ethel was brought out of trance rather quickly.

"My hip," she complained. "I don't think I can move."

"Passing conditions" or symptoms the ghost brings are sometimes present for a few moments after a medium comes out of trance. It is nothing to be alarmed about.

I closed Ethel's eyes again, and sent her back into trance, then brought her out again, and this time all was "clear." However, she still recalled a scream in a passage between the two rooms.

I wondered about the Indian nature of the ghost. Were there any Indians in this area?

"Certainly," Mr. Waldron replied. "They are of mixed blood, often Negro blood, and are called Jackson Whites. Many of them worked here as servants."

The footsteps the superintendent had heard on the floor below were of two persons, and they could very well have come from this area, since the room we were in was almost directly above his offices.

There was, of course, no record of any servants named Jeremiah or Lucy. Servants' names rarely get recorded unless they do something that is most unusual.

I asked Mrs. Tholl about ladies who might have fitted the description of the haughty lady who had spoken to us through Ethel Meyers in trance.

"I associate this with the Hewitt occupancy of the house," she explained, "because of the reference to a passage connecting two parts of the house, something that could not apply to an early structure on the spot. Amelia Hewitt, whose bedroom we had come through, was described in literature of the period as 'all placidity and kindliness.' Sarah Hewitt, however, was quite a cut-up in her day, and fitted the character of 'the lady' more accurately."

But we cannot be sure of the identity of the ghost-lady. She elected to keep her name a secret and we can only bow to her decision and let it remain so.

What lends the accounts an air of reality and evidence is, of course, the amazing fact that Ethel Meyers spoke of "Jackson Whites" in this house, an appellation completely new to her and me.

I am also sure that the medium had no knowledge of Indians living in the area. Then, too, her selecting a room above the spot where the ghostly steps had been heard was interesting, for the house was sprawling and had many rooms and passages.

Return to Clinton Court

When I investigated Clinton Court, New York, in 1960, and wrote about it in *Ghost Hunter*, I never dreamed I'd have to come back and talk to a ghost again. But sometimes the dead won't stay still. Our first visit had been somewhat impaired by a nervous real estate firm who wanted us out of the house as quickly as possible. Ethel Johnson Meyers went into trance in the lower portion of what was once the stables and carriage house of Governor Clinton. Now located in the heart of Hell's Kitchen, it was then a rural neighborhood in which the Clinton Mansion, now gone, was surrounded by fields and woodlands close to the North River.

Ethel Meyers' trance was fully described in the chapter called "The Clinton Court Ghosts" in *Ghost Hunter*. When we left the downstairs apartment where Ethel and I had spent a quiet hour, I was pretty sure there would be no further need for our services. The apartment was then in a state of disrepair, there was no tenant as yet, and all we had to sit on were a bench and a completely worn-out chair someone had left behind.

I thought no more of charming Clinton Court so neatly tucked away behind an iron gate and probably unknown to most New

Yorkers, until 1964, when a Miss Alyce Montreuil wrote to me of her experiences in the house at 422½ West Forty-sixth Street, New York.

As a friend of the tenants who had taken one of the two apartments making up the former carriage house, she had had her brush with the uncanny. I reported this in detail in *Ghosts I've Met*; how the upstairs door near the porch atop the stairs would not stay closed, how the door seemingly unlocked itself, and how her dogs would freeze when approaching the staircase leading to the upper apartment.

Again I thought I had done my duty to restless Clinton Court by reporting these later developments during the tenancy of Danny Brown and Frank Benner, between 1959 and 1963. Meanwhile, the lower apartment had also acquired new tenants, Mr. and Mrs. Dan Neary, who had lived there since 1963.

Somehow Clinton Court would not leave me alone. A young student of the occult named Bob Nelson wrote to me of doors opening by themselves. But he had read my book, and I was afraid it might have inspired him to look for these things. Then in February of 1965, Mrs. Leo Herbert contacted me after seeing Sybil Leek and myself "de-ghosting" (or trying to "de-ghost") June Havoc's house, situated behind theirs, on Miss Havoc's television program.

Her husband, a direct descendant of Victor Herbert, was property master for all David Merrick shows, and Mrs. Herbert was a dancer. They had lived in the two top floors composing the upper apartment since 1964. There were some odd things going on in the place, and would Sybil Leek and I please come and have a talk with whoever it was who was causing them?

No sooner said than done. On March 28, about a dozen people assembled in the upstairs living room of the Herberts. They included the downstairs neighbors, the Nearys; some people living in the front, or un-haunted section of Clinton Court; Bob Nelson, Carl Gewritz, the Herbert children, and Mr. and Mrs. Biff Liff; Gail Benedict, public relations director, Bill Hazlett, and Peter Hahn of

North American Newspaper Alliance; Catherine and I; and, of course, Sybil Leek, resplendent in purple dress, stockings, and cape.

Promptly at nine, we dimmed the lights and grouped ourselves around the room roughly in a circle, with Sybil stretching out on a chair in the upper center.

After the usual few moments of hypnosis, I had Sybil safely entranced, and I waited for the ghost to make himself or herself known. I knew there were several layers of consciousness in the place, and I could not be sure about the ones who would break through the barrier and use Sybil's vocal cords to communicate with us.

Her lips moved silently for a few moments while I strained not to miss the first words. Gradually the sounds became intelligible and I moved closer.

"What is your name?" I asked.

"Walker."

I asked the ghost to speak up.

"George . . . Walker," the voice said, plainly now.

"Is this your house?"

"No. George . . . I have blood in my mouth . . . hurt."

"Who hurt you?"

"Don't know . . . dying . . . I'm dying . . . too late . . . "

"Do you live here?"

"No . . . Brice."

"What street?"

"No street. Brice. South."

"What year is this?"

"Ninety-two."

"What can we do to help you?"

"I want to live . . . doctor."

"Which doctor do you want us to call?"

"Warren. East . . . Easton."

It sounded like East Hampton to me, but I wasn't sure. The voice had difficulty maintaining an even tone.

"How did you get to this house?" I inquired.

"Went to the river . . . everybody . . . friends, soldiers . . . Alfred . . . came to rest . . ."

"Why did you come to this house?"

"I like it . . . remembered . . . coming here to see George . . . two Georgies."

"What is this other George's name?"

"Clinton. George Clinton . . . I die . . . "

"Are you a soldier?"

"Yeah . . . Colonel . . . George . . . Walker."

"What regiment?"

"Two-Four."

"Who is the commanding general?"

"Wilson."

"First name?"

"Amos . . . nobody bothers . . ."

"Yes, I do. I will help you. Who attacked you?"

"I don't know."

I asked what he wanted in this house.

"I want to stay . . . no house, field! Can't get to the house."

"Where were you born?" I changed the subject before the ghost could get too upset to give us information.

"Brice . . . Carolina . . . "

"When did you come up here?"

The voice hesitated.

"Eight-three . . . no, ninety-three . . . eighty-eight."

"How did you get hurt?"

"Blood in my chest . . . knife . . ." He added that it was a man, a soldier, but he did not recognize him.

Suddenly, the jaws of the medium started to quiver and the voice began to give out.

"Can't talk . . ." I calmed him, and his tone became once more steadier.

"What other regiments were here?" I resumed.

"Queens . . . Nine . . . "

"Were you in any campaign?"

"Brice . . . "

"What town is Brice near?"

"Pike's Hill."

"What colony?"

"Carolina . . . North Carolina."

"Any other town it is near to?"

"Pike's Hill, Three Hills . . . "

I asked him whether he knew anyone else here, but the ghost replied he couldn't see things in the "field," only smoke.

"The house is too far. I can't get there," he repeated.

"What is your wife's name?"

"Martha . . . Brice."

"Children?"

"Three."

"Your father's name?"

"Stephen . . . Brice . . . Burnt Oak . . . ."

"Is that the name of a house?"

"Yes . . . "

"Is he alive or dead?"

"Dead."

"When did he die?"

"Fifty-nine."

"Where is he buried?"

"Burnt Oak."

"Cemetery?"

"In the garden."

"What denomination was he?"

"Catholic."

"Were you Catholic?"

"Yes . . . French Catholic."

"Were you baptized?"

"St. Theresa."

"Where is this?"

"Pike Hill."

"What year were you born?"

"Thirty-four."

"Any brothers who were officers?"

"Clifford . . . Colonel . . . fourteenth regiment, stationed Pike Hill."

"Cavalry or infantry?"

"Infantry."

"Any other brothers who were officers?"

"Aaron . . . Captain . . . "

"Where stationed?"

"Don't know."

I felt it was time to release this unhappy one. Gently, I suggested his pain was no more, and asked him to join his loved ones.

A moment later he slipped away. I then asked that Sybil Leek, still deeply entranced, answer my questions, without awakening. This is actually switching from deep trance to clairvoyant trance in the middle of the séance, but Sybil has extraordinary powers of the mind and is a disciplined medium. Sybil's own voice responded to me now. She sounded somewhat sleepy and wasn't her usual crisp self, but nevertheless she was clearly audible.

I asked her to look around and report what she saw. Sybil's etheric body was now "on the other side" for the time being, and she was able to see the same things a permanent resident of that other world would be seeing.

She described a house with three windows, with a "sort of office" inside.

"There are people here who should not be here . . . girls!" she said.

"What happens here?" I asked.

"Something to do with the staircase . . . something happened . . . trying to see . . . I don't like it . . . someone hanging . . . don't like it . . . a man . . . "

"What does he look like?"

"Six . . . young men . . . gray clothes . . . someone hung *him* . . . I don't want to look . . . ."

"Is there anyone else on the staircase?" I inquired.

"Yes," Sybil said in halting tones. "That girl."

"How old is she?"

"Twenty-five, twenty-six."

"What is she doing on the staircase?"

"She has seen *him*. Doesn't care. She wants someone to take him away, but then she forgets about it. She was wrong about the man . . . liking him . . . I see her living in this house and she is very happy, until she gets frightened by the man. She doesn't like the staircase. Someone takes the staircase and *puts it somewhere else* . . . I don't want to stay here . . . bad house."

"What about the staircase?" I pressed Sybil.

"She moved the staircase and then got to go back to the old staircase and then they caught up with her."

"Who caught up with her?"

"The man's friends. The man who was hung. She was very ill. He had her move the staircase. They knew it was there. And so she kept going back. And then she died . . . *somebody pushed her*. And she hurt her back, she couldn't walk, bad house."

"The girl — because she's frightened. She throws things onto the ground. She runs up the stairs — the other stairs — trying to get away — she doesn't like music — reminds her of sad song — the music starts things off here."

"How long ago did she die?"

"Eighteen-four-o — about . . . "

"Is she causing all the disturbances in this house?" I asked.

"No . . . a man, and she, and others . . . lot of people pass through . . . to the river."

"Anyone else on the staircase?"

"No."

"Look at the door. Is anybody at the door?"

"Animal . . . dog . . . scratching . . . nobody there to let it in . . . she's inside."

"Is this her house?"

"Sort of. Lives here . . . .Goes to the door because of the scratching noise."

"Is it her dog?"

"Dog lives in the house . . . strange, she wants to go, and she can't."

"Why?"

"Because she would have no money. She is wanting to open the door, let the dog in."

"Is the woman on the other side?"

Sybil's voice was somewhat puzzled.

"*I'm* on the other side."

Of course she was . . . temporarily.

"Is she the same girl you saw on the stairs?"

"Yes."

"Is there anyone else here?"

"No."

"Do you see any children here?"

"Four children. Not here now. Not very strong."

"Look at the staircase once more. Was there any kind of tragedy on this staircase?"

"I see someone who falls. Older man. The girl . . . is used to the staircase now. She keeps *staying* on this staircase."

"You mean like the man who was hanged?"

"Yes. It is very confusing. She is on the staircase waiting for something else, I think. Someone and something else to happen. Someone to come, she is very confused."

I felt Sybil had been "under" long enough and decided to bring her out of her trance. This was accomplished quickly. When Sybil awoke, she remembered very little, as usual.

The group was animated now as everyone sought to sum up reactions and feelings. Our bearded host, Leo Herbert, who was next to Sybil with the entrance door at his back, was the first to speak.

"It is very strange, but just before Hans put Sybil under, I felt that there was a draft. I got up, and shut the door, but I could still feel this coldness, right here, on me. It just never left, and feels pretty much like that this moment, though not with the intensity it had when you were hypnotizing Sybil. I had the feeling if I moved out of this spot, Sybil would talk louder."

Sybil's entranced voice was not loud on this occasion, and some of the group farther back in the room had difficulty hearing her.

"Did you have any psychic experiences in this house prior to our session tonight?" I asked Leo Herbert.

"I have heard noises from upstairs, where I sleep, and I came down here to investigate and found no one here," Herbert said, "but I had the feeling of a *presence* here. As if somebody had just been here. This was only two and a half weeks ago. The first time when I awakened, I thought that I heard footsteps down here, and I waited a long time and heard nothing, and after fifteen minutes, I went back to bed. An hour later I was awakened again, went directly down, checked the windows and door and found them all locked. Yet I felt someone had been present here."

I then turned to Mrs. Herbert, who was sitting on the comfortable couch next to Catherine.

"What about you — have you had any uncanny experiences here?"

"About a year ago, I was alone in the apartment," the slender brunette answered, "when I was sure someone was throwing pebbles against the skylight of the roof above our bedrooms. I also heard footsteps on the roof."

"Did you look to see who it was?"

"No, I was terrified."

"Did you find any pebbles on the roof?"

"No, nothing. I went up the next morning, but there was nothing on the roof. No pebbles."

I thanked Mrs. Herbert and approached the Nearys, who live below the Herberts. Mrs. Neary was quite willing to talk to me, although she had originally been a skeptic about ghosts.

"The sounds in the house are so much more varied than ever before," she volunteered. "I have heard a bell ringing, yet there is no bell. On at least six occasions lately, I have felt someone brush past me, yet nobody could be seen. I have had a sense of shadow. There are all sorts of strange noises. Primarily in the area of the wall between the living room and kitchen. Sometimes there is ticking in the wall."

I asked for quiet, and read aloud Miss Montreuil's letter to me, relating the experiences she had had at the house while a guest of previous tenants. I stressed that Sybil Leek did not know where we would be going that evening. She had no advance information, because we never discuss cases beforehand. I had directed the driver to take us to 420 West Forty-Sixth Street, carefully avoiding the use of "Clinton Court." On arrival, I had hustled her upstairs, so that she had no chance to study the house or familiarize herself with it.

And yet much of what came through Sybil Leek's entranced lips matched the earlier testimony of Ethel Johnson Meyers. Much was new, too, and could be checked without much difficulty. I felt Ethel had "sensed" a girl on the staircase, and so had Sybil.

That the stairs had been moved was unknown to both Ethel and Sybil at the time, yet both said they had been. Sybil spoke of a man hanged on the stairs, which might very well refer to Old Moor, the sailor hanged for mutiny on the Battery, but buried here in Potter's Field. Clinton Court was built above the old Potter's Field.

The girl, waiting for someone and for something to happen, was felt by both mediums. And the story of the pebbles and footsteps on the roof meshes with Mrs. Meyer's tale of a girl pushed off the roof to her death.

The officer named Walker was a new character in the ever-expanding ghostly cast of Clinton Court. Could he be traced?

Sometimes it is even difficult to trace a living officer, and tracing a dead one isn't easy. I did not expect to be completely successful, but I had hoped that at least one or two names could be traced or proved correct.

Sybil, in trance speaking with the voice and mind of Col. George Walker, had referred to a commanding officer by the name of Amos Wilson. He also said his doctor was one Dr. Warren, and that he had come to New York in 1788. We don't know, at least from the psychic end, whether he was still on active duty in 1792, when presumably his death occurred. He might have been retired and his visit to New York might not have been connected with his military career at all.

It was therefore with considerable interest that I found in Heitman's *Historical Register of Officers of the Continental Army* that a George Walker had been a Second Lieutenant, serving in that capacity to 1783, and that one Amos Wilson, First Lieutenant, had served at least in 1776; also, one John Warren, Surgeon, is recorded for the period from 1777 to 1783. These officers served with Northern regiments, while Walker claimed North Carolina as his home. However, it was not unusual for officers, or men, for that matter, to serve in regiments based in other regions of the country than their own colony. Many Southerners did indeed come north during the revolutionary and post-revolutionary period to serve with established "Yankee" regiments.

In trance, Walker claimed to have had a brother named Aaron Walker, with the rank of Captain. I found a Lt. Aaron Walker, attached to a Connecticut regiment in 1776. George Walker — the one I found listed — served in New Jersey, incidentally, which could have brought him into nearby New York.

I did not locate Walker's other brothers, nor did I come across his father or wife, but we must keep in mind that the records of the period are not complete. Certainly the claimed friendship with George Clinton fits in chronologically. The ghost also spoke several times of a place called Brice, North Carolina, and described it as being near Pike's Hill. There is a Pikes*ville*, North Carolina.

As for Brice, North Carolina — or perhaps Bryce, as the spelling was never given — this took a bit more searching. Finally, the reference librarian of the North Carolina State Library in Raleigh, Mrs. Helen Harrison, was able to supply me with some information.

The *Colonial Records*, which is a list of incorporated towns, early maps, postal guides, etc., revealed nothing about such a place. The State Department of Archives and History also checked their files without success. But in *Colonial Records*, vol. IV, page 16, there is *mention* of a sawmill being erected at Brice's Creek, Newbern, in 1735, and of Samuel Pike receiving a land grant at Newbern in 1748.

"Brice started to acquire land grants as early as 1707," Mrs. Harrison pointed out, "and it is known that Brice built a fort on his plantation and that patents were granted for land on Brice's Creek as late as 1758. It seems possible that this settlement may be the Brice to which you refer."

What about Pike's Hill and Three Hills, which the ghost said were close to each other and to Brice?

"In 1755," Mrs. Harrison stated, "there was a movement to build the capital at Tower Hill, Craven County, N.C. It interested me to find that *all three* of these places are located in Craven County, though Tower Hill may have no connection with Three Hills."

On re-hearing the tapes, I find I cannot be absolutely sure whether the ghost said Tower Hill or Three Hills. It could have been either.

So there you have it. How could Sybil Leek (or I, for that matter) know these minute details that are so obscure even a local historian had difficulty tracing them?

Not a ghost of a chance, I think.

The Teen-Agers and the
Staten Island Ghost

I receive a great many letters from people between the ages of twelve and eighteen who have a serious, often very inquisitive interest in extrasensory perception. Sometimes they have a case of their own to report.

Such was the case when I first heard from Carolyn Westbo, who lived on Staten Island. It seemed that her aunt, Mrs. Carol Packer, had lived in a house on Staten Island where a poltergeist had also taken up residence. Poltergeists are ghosts who like to make noises or move objects around.

Carolyn's aunt no longer lived at the house. I asked the new owners, a family by the name of Goetz, for permission to visit.

What I liked about Carolyn Westbo, who was seventeen and very serious, was that she herself was doubtful about her experiences and wondered if they weren't all due to imagination or, as she put it, "self-delusion." But deep down she knew she was psychic, and had already accepted this knowledge.

"When were you at the house on Henderson Avenue the last time, Carolyn?" I asked.

"The last time I was at the house was in January of 1965," she answered. "My aunt was in the process of moving out, and the house was in an uproar. I stood against the wall and watched the proceedings. My left side was turned to the wall, and I was reminiscing about the wonderful times I had had on New Year's Eve, and somehow smiled to myself. All of a sudden, my *right side*, the right side of my head, felt very depressed and a feeling of great despair came over me. I felt like wringing my hands and was very distraught. It only stayed with me a few moments, but I had the distinct feeling of a woman who was very worried, and I could almost feel something or someone pressing against the right side of my head. And then I saw a mist, in the large downstairs dining room of the house."

"A mist? What sort of mist?"

"It had a shape, rather tall and thin. It did not have a face, and looked kind of ragged. *But I did see hands wringing.*"

Carolyn had told her aunt about her uncanny experience, even though she was afraid she would be laughed at. Her own family had pooh-poohed the whole thing, and Carolyn did not like to be laughed at, especially when she *knew* she had seen what she had seen. But her aunt did not laugh. She, too, had observed the misty shape when she was alone in the house, yet she had always felt great comfort with the ghost, whoever it was.

It was then that Carolyn learned about the poltergeist on Henderson Avenue. Objects were moving by themselves, her aunt admitted, such as things falling from a table and other objects that hadn't been touched. On one occasion she heard a loud crash downstairs — the house had three stories — and found a freshly baked pie upside down on the floor. She had placed it far back on the shelf in the pantry. Pots and pans around the pie had not been touched, and no trucks were passing by outside that might account for the vibration that could have caused the pie to fall. There had been nobody else in the house at the time. The aunt, Carol Packer, now lives in upstate New York. She had never accepted the idea of a ghost, and yet could not offer any explanation for the strange happenings in the house.

"Have you had other experiences of a psychic nature?" I asked the young girl.

"Nothing really great, only little things, such as knowing what my teacher would ask the next day, or what people are wearing when I talk to them on the telephone or dream about them. I see things happening and a week later or so, they do happen."

Carolyn and her aunt had looked into the history of the house. They found that three families prior to Mrs. Packer's stay in the house, a woman had dropped dead on the front porch. They never knew her name or anything else beyond this bare fact.

There the matter stood when our little expedition consisting of Sybil Leek and myself, book editor Evelyn Grippo, and CBS news-caster Lou Adler and his wife, arrived at the Victorian structure where the ghost was presumably awaiting us. Mr. Adler brought along a CBS radio car and an engineer by the name of Leon, who we almost lost on the way over the Verrazano Bridge. It was a humid Sunday evening in May of 1965. Fifteen people had assembled at the Goetzes' to celebrate some kind of anniversary, but I suspect they were very curious about our investigation as an added attraction. We could hear their voices as we mounted the steep wooden steps leading to the house from Henderson Avenue, a quiet street lined with shade trees.

While the CBS people set up their equipment, I politely put the celebrants into the front room and collected those directly concerned with the haunting around a heavy oak table in the dining room on the first floor of the sturdy old house. Carolyn Westbo, her younger sister Betsy, Mr. and Mrs. Goetz, their son and a married daughter,

Mrs. Grippo of Ace Books, the Adlers, and I formed a circle around the table. I had asked Sybil to wait in another room, where she could not possibly overhear a single word that was said in the dining room. Afterwards, skeptical reporter Lou Adler admitted that "unless she had some sort of electronic listening device by which she could listen through walls, or unless you and Sybil set this up to trick everybody — there is no alternative explanation for what occurred this evening." Needless to say, we did not use electronic devices. Sybil could not hear anything, and neither she nor I knew anything of what would happen later.

As soon as Sybil Leek was out of earshot, I started to question the witnesses among those present. Carolyn Westbo repeated her testimony given to me earlier. I then turned my attention, and my microphone, to Betsy Westbo.

Betsy had been to the house a number of times. Had she ever felt anything unusual in this house?

"One time I walked in here," the serious young girl said in response. "My mother and my cousin were in the kitchen downstairs, in the rear of the house, and I walked into the hall. It was dark, about sunset, and I suddenly felt as if someone were staring at me, just looking at me. I was sure it was my cousin, so I asked him to come out. He had played tricks on me before. But he wasn't there, and I went into the kitchen, and he had not left it at all."

"Any other experiences bordering on the uncanny?" I asked.

This 15-year-old girl was calm and not at all given to imagination, I felt, and she struck me as mature beyond her years.

"The time my aunt moved out, I was here, too. I felt as if someone were crying and I wanted to cry with them. I was just walking around then, and it felt as if someone were next to me crying and saying, 'What's going to happen to me?'"

Betsy had also had psychic experiences in her young life. Not long before in her family's house, just down the street from the haunted house her aunt used to call home, Betsy was asleep in bed around 11 P.M., when she awoke with a start.

"I heard a screech and a dog yelping, as if he had been hurt. I was sure there had been an accident, and we looked out the window, but there was nothing, no car, no dog."

"What did you do then?"

"We couldn't figure it out," Betsy answered, "but the very next evening, again at eleven o'clock, we heard the same noises — my sister was with me in the room this time. We checked again, and this time there was a dog. I had seen the entire accident happen, *exactly as it did, twenty-four hours before!*"

"Amazing," I conceded. "Then you are indeed clairvoyant."

Mrs. Mariam Goetz, a pleasant-looking, vivacious woman in her middle years, had been the lady of the house since February of 1965. She had not seen or heard anything uncanny, and she felt very happy in the house. But then there was this strange business about the silver —

"My silver spoons disappeared, one by one, and we searched and searched, and we thought someone was playing a prank. Each blamed the other, but neither Mr. Goetz, nor my son, nor my young married daughter, Irene Nelson, who lives with us, had hidden the spoons. The wedding gifts were displayed in Grandmother's room upstairs, including some pretty silver objects. One evening, after about a week of this, we discovered in each bowl — a silver spoon! Of course we thought Grandmother had been playing a trick on us, but she assured us she had not."

The rest of the spoons turned up in the drawers of the room, carefully hidden in many places. Although the grandmother was quite aged, she was in good mental condition, and the Goetzes really had no proof that she hid the spoons.

"Irene, my married daughter, had come to sleep with me several nights, because she hadn't felt very secure in her own bedroom," Mrs. Goetz added.

Mrs. Irene Nelson was a young woman with dark eyes and dark hair, not the dreamer type, but rather factually minded and to the point. She had been in the house as long as her parents, four months to the time of my investigation.

Had she noticed anything unusual?

"Yes," the young woman said. "One night I was sitting in the kitchen at the table, with two friends of mine, and as we sat there and talked, some screws were falling to the floor from the kitchen table, by themselves, one by one. My friends left. I got up to gather my things, and the table collapsed behind me. One of its legs had come off by itself. But the table was not wobbly, or any of the screws loose, just before we used it, or we would have noticed it. There was nobody else in the house who could have loosened the screws as a prank, either."

"And poor Grandmother can't be blamed for it, either," I added. The octogenarian did not get around very much any more.

"Anything else?" I asked, crisply.

"One night, about four in the morning," Mrs. Nelson said, "I woke up with a sudden start and I opened my eyes and could not close them again. Suddenly, I felt pin-prickles all over my body. I felt chilly. I felt there was someone in the room I could not see. I heard a strange sound, seemingly outside, as if someone were sweeping the sidewalk. This was in my bedroom directly above the living room. The feeling lasted about ten minutes, and I just lay there, motionless and frightened. I had several bad nights after that, but that first time was the worst."

"Have you ever felt another presence when you were alone?"

"Yes, I have. In different parts of the house."

The house, along with the building next door, was built at the turn of the century. It was Victorian in architecture and appointments. Heavy wooden beams, many small rooms on the three floors, high ceilings, and solid staircases characterized the house on Henderson Avenue.

It was time to bring Sybil Leek into the dining room and start the trance.

Had anything happened to her while she was waiting outside in the kitchen? Sybil seemed somewhat upset, a very unusual state for this usually imperturbable psychic lady.

"I was standing by the refrigerator," she reported, "and the kitchen door opened about two inches. It disturbed me, for I did not want anyone to think I was opening the door to listen. There was someone there, I felt, and I could have easily gone into trance that moment, but fought it as I never do this without you being present."

Imagine — a ghost too impatient to wait for the proper signal!

"I wanted to run outside, but restrained myself," Sybil added. "I never moved from the spot near the refrigerator. I was terrified, which I rarely am."

We sat down, and soon Sybil was in deep trance. Before long, a faint voice made itself heard through Sybil's lips.

"What is your name?" I asked.

"Anne Meredith." It came with great difficulty of breathing.

"Is this your house?"

"Yes . . . I want to get in. I live here. *I want to get in!*"

"What's wrong?"

"I . . . have . . . heart trouble . . . I can't get up the steps."

Sybil's breathing was heavy and labored.

"How long have you lived here?"

"Thirty-five."

"What year did you move in?"

"Twenty-two."

"Were you alone in this house?"

"No . . . James . . . these steps . . . James . . . son."

"What is it you want?"

"I can't stay here . . . want to get in . . . the steps . . . can't get to the door . . . *door must be opened.*"

"How old are you?"

"Fifty-two."

"Where did you go to school?"

"Derby . . . Connecticut."

"Your father's name?"

"Johannes."

"Mother's?"

"Marguerite."

"Where were you baptized?"

"Derby . . . my lips are sore . . . I bite them . . . I have pain in my heart."

I started to explain her true status to her.

"You passed out of the physical life in this house," I began. "It is no longer your house. You must go on and join your family, those who have passed on before you. Do you understand?"

She did not.

"I have to get up the stairs," she mumbled over and over again.

As I repeated the formula I usually employ to pry an unhappy ghost away from the place of emotional turmoil in the past, Sybil broke out of trance momentarily, her eyes wide open, staring in sheer terror and lack of understanding at the group. Quickly, I hypnotized her back into the trance state, and in a moment or two, the ghost was back in control of Sybil's vocal apparatus. Heavy tears now rolled down the medium's cheeks. Obviously, she was undergoing great emotional strain. Now the voice returned slowly.

"I want to come in . . . I have to come back!"

"You died on the steps of this house. You can't come back," I countered.

"Someone's there," the ghost insisted in a shaky voice. "I have to come back."

"Who is it you want to come back to?"

"James."

I assured her James was well taken care of, and she need not worry about him anymore.

"Don't leave me outside, I shall die," she said now.

"You *have* died, dear," I replied, quietly.

"Open the door, open the door," she demanded.

I took another tack. Suggesting that the door was being opened for her, I took her "by the hand" and showed her that someone else lived here now. No James. I even took her "upstairs" by suggestion. She seemed shocked.

"I don't believe you."

"This is the year 1965," I said.

"Fifty-five?"

"No, sixty-five."

There was disbelief. Then she complained that a dog kept her up, and also mentioned that her mother was living upstairs.

What was the dog's name?

"Silly dog . . . Franz." A dog named Franz was unusual even for a ghost, I thought. Still, people do like to give their pets strange names. The Goetzes had named their aged spaniel Happy, and I had never seen a more subdued dog in my life.

Why was she afraid of the dog? I asked the ghost.

"I fall over him," she complained. "My heart . . . dog is to blame."

"But this happened in 1955, you say."

"Happened *today*," she answered. To a ghost, time stands still. She insisted this was 1955. I strongly insisted it was 1965. I explained once more what had happened to her.

"Not dead," she said. "Not in the body? That's silly."

Unfortunately, very few ghosts know that they are dead. It comes as a shock when I tell them.

"I'm going upstairs and neither you nor that dog will stop me," she finally said resolutely.

I agreed to help her up the stairs.

"Lift me," she pleaded.

Mentally, we opened the door and went upstairs.

"Where is my mother?" she said, obviously realizing that her mother was not there. I explained she had died. The truth of the situation began to dawn on Anne Meredith.

I took advantage of this state of affairs to press my point and suggest her mother was awaiting her outside the house.

"May I come back sometime?" the ghost asked in a feeble voice.

"You may if you wish," I promised, "but now you must join your mother."

As the ghost faded away, Sybil returned to her own body.

She felt fine, but, of course, remembered nothing of what had come out of her mouth during trance. Just before awakening, tears once more rolled down her face.

I thought it rather remarkable that Sybil, in her trance state, had brought on a female personality who had died of a heart attack on the outside steps leading to the house. Sybil had no way of knowing that such a person actually existed and that her death had indeed taken place some years ago as described.

What about the names Anne Meredith and James?

Carolyn Westbo checked with the lady who had owned both houses and who lived in the one next door, a Miss Irving. Quite aged herself, she did not recall anyone with the name of Anne Meredith. By a strange coincidence, her own first names were Anne Adelaide. Derby, Connecticut, exists.

Checking church registers is a long and doubtful job at best. Finding a record of Anne Meredith would be wonderful, of course, but if I didn't find such a record, it didn't mean she never existed. Many tenants had come and gone in the old house atop the hill on Henderson Avenue. Perhaps Anne and Meredith were only her first and middle names.

Time will tell.

Meanwhile, it is to be profoundly hoped that the hand-wringing lady ghost of Staten Island need not climb those horrible stairs any longer, nor cope with dogs who have no respect for ghosts — especially ghosts who once owned the house.

The Phantom Admiral

I had never heard of Goddard College until I received a letter from Jay Lawrence, a second-semester student at Goddard College in Plainfield, Vermont. Mr. Lawrence was serious about his interest in psychic phenomena and he had some evidence to offer. He did more than ask me to speak at the college on extrasensory perception; he invited me to come and have a look at a ghost he had discovered in Whitefield, New Hampshire, about two hours' drive from Goddard.

The haunted house in Whitefield belonged to the Jacobsen family who used it as a summer home only. The younger Jacobsen, whose first name was Erlend — they're of Norwegian descent — invited us to come stay at the house, or at least have a look at it. The Goddard College boys offered to pick us up in Boston and drive us up through the scenic White Mountains to Whitefield.

We arrived at dusk, when the country tends to be peaceful and the air is almost still. The house was at the end of a narrow, winding driveway lined by tall trees, hidden away from the road. There was a wooden porch around three sides of the wooden structure, which rose up three stories.

We were welcomed by Erlend Jacobsen, his wife, Martha, and

their little boy Erlend Eric, a bright youngster who had met the ghost, too, as we were to find out.

Inside the house with its spacious downstairs dining room and kitchen, decorated in a flamboyant style by the Jacobsens, we found Mr. and Mrs. Nelson, two friends of the owners, and Jeff Broadbent, a young fellow student of Jay Lawrence.

Sybil puttered around the house, indulging her interest in antiques. I mounted my tape recorder to hear the testimony of those who had experienced anything unusual in the house. We went upstairs, where Sybil Leek could not very well hear us, and entered a small bedroom on the second floor, which, I was told, was the main center of ghostly activities, although not the only one.

The house was called "Mis 'n Top" by its original owner and builder. I lost no time in questioning Erlend Jacobsen, a tall young man of thirty on the Goddard College faculty as an instructor, about his experiences in the old house.

"When my parents decided to turn the attic into a club room where I could play with my friends," Erlend Jacobsen began, "they cut windows into the wall and threw out all the possessions of the former owner of the house they had found there. I was about seven at the time.

"Soon after, footsteps and other noises began to be heard in the attic and along the corridors and stairs leading toward it. But it was not until the summer of 1956, when I was a senior in college and had just married, that I experienced the first really important disturbance."

"1955, Erlend," the wife interrupted. Wives have a way of remembering such dates. Mr. Jacobsen blushed and corrected himself.

"1955, you're right," he said. "That summer we slept here for the first time in this room, one flight up, and almost nightly we were either awakened by noises or could not sleep, waiting for them to begin. At first we thought they were animal noises, but they were too much like footsteps and heavy objects being moved across the floor overhead, and down the hall. We were so scared we refused to move in our beds or turn on the lights."

"But you did know of the tradition that the house was haunted, did you not?" I asked.

"Yes, I grew up with it. All I knew is what I had heard from my parents. The original owner and builder of the house, an admiral named Hawley, and his wife, were both most difficult people. The admiral died in 1933. In 1935, the house was sold by his daughter, who was then living in Washington, to my parents. Anyone who happened to be trespassing on his territory would be chased off it, and I imagine he would not have liked our throwing out his sea chest and other personal possessions."

"Any other experience outside the footsteps?"

"About four years ago," Erlend Jacobsen replied, "my wife and I, and a neighbor, Shepard Vogelgesang, were sitting in the living room downstairs discussing interpretations of the Bible. I needed a dictionary at one point in the discussion and got up to fetch it from upstairs.

"I ran up to the bend here, in front of this room, and there were no lights on at the time. I opened the door to the club room and started to go up the stairs, when suddenly I walked into what I can only describe as a *warm, wet blanket,* something that touched me physically as if it had been hung from wires in the corridor. I was very upset, backed out, and went downstairs. My wife took one look at me and said, 'You're white.' 'I know,' I said. *'I think I just walked into the admiral.'*"

"I suppose he didn't enjoy your bumping into him in this fashion either," I commented. "Anything else?"

"I was alone in the house, in the club room, which is designed like a four-leaf clover — you can see into the section opposite you, but you can't see into the other two. I was lying there, looking out the window at sunset, when I heard someone breathing — rhythmically breathing in, out, in, out."

"What did you do?"

"I held my own breath, because at first I thought I might be doing it. But I was not. The breathing continued right next to me! I became terrified, being then only fifteen years of age, and ran out of the house until my parents returned."

I asked him again about the time *he touched the ghost*.

How did it feel? Did it have the touch of a human body?

"Nothing like it. It was totally dark, but it was definitely warm, and it resisted my passage."

"Has anything happened to you here recently?"

"About two and a half weeks ago, I walked into the house at dusk and I heard very faint crying for about fifteen or twenty seconds. I thought it might be a cat, but there was no cat in the house, and just as suddenly as it had started, the crying stopped. It sounded almost as if it were outside this window, here on the second floor."

"Is there any record of a tragedy attached to this house?"

"None that I know of."

"Who else has seen or heard anything uncanny here?"

"My parents used to have a Negro maid who was psychic. She had her share of experiences here all right. Her name is Sarah Wheeler and she is about seventy-five now. The admiral had a reputation for disliking colored people, and she claimed that when she was in bed here, frequently the bedposts would move as if someone were trying to throw her out of bed. The posts would move off the floor and rock the bed violently, held by unseen hands, until she got out of bed, and then they would stop. She was a Catholic and went to the church the next day to fetch some Holy Water. That quieted things down. But the first night of each season she would come without her Holy Water and that was when things were worst for her."

"Poor Sarah," I said.

"She was psychic, and she had an Indian guide," Erlend Jacobsen continued. "I did not put much stock in some of the things she told us, such as there being treasure underneath the house, put there by the old admiral. But eight or nine years ago, I had occasion to recall this. The house has no cellar but rests on stone pillars. We used to throw junk under the house, where wooden steps led down below. I was cleaning up there with a flashlight, when I saw something shiny. It was a cement block with a silver handle sticking out of it. I chipped the cement off, and found a silver bowl, with 'A.H.' engraved on it."

I turned my attention to Mrs. Jacobsen. She had three children, but still gave the impression of being a college sophomore. As a matter of fact, she was taking courses at Goddard, where her husband was an instructor.

It was ten years to the day — our visit was on June 11 — that the Jacobsens had come to this house as newlyweds.

"We spent one night here, then went on our honeymoon, and then came back and spent the rest of the summer here," Martha Jacobsen said. "The first night I was very, very frightened — hearing this walking up and down the halls, and we the only ones in the house! There was a general feeling of eerieness and a feeling that there was someone else in the house. There were footsteps in the hall outside our bedroom door. At one point before dawn, the steps went up the stairs and walked around overhead. But Erlend and I were the only ones in the house. We checked."

Imagine one's wedding night interrupted by unseen visitors — this could give a girl a trauma!

"Two weeks later we returned and stayed here alone," Mrs. Jacobsen continued, "and I heard these footsteps several times. Up and down. We've been coming here for the last ten years and I heard it again a couple of weeks ago."

"Must be unnerving," I observed.

"It is. I heard the steps overhead in the club room, and also, while I was downstairs two weeks ago, the door to the kitchen opened itself and closed itself, without anyone being visible. Then the front door did the same thing — opened and shut itself.

"Along with the footsteps I heard things being dragged upstairs, heavy objects, it seemed. But nothing was disarranged afterwards. We checked."

"Any other events of an uncanny nature?" I asked as a matter of record. Nothing would surprise me in *this* house.

"About ten years ago, when we first moved in, I also heard the heavy breathing when only my husband and I were in the house. Then there was a house guest we had, a Mrs. Anne Merriam. She had this room and her husband was sleeping down the hall in one of the single rooms. Suddenly, she saw a figure standing at the foot of her bed."

"What did she do?"

"She called out, 'Carol, is that you?' twice, but got no answer. Then, just as suddenly as it had come, the figure dissolved into thin air.

"She queried her husband about coming into her room, but he told her that he had never left his bed that night. When this happened on another night, she attempted to follow the figure, and found her husband entering through another door!"

"Has anyone else had an encounter with a ghost here?" I asked.

"Well, another house guest went up into the attic and came running down reporting that the door knob had turned in front of his very eyes before he could reach for it to open the door. The dog was with him, and steadfastly refused to cross the threshold. That was Frank Kingston and it all happened before our marriage. Then another house guest arrived very late at night, about five years ago. We had already gone to bed, and he knew he had to sleep in the attic since every other room was already taken. Instead, I found him sleeping in the living room, on the floor, in the morning. He knew nothing about the ghost. 'I'm not going back up there any more,' he vowed, and would not say anything further. I guess he must have run into the admiral."

What a surprise that must have been, I thought, especially if the admiral was all wet.

"Three years ago, my brother came here," Mrs. Jacobsen continued her report. "His name is Robert Gillman. In the morning he complained of having been awake all night. A former skeptic, he knew now that the tales of ghostly footsteps were true, for he, too, had heard them — all night long in fact."

Jeffrey Broadbent was a serious young man who accompanied Jay Lawrence to the house one fine night, to see if what they were saying about the admiral's ghost was true.

They had sleeping bags and stayed up in the attic. It was a chilly November night in 1964, and everything seemed just right for ghosts. Would they be lucky in their quest? They did not have to wait long to find out.

"As soon as we entered the room, we heard strange noises on the roof. They were indistinct and could have been animals, I thought at first. We went off to sleep until Jay woke me up hurriedly around six in the morning. I distinctly heard human footsteps on the roof. They slid down the side to a lower level and then to the ground where they could be heard walking in leaves and into the night. Nothing could be seen from the window and there was nobody up on the roof. We were the only ones in the house that night, so it surely must have been the ghost."

Jay Lawrence added one more thing to this narrative.

"When we first turned out the flashlight up in the attic, I distinctly heard a high-pitched voice — a kind of scream or whine — followed by footsteps. They were of a human foot wearing shoes, but much lighter than the normal weight of a human body would require."

Jerry Weener also had spent time at the haunted house.

"In early March of 1965, Jay and I came over and had dinner at the fireplace downstairs. We decided to sleep downstairs and both of us, almost simultaneously, had a dream that night in which we met the admiral's ghost, but unfortunately on awakening, we did not recall anything specific or what he might have said to us in our dreams. A second time when I slept in the house, nothing happened. The third time I came over with friends, I slept in the attic, and I heard footsteps. We searched the house from top to bottom, but there was no one else who could have accounted for those steps."

Erlend Eric, age eight going on nine, was perhaps the youngest witness to psychic phenomena scientifically recorded, but his testimony should not be dismissed because of his age. He had heard footsteps going up and down and back up the stairs. One night he was sleeping in the room across the hall when he heard someone trying to talk to him.

"What sort of voice was it?" I asked. Children are frequently more psychic than adults.

"It was a man's," the serious youngster replied. "He called my name, but I forgot what else he said. That was three years ago."

Miriam Nelson was a petite young woman, the wife of one of Erlend Jacobsen's friends, who had come to witness our investigation that evening. She seemed nervous and frightened and asked me to take her to another room so I could hear her story in private. We went across the hall into the room where the figure had stood at the head of the bed and I began my questioning.

"My first experience was when Erlend and I brought a Welsh Corgi up here; Erlend's parents were here, too. I was downstairs in the library; the dog was in my lap. Suddenly I felt another presence in the room, and I could not breathe anymore. The dog started to bark and insist that I follow him out of the room. I distinctly felt someone there.

"Then on a cold fall day about four years ago, I was sitting by the stove, trying to get warm, when one of the burners lifted itself up about an inch and fell down again. I looked and it moved again. It could not have moved by itself. I was terrified. I was alone in the house."

I had heard all those who had had an encounter with the ghost and it was time to get back downstairs where the Jacobsens had laid out a fine dinner — just the right thing after a hard day's drive. A little later we all went up the stairs to the top floor, where Sybil stretched out on a couch near the window. We grouped ourselves around her in the haunted attic and waited.

"I had a feeling of a *middle* room upstairs," Sybil said, "but I don't feel anything too strongly yet."

Soon Sybil was in deep trance as we awaited the coming of the admiral — or whoever the ghost would be — with bated breath. The only light in the attic room was a garish fluorescent lamp, which we shut off, and replaced with a smaller conventional lamp. It was quiet, as quiet as only a country house can be. But instead of the ghost speaking to us directly and presumably giving us hell for trespassing, it was Sybil herself, in deep trance "on the other side," reporting what she saw — things and people the ordinary eye could not perceive.

"I'm walking around," Sybil said. "There is a man lying dead in the middle room. Big nose, not too much hair in front, little beard cut short now. There is a plant near him."

"Try to get his name, Sybil," I ordered.

"I'll have to go into the room," she said.

We waited.

"He is not in here *all* the time," she reported back. "He came here to die."

"Is this his house?"

"Yes, but there is another house also. A long way off. This man had another house. Hawsley . . . Hawsley."

Almost the exact name of the admiral, I thought. Sybil could not have known that name.

"He went from one house to another, in a different country. Something Indian."

"Is he still here and what does he want?"

"To find a place to rest because . . . he does not know in which house it's in!"

"What is he looking for?"

"Little basket. Not from this country. Like a handle . . . it's shiny . . . silver . . . a present. It went to the wrong house. He gave it to the wrong house. He is very particular not to get things confused. It belongs to Mrs. Gerard at the other house. He usually stays in the little room, one flight up. With the fern. By the bed."

"But what about Mrs. Gerard? How can we send the package to her unless we get her address?" I said.

"It's very important. It's in the wrong perspective, he says," Sybil explained.

"What did he have for a profession?" I tried again.

"He says he brought things . . . seeds."

"What are his initials or first name?"

"A. J. H."

Sybil seemed to listen to someone we could not see.

"He's not troublesome," she said. "He goes when I get near to him. Wants to go to the other house."

"Where is the other house?"

"Liang . . . Street . . . Bombay."

"Does he know he is dead?"

"No."

I instructed her to tell him.

"Any family?"

"Two families . . . Bombay."

"Children?"

"Jacob . . . Martin."

It was not clear whether the ghost said Jacob or Jacobsen.

"He is shaking himself," Sybil now reported. "What upset him? He worries about names. A. J. A. name on something he is worried about. The names are wrong on a paper. He said Jacobsen is wrong. It should be Jacob Hawsley son."

Evidently the ghost did not approve the sale of his house by his executors, but wanted it to go to his son.

"Because of two houses, two families, he did not know what to do with the other."

"What does 'A' stand for in his name?"

"Aaron . . . Aaron Jacob."

"Does he have any kind of title or professional standing?"

"A-something . . . A-D-M . . . can't read . . . Administrator A-D-M . . . it's on the paper, but I can't read the paper."

Still, she did get the admiral's rank!

I promised to have the gift delivered to Mrs. Gerard, if we could find her, but he must not stay in this house any further.

"Who waters the plants, he asks," Sybil said.

I assured him the plants would be taken care of.

"But what about the other house, who waters the plants there?" the ghost wanted to know.

"How does he go there?" I asked in return.

"He sails," Sybil replied. "Takes a long time."

Again I promised to find the house in India, if I could.

"What about a date?" I asked. "How long ago did all this happen?"

"About 1867," Sybil replied.

"How old was he then?"

"Fifty-nine."

I implored the admiral not to cause any untidiness in the house by upsetting its inhabitants. The reply via Sybil was stiff.

"As a man with an administrative background, he is always tidy," Sybil reported. "But he is going now."

"He is going now," Sybil repeated, "and he's taking the ferns."

I called Sybil back to her own body, so as not to give some unwanted intruder a chance to stop in before she was back in the driver's seat, so to speak.

None the worse for her travels in limbo, Sybil sat up and smiled at us, wondering why we all stared at her so intently. She remembered absolutely nothing.

Erlend Jacobsen spoke up.

"That basket she mentioned," he said. "When my parents first bought the house, there was hanging over the dining room, on a chain, a stuffed armadillo, which had been shellacked from the outside. It had straw handles and had been turned into a *basket*. It was around the house until about five years ago, but I have no idea where it is now. For all we know, it may still be around the house somewhere."

"Better find it," I said. "That is, if you want those footsteps to cease!"

Just as we were leaving the house, the senior Jacobsens returned. Mr. Eric Jacobsen does not care for ghosts and I was told not to try to get him to talk about the subject. But his wife, Josephine, Erlend's mother, had been pushed down the stairs by the ghost — or so she claims. This is quite possible, judging by the way the admiral was behaving in his post-funeral days and nights.

Our job in Whitefield seemed finished and we continued on to Stowe, Vermont, where we had decided to stay at the famous Trapp Family Lodge. Catherine had become interested in Mrs. Trapp's books, and from *The Sound of Music*, we both thought that the lodge would provide a welcome interlude of peace during a hectic weekend of ghost hunting.

The next morning we rested up from the rigors of our investigation and found the world around us indeed peaceful and promising. The following morning we would go down to Goddard College and address students and teachers on the subject of ghosts, which would leave us with a pleasant afternoon back at Stowe, before flying back to Manhattan. But we had reckoned without the commercial spirit at the lodge. Like most overnight lodgings, they wanted us out of our rooms by eleven o'clock Sunday morning, but finally offered to let us stay until two. I declined.

After my talk at the college, we were taken to one of the girls' dormitories where uncanny happenings had taken place. The college was situated on the old Martin farm, and the manor had been turned into a most elegant girl students' residence, without losing its former Victorian grandeur. Reports of a dead butler still walking the old corridors upstairs had reached my ears. Two students, Madeleine Ehrman and Dorothy Frazier, knew of the ghost. The phenomena were mainly footsteps when no one was about. A teacher who did not believe in ghosts set foot in the manor and later revealed that the name Dawson had constantly impressed itself on her mind. Later research revealed that a butler by that name did in fact live at the manor house long ago.

Sue Zuckerman was a New York girl studying at Goddard.

"One night last semester," she said, "I was up late studying when I heard footsteps approaching my room. After a few seconds I opened my door — there was nobody there. I closed the door and resumed studying. I then heard footsteps walking away from my door. I looked again, but saw nothing.

"During this time for a period of about three weeks, my alarm clock had been shut off every night. I would set it for about seven-thirty, but when I woke up much later than that, the alarm button was always off. I began hiding my clock, locking my door — but it still happened.

"Back in 1962, I was toying with a Ouija board I had bought more in fun than as a serious instrument of communication. I had never gotten anything through it that could not have come from my own mind, but that Friday afternoon in 1962, I worked it in the presence of three other friends, and as soon as we put our hands on it, it literally started to leap around. It went very fast, giving a message one of us took down: 'I am dead . . . of drink.'" Are you here now in the Manor?' 'One could speak of my presence here.' There was more, but I can't remember it now.

"Afterwards, a strange wind arose and as we walked past a tree outside, it came crashing down."

I don't know about strange "wind," and Ouija boards are doubtful things at times, but the footfalls of the restless butler named Dawson must have been a most unusual extracurricular activity for the co-eds at Goddard College.

The Somerville Ghost

"**I'**m Mrs. Campano," the letter read in a large, clear handwriting, "and I've been living in this house for four months now." The woman had heard me on station WBZ, Boston, and wanted to report a haunted house.

I called her and found Mrs. Campano a reasonable, well-spoken lady in her middle years. Her elder daughter had recently married and her son was grown, and it made sense for the mother to move to a smaller house. But at the moment she was still at the haunted house on Washington Avenue in Somerville, Massachusetts.

The first impression that something strange went on in her house was when she noticed her dog's unusual behavior. The dog barked constantly and kept running up and down the stairs to the upper floor. When the daughter moved out, she took the dog with her, and Mrs. Campano's house became quiet *except for the ghost.*

There was a light in the downstairs living room of the wooden house, so she found it unnecessary to turn on any additional lights when she wanted to mount the stairs. One night in 1964, when she passed the stairway, she heard someone crying. She entered the bathroom, and when she came out she still heard the sound of someone crying as if hurt. She walked up the stairs, thinking it was one of her children having a nightmare, but when she got to the top of the stairs, the crying stopped.

She checked all the rooms upstairs, and the children were fast asleep. She went back to bed downstairs. Then, above her head, she distinctly heard the shuffling of feet, as if two people were fighting and struggling. She had a puppy, who started to act strangely just as the larger dog had done.

The experience upset Mrs. Campano no end, and she talked it over with her elder daughter, Marsha, now married. The girl was sympathetic, for she, too, had heard the crying and at one time footsteps of someone going up and down the stairs, with the crying continuing for about twenty minutes. It sounded like a woman.

They decided to do something about the noises. A group of young boys, friends of her son's, stayed overnight at the old house. They took the upstairs room where most of the disturbances centered. At first, everything was quiet. The youngest girl and some of her friends went to sleep in another room upstairs. Soon the boys heard tapping and crying, but thought the girls were trying to put over a practical joke. They jumped from their beds and raced across the hall only to find the girls fast asleep in their room.

Mrs. Campano turned to the church for relief, but the local priest refused to come. A friend supplied her with Holy Water but the relief was short lived. A week later, noises started up again.

When Marsha, the elder daughter, had the bedroom to the right upstairs, she often heard the crying and felt as though someone were touching her. But she had kept quiet about these sensations. After she had moved out, the younger daughter, who had the room now, also reported that she felt a presence in her room, and something or someone unseen touching her feet as if to rouse her!

The eighteen-year-old son also had heard the footsteps and crying and had decided to check on the source. When he had reached the hallway, the crying suddenly stopped, but the puppy, which had come with him, kept on growling. Ten minutes later the noises started up again, this time from the cellar.

One more thing Mrs. Campano found strange about the house: on the wall of the room upstairs there was a red spot that looked like blood.

I reached Jim Tuverson, of WBZ's "Contact" program, to arrange for a visit to the haunted house on Washington Avenue, Somerville.

There was a problem, though. Mrs. Campano had decided to move out on May 31, 1965, and our visit would be in June. We took it up with the landlord, Costa & Sons. This is not so easy as it sounds. How do you tell a real estate man one of his properties is haunted? You don't tell him, that's how. You do tell him you've got an interest in old New England houses and could you do a little historical research?

When we arrived at the house I realized immediately how funny the request must have sounded to Mr. Costa. The house was a ramshackle, run-down structure. Since Mrs. Campano had moved, we agreed to see her *after* the investigation and trance session.

It was a warm day for Boston when we met Jim Tuverson and Bob Kennedy of WBZ at Logan Airport. Sybil Leek had flown in directly from San Francisco — using an airplane of course — and joined us for the ride to the haunted house. She knew nothing whatever about the case, not even the location of the house. We left our cars in front of the house where a few curious people had gathered. They rarely saw two radio cars pull up in this unglamorous section of town.

Quickly we went inside the house where a lady from the real estate firm of Costa & Sons was expecting us. The house had been stripped of all its contents except the dirt, which was still around in generous quantities. The aroma was somewhat less than heavenly and it was my fondest wish to get out of there as soon as possible. It was about four in the afternoon and bright, but Sybil never lets such things bother her when we investigate a place.

We hastily borrowed a chair from the house across the street and assembled in the kitchen downstairs. Sybil took to the chair, and I began the session by asking for her impressions of this dismal house.

"As you know, I came in and walked right out again and got a drink next door — that's always a bad sign for me. I don't like this place at all, and I don't think we're in the right room. The upstairs room is the right place."

"What do you feel about the upstairs?"

"There is a strange smell in one of the rooms upstairs, not just a physical smell, but something beyond that. I always associate this smell with something quite evil and I don't think I'm in for a good time."

"What do you think has taken place in this house?" I asked.

"I think there has been some violence here," Sybil replied without hesitation, "the right hand room upstairs."

"Do you feel any presence in this house?"

"I feel a very bad *head* right now," Sybil said and touched the back of her own head as if she felt the pain herself. "My head is very bad. There is some lingering evil which pervades not only the inside of the house, but even the outside is not immune."

I then asked Sybil to relax as well as she could under these uncomfortable circumstances, and to allow whatever entity might be hovering about to communicate through her.

Outside the warm air was filled with the distant noises of a bustling city, but inside the drab, dirty house, time seemed to stand still as we tried to wedge open a doorway into another dimension.

"Things are different today," Sybil finally said. "I'm looking in at the house — but nobody can speak through me."

We should have gone upstairs to the room Sybil thought was the center of the haunting, I thought. Still, one never knows. Sometimes just being in a house, any place within the walls, is sufficient to make contact.

I instructed Sybil to remain in trance and to report back anything she could find.

"Right hand side," Sybil said in a quiet, slow voice, different from her habitual speech. "There's someone in the house . . . it's a girl."

"What do you see upstairs?"

"I see the girl on the bed. She's got long, wavy hair, she can't get up, her head is very bad."

"Is she injured?"

"Yes . . . in the back. She's dead. There's a child or a dog, a child . . . this is 1936 . . . I keep going outside the house, you see, because there's someone around . . . I can't find him."

"Can you speak to the woman on the bed?"

"She worries about the child."

I explained about her true status and where the child now was.

"She's getting angry," Sybil reported. "She does not believe you."

I told Sybil to instruct the woman how to call for her child. But the ghost was very confused. We tried to get her to follow Sybil out of the house. I kept explaining what had happened to her.

"She won't leave until she finds the child," Sybil explained and I kept thinking of the scurrying footsteps on those stairs, the crying — it all fitted in with a mother trying to find her baby!

"What is her name?" I asked.

There was silence as we waited for more evidence from Sybil's lips.

"Linda Mathews," Sybil said, clearly and distinctly.

"And the child's name?"

"Margaret."

I had never heard these names before in connection with this case, nor had anyone else in the room. Mrs. Campano had not mentioned them to me either.

I instructed Linda to call for her child and then leave the house. But she wouldn't budge.

"She's waiting for someone . . . Robert Shaw was here, she says."

"Did *he* hurt her?"

"She'll kill him, because she hates him enough. He hurt her. He hit her."

"Did he kill her?"

"She doesn't know."

"Did her husband kill her?"

"She doesn't know."

Again Sybil, on my urging, explained her situation to the ghost.

"She's coming a little closer now," Sybil reported. "I think she's Scotch. Country type. She's moving now, off the bed. I'm with her. She's very weak."

I told Sybil to withdraw as soon as the ghost was safely outside the house. Quickly I brought her out of trance.

"Quite an ordeal, somehow," Sybil said, although she did not remember anything that had come through her while in trance. I sent her and my wife on to the radio station with Bob Kennedy, while Jim Tuverson and I drove in his car to Mrs. Campano's new house, a few blocks down Washington Avenue.

The new house was much smaller and the Campanos occupied only a part of it, but it was brighter and much more cheerful than the house we had just left.

A sudden idea struck me. I walked into the Campano living room, and shot a question at Mrs. Campano —

"Have you ever heard of Linda Mathews?"

"Yes," Mrs. Campano replied with surprise. "I used to get her mail at the old house all the time, and always sent it back. She used to live in the house. In fact, she died there. But I don't know any more than that."

Here we had immediate corroboration of a name — not a common name like Jones or Smith, but a definite name not easily guessed — and information concerning this name had not been known to anybody in the haunted house while we were there!

Thus Sybil could not have gotten the name from the unconscious minds of any of us in the house, not indeed from me, since I had only learned of the Mathews matter this minute. Jim Tuverson was visibly impressed. Here was proof of the kind that would stand up in any court of law. Sybil had really done a superb job.

I questioned Mrs. Campano about her experiences at the house. Was there anything she had not told me prior to my coming to Somerville?

"It was like a woman crying as if she had been hurt," she reiterated. "Then one night I was the last one to go to bed and everything seemed perfectly normal. In the morning, however, I discovered a series of pictures, which I have in the room between bookends, placed on the floor as if by human hands. Nobody could have done this."

I thought perhaps the unfortunate woman ghost had been trying to get her attention.

"What about your husband?" I asked. "Has he ever heard anything unusual?"

"Yes. One morning we came in around 3 A.M., and we were in the kitchen downstairs cooking, when we both heard someone coming down the stairs. He thought one of the children had smelled the food and was about to join us, but, of course, nobody appeared."

"What about you and your son hearing those footsteps coming up from the cellar?" I asked.

"It sounded like someone in heavy boots coming up the cellar steps," Mrs. Campano explained, "and then we heard the noise of someone handling pots and pans in the kitchen."

"Were they actually moved around?"

"Yes. The next morning we found the kitchen in disorder, but nobody had been in who could have done this. No burglars, either."

I began to wonder if the cellar at the Washington Avenue house did not hold the bodies of two murdered people.

"Did you check the cellar?" I asked.

"The next day," Mrs. Campano replied, "but we found nothing."

Mrs. Campano's father, Peter Cagliano, 73, is a mystic and probably psychic. He came to the house, and for a while things became quiet after that.

Evidently, Mrs. Campano also had inherited some of her family's psychic talents. Her first psychic experience took place when she was 17 years old. She then lived in a house where a murder had been committed and witnessed the noises and physical phenomena accompanying the haunting. Seven years ago, she saw the apparition of a woman known to have died, by the name of Jehasses, but no communication ensued.

"What do you know about a murder committed in the house you just left?" I finally asked her.

"The husband killed his wife and baby, and then himself," she replied, *"with an ax, up in one of the rooms."*

Exactly what Sybil had said in trance!

There was one more witness I wanted to question: Mrs. Campano's married daughter, Marsha Parmesano, who used to sleep in the haunted room upstairs.

"When I was asleep," she said, "I used to feel someone breathing over me, but when I turned around there was nobody there. At the edge of my bed I felt someone sitting there, like gettin' up and sittin' down, but there was no one there. That was the room to the right, upstairs. I felt it a couple of times."

After all, she was occupying Linda Mathews' bed — and adding discomfort to the ghost's unhappy state.

We left the Somerville ghost house with the conviction that the next tenant would have nothing to worry about. No more footsteps, no more crying. That is, unless there is something — or somebody — buried in the cellar that needs to be discovered.

But I doubt it even then. Sybil Leek managed to lead the murdered woman out of her self-imposed prison to join her child. Unless the allegedly guilt-laden husband is still outside the walls of the old house, unable to leave the place of his crimes, everything should be peaceful on Washington Avenue.

Come and Meet
My Ghost!

Margaret Widdemer was a spirited lady in her sunny years, a famed author and prize winner, who had for years made her home in the New York studio building on West Sixty-seventh Street called the Hotel des Artistes. It was the sort of place that cries out for a ghost, modeled on European studios and full of eerie, half-lit corridors and nooks. The tenants are painters, writers, and teachers.

Miss Widdemer lived in a roomy duplex, with a pleasantly crammed living room downstairs, and a wooden staircase winding to the upper story, which was divided unevenly between her workroom and a small bedroom.

All her life, Margaret Widdemer, poet and novelist, had had psychic experiences of one kind or another. Pennsylvania-born, she had visions of the dead many times.

Miss Widdemer bought her apartment in the mid-1940s, from a Mrs. Gertrude F., who had since passed on. Mrs. F. had another apartment a few doors away herself; she, her husband, and a daughter were among the original shareholders of the building, built around 1910.

Elizabeth Byrd, a mutual friend, had told me of her uncanny feelings in Margaret Widdemer's apartment.

It intrigued me sufficiently to make an appointment for a visit, but I did not feel that the presence of a medium was required — the evidence was too slender. Thus I arrived at the Hotel des Artistes on a damp night in February, 1965, accompanied only by my tape recorder and immense good will toward whoever it was who was present in the place!

I asked Miss Widdemer what her unusual experiences in the apartment had been.

"There have been unexplained noises, bangings of doors and such, and my cleaning woman would say, 'I thought you were in.' She would say 'I just saw someone walk up the stairs' — but, of course, I was not in. The same thing would happen to me. I was here alone, and I thought my maid had come in, because I heard footsteps going up and down the stairs, but on checking I found she hadn't come in at all."

Present were Elizabeth Byrd, Mrs. L. (a psychic neighbor from across the hall), and Barrie Gaunt, the young English designer and actor whose own haunted apartment we had visited not long before down on Charles Street.

For the past few minutes, Barrie had been restless and I saw him wandering about the place, up and down the stairs, as if searching for something or someone. The house was strange to him, of course, and I thought he was just exploring with the natural curiosity of the artist. But he seemed perplexed, and I began to wonder if he had sensed anything out of the ordinary.

"Someone came up these stairs," he finally said, "stopped about here and turned around — hate in the eyes. It's a woman."

His left hand felt strangely stiff, he added. And he had a feeling that someone was murdered here.

Elizabeth Byrd, too, had had an unusual experience in the apartment in April.

"I was having dinner with Margaret, and at one point wanted to go to the powder room. I went up the stairs, and the minute I got to the top of the stairs, I was seized with fear. I blundered into the other rooms before I could get my bearings. I didn't want to yell for help, because Margaret walks with a cane and would have had to scramble up the stairs to help me. I couldn't get down again fast enough. I was really scared, and I don't scare easily."

I turned my attention once more to Barrie Gaunt.

"I feel a great tragedy here," he said, "especially on the staircase where the curve is. I feel an agonizing screaming. In the room directly above this, there is a complete turmoil. A very beautiful woman, I feel, also a man, and I feel there's been a death here, a death by violence. The woman is fighting for her life, but not physically. Rather, she is fighting for *her mentality*. The person who is dead in this apartment is the man."

Everybody stared at Barrie now, as it turned out that we had a medium among us, after all, even though I had not brought one.

"Go on," I said, but it was hardly necessary. Barrie was engrossed in his impressions.

"The tragedy involved both people in this apartment. I just know it." Still shaken with the eerie feelings that had beset him on the stairs, Barrie reiterated his conviction of a terrible struggle going on and the woman's agony stood vividly etched on his expressive face.

I decided it was time to break up our meeting, and thanked our hostess. A few days later, Margaret Widdemer was able to supply some of the answers to the questions raised by Barrie Gaunt.

"The F. girl, Christy, was a tall, very beautiful blonde with great blue eyes," she said. "When she was around seventeen, she suddenly went raving mad, and became so violent that she had to be removed.

There was a history of disturbance on both sides of the family, it is alleged, and her hatred directed itself, for reasons unknown, against her own mother. She was placed in an insane asylum at Middletown, New York. Her mother could not even visit her, so violent was the poor girl's reaction."

"Then the girl lived here for a while, before they removed her?" I asked.

"Evidently so," Miss Widdemer said, and explained that Mrs. L., her neighbor, had helped her gather this information.

Was it the father restraining his raving daughter that Barrie had sensed on the stairs? He was dead now, and no information on how he died was available.

The question now: Was the girl still living at the asylum? A few days later, that question, too, was answered. She had died some time ago, still raving mad.

Barrie Gaunt, of course, could not have known any of these facts. I took a series of photographs in the apartment, none of which showed anything unusual. Was it an etheric impression then that Barrie had sensed, a re-enactment of the emotional events of the past? Or was the ghost of the poor girl still holding on to her one-time home, struggling against the brute force that was to take her away from it forever?

Country House Ghosts

In May of 1964, I received a telephone call from a lady who identified herself as Doris Armfield. She had read my book *Ghost Hunter*, and wanted to invite me to a house at Rehoboth, Massachusetts, where a poltergeist had taken up residence.

I asked her to give me a detailed account of her experiences.

"My husband and I purchased the house sometime around 1940. It was purported to be more than 200 years old. We have never heard that it was haunted or that any violent death had occurred in it, but the legend has persisted that this was the house that had a fortune buried somewhere in a stone wall, and we treated this story as an old-time tale.

"We have had many odd happenings at the house during the years, but the noises heard in the kitchen are what concern me. The original house was a regular Cape Cod consisting of four rooms downstairs and an attic upstairs. One hundred years after the original house was built, a kitchen ell was added, consisting of the kitchen, a small room off the kitchen, and a large back hall. Our current postmaster in town lived in the house at one time and he added dormers upstairs. We put a porch along the ell. There is also a small barn used as a garage. These constitute the physical plan of the house. We own about 100 acres on both sides of the street.

"Shortly after we moved in, the first event happened. My husband and I were eating supper in the kitchen when a sound like an explosion made us both bound from our chairs. We found that a glass dish in the kitchen cupboard on the top shelf had shattered. We decided that maybe a change of temperature had made the dish break and left it at that. However, this particular noise has been the only one where we found physical evidence of breakage.

"About two years after this, my husband joined the Navy in World War II and his aunt came to stay with me for a week or two. The first night as we sat down to supper in the kitchen, my dog Dusty sat beside my chair, and all of a sudden he started to growl very deeply. The hackles rose on his back, he bared his teeth, and scared me half to death, because I had never seen him do this unless he thought my husband or I was threatened. He was *staring at an empty chair* to my left, but I thought his growl meant someone was around the house. I went out and looked around, but no one was there.

"My aunt went home to her own house after a week or so and I lived alone in the house with the dog and some assorted cats. One night I was reading in bed, with the dog at my feet. I reached up to put off the bed lamp when I heard a tremendous crash and the sound of dishes banging, crashing, and shattering. I knew immediately that the dish cupboard in the kitchen had fallen loose from the wall and that it had hit the counter beneath it and just spewed all the hundreds of dishes across the floor and smashed them to smithereens. The dog and I flew into the kitchen only to find everything was intact. I took a flashlight and went all over the house from cellar to attic, knowing all the while that the only big quantity of dishes were in that kitchen cupboard.

"We decided to make a three-room apartment upstairs for a

girlfriend of ours who had lost her husband a few years before. She moved in, and the years went by, eighteen years, in fact.

"One evening at 5 P.M., she came home from work, and walked upstairs to her apartment. She had her foot on the last step when she just stood there unable to believe that horrible crashing and clattering of dishes being broken.

"Naturally, she expected to see the three-shelved kitchen cupboard torn away from the wall, figured it had hit the counter beneath it, and that every dish had fallen, breaking and rolling along the floor. She stood there in amazement when she found nothing was disturbed.

"We went home the next weekend, and as we compared noises, we found we had both had the same impression of what had happened, and the noises were identical. This happened about two years ago.

"About two months ago, a neighbor and myself were singing, and also playing the piano in the dining room, and were also tape recording our efforts. My husband was in the room behind the kitchen, and my sister was reading in the living room. At the end of a song we heard a crash of dishes or glasses and we all converged on the kitchen. I thought our Siamese cat had climbed onto a shelf on the hutch and possibly knocked off three or four plates that had then broken. Once again we all looked at each other and couldn't believe that nothing was broken. I then thought of the fact that the crash was on the tape, and we played it back and sure enough, we heard it loud and clear."

Immediately after I received Mrs. Armfield's report, I telephoned her at her weekday residence in Connecticut. The house at Rehoboth, Massachusetts, where the uncanny phenomena had taken place, was a weekend retreat.

I offered to come out to have a look at the house on my next trip to Boston.

"Everything is quiet for the moment," she replied, "but you're welcome any time."

Somehow the trip never occurred, and it was not until April, 1965, when I finally got around to reaching the Armfields again. I have no staff to help me, and cases just pile up until I can get around to them myself. This time my note was answered by Doris' husband, Richard Armfield. His wife had passed away in January of 1965. Under the circumstances, I decided not to trouble him, hoping that Mrs. Armfield herself might have discovered what or who it was who caused the uncanny noises in the Rehoboth house — from *her* side of the veil.

....

Charles Demers, who described himself as a combat veteran and unafraid of anything, lived with his family in an old house in Hampstead, New Hampshire. He bought the house in 1959. His two older girls — he had three children — slept upstairs in a finished room at the rear of the attic. Right away, they complained about noises in the attic. When he went to investigate, he himself heard the footsteps of a heavy person walking across the floor, night after night, at 10 P.M. The two children were moved downstairs, and Demers himself took the room in the attic.

"I have stared death in the eye many times, Mr. Holzer," Demers said, "and I was not afraid. I listened hard and sure enough, *it* was coming to the door of the bedroom. I gently slid out of bed and turned on the light, waiting. The ghost was just outside the door. I looked at the door knob, and *it was being turned slowly*. I did not panic, but nothing further was heard."

No footsteps going down, for instance.

....

Another New Hampshire case concerned a certain Mrs. V., who had been subject to the uncanny all her life. On more than one occasion she had seen an apparition of her own father, especially when she was in some sort of difficulty. The house she and her second husband occupied in a small town in New Hampshire was very old. There was a little door leading up to the attic. A narrow staircase ascended to the attic, and for no apparent reason, the door kept opening by itself. Someone walking about in the attic, softly, as if in stocking feet, had become an almost daily occurrence. Finally, she asked around, and found out that the house had once belonged to an old man who had been abused and put into the attic. The man finally cut his throat, and was buried in the family cemetery nearby. It was his house once, but his people apparently took it away. And now he was back in command once more.

....

Mae Ramirez was a widow in her late thirties, with three children, who lived in a small town in the Cape Cod area. I talked to her on the telephone at length and she struck me as pretty level-headed, although she seemed scared of ghostly visitations. Small wonder, with the ones she had.

There was a certain young man her father disliked very much. She stopped seeing him when she got married, but after her divorce many years later, she took up with him again.

Her father had died in 1945, and Mrs. Ramirez left Massachusetts soon after, only to return in 1954. Shortly after she had placed some flowers on her father's grave after her return to Cape Cod, she woke one night from deep sleep with the fearful feeling that she was not alone in the room. Groping for some matches she had put under the pillow, she was unable to find them. In the semi-darkness her eyes fell upon the left side of her pillow where she distinguished the outline of a man. Finally she overcame her fears, and sat up in bed. Before her stood her late father, dressed in dark clothes, looking directly at her. Without saying a word, he left slowly and quietly.

"I heard the steps," Mrs. Ramirez said, "but when he reached the stairs, he did not go down, *but through the wall.* Afterwards I went downstairs, and checked the doors, looked in closets, and there was no one there."

After she stopped seeing the young man her father had disapproved of, the ghost of her father never returned.

....

Jane Morgan had a house in Kennebunkport, Maine, that was full of ghosts. I had talked to her time and again, offering my services and those of Sybil Leek to help her get relief. But she didn't want to free her house from its ghosts. To begin with, her brother, who shared ownership in the house with the talented singer, had for years insisted that there was nothing to the story.

"You may have discussed the hauntings in my house with my sister," he said cheerily, "but I live here and I assure you there ain't none!"

I thanked Mr. Currier — Currier is Jane Morgan's real name — and forgot all about it, for, let's face it: I've got more unsolved hauntings to take care of than an army of parapsychologists could handle. But the whole controversy — was there or wasn't there a ghost at Jane Morgan's place — was brought to mind again when the *New York Daily News*, November 16, 1964, quoted the singer as saying:

"I don't want to have them exorcised. That would be cruel. They might have no other place to go . . . and besides, I'd miss these friendly spirits."

Having read *Ghost Hunter*, Miss Morgan knew perfectly well what happens to a freed ghost, and that the "place" they are helped to reach is infinitely more joyous than a musty New England mansion.

Because of an exciting séance I held with Ethel Johnson Meyers in a New York apartment, a piece appeared in the *New York World Telegram* in which columnist Norton Mockridge described the procedure we used. He was swamped with mail from people with similar problems, he says, although I never saw the letters. But he did manage to follow up his first piece with an interview with Jane Morgan in which she unburdened herself of the whole story of her ghosts.

Ned, a revolutionary soldier, had killed his girlfriend Nellie's other lover, and since that time, he and his lady-love had cavorted in the old house, kept there, presumably, by their guilt feelings. Their laughing and moaning had been heard by many. Doors opened and closed by themselves at night and spectral figures had been seen flitting from room to room. Visitors, it was alleged, had spoken of a "lady in gray" in the hall who did not return their greetings, and there was a sealed coffin in the cellar of the house.

"I had a medium at the house," Miss Morgan told me, but when she mentioned her name, I confessed I had never heard of her.

"She refused to stay at the house," Jane Morgan continued, and explained that for that reason anyone else would not be likely to succeed either. I patiently explained the rather considerable difference between a successful parapsychologist and a timid medium who runs at the first chilly sign of a *real* ghost!

All the same, Jane Morgan refused to allow us to have a go at it. Meanwhile, Norton Mockridge reported that playgoers at the nearby Kennebunkport Playhouse frequently saw a man in Colonial uniform and a woman framed in the window of the haunted house across the road. They usually took them for actors rehearsing for the next week's play.

The Curriers have, however, abandoned the house for another place not far away. The new tenants didn't complain about any ghostly visitations. But then Ned and Nellie may have needed some time to get used to their new keepers.

....

The John Jay House near Bedford Village, Westchester, New York, was a museum maintained by the county. Restored exactly as it was when one of America's founding fathers, Chief Justice John Jay, lived in it, it had the reputation of being haunted. "Was there anything to it?" I asked the curator, Lewis Rubenstein.

"According to family tradition," the curator explained, "Mrs. William Jay, wife of the second of the Jays to live permanently at Bedford, saw the ghost of her mother-in-law in one of the bedrooms. Two guests at widely spaced intervals are also reported to have seen the apparition."

Although he personally did not put stock in such stories, Mr. Rubenstein extended a cordial invitation for me to visit the house.

"We know that discovery of a ghost would be good for business," he said, "but we would prefer that people came to see the site for its real historic value rather than for its other somewhat tenuous merits."

When I finally got around to making an appointment to see the house in the company of a good medium, Mr. Rubenstein got cold feet, it seems. Retracting his invitation, he referred the decision to the trustees. Otto Koegel, board chairman, informed me curtly that I was not welcome. Maybe the ghostly mother-in-law was afraid I'd dislodge her.

The Girl Ghost
on Riverside Drive

One day in January of 1965, a gentleman named H. D. Settel called me on the phone to report a ghost in his Victorian apartment on Riverside Drive in New York City. Since I also live on the Drive, it seemed the neighborly thing to do to go have a look. Mr. Settel, who was in his late twenties or early thirties, had lived in the fourth floor walk-up apartment of what was once a small townhouse for some time. He got married and his wife joined him there in October of 1964.

Since moving in, his normally cheerful wife had gone into fits of despondency for which there seemed to be no rational explanation. Spending a lot of time at home, she felt a great anxiety at times, as if something momentous were about to happen. Gradually, the sensation changed to one of dissociation, a desire to leave her physical body. Fighting this tendency, she reported the strange sensations to her husband, who was sympathetic, and suggested she stop fighting the "take-over." When she followed his advice, she found herself crying for no apparent reason.

This was followed by most unusual behavior on her part. In the middle of the night, she sat up in bed and started to talk in a most irritated fashion. Unfortunately, neither of the Settels remembered the substance of her outbreak.

About mid-January, Mrs. Settel was on the threshold of sleep when she heard a curious tapping sound on the dresser. Quickly she turned on the light and the tapping stopped, but she had the fleeting impression that there was someone else in the apartment, and the strange, floating sensation came back.

Her husband also had an unusual experience. He awoke one night toward five in the morning, and asked his wife whether she had screamed. She assured him that she hadn't. Trying to get hold of himself, Settel explained that he had just heard a young girl scream. He had seen a girl dressed in a maid's uniform standing in the doorway of the two-room apartment, looking into the bed-room, and holding a large white dog on a leash. *Her look was one of pure evil.*

Somehow he had the impression that her name was Eudrice, and he felt himself compelled to write down the words "Eudrice was a girl of young looks." Neither phrasing nor handwriting was his own. The Settels had never heard of anyone named Eudrice, so they called the public library and were told that it was a Colombian form of the Greek name Eurydice.

I asked whether either of them had had psychic experiences before coming to the house on Riverside Drive.

On their honeymoon, Mr. Settel saw a very old lady during the night, and described the vision in great detail to his wife the next morning. From the details of appearance, dress, brooch, room, and chair in which he saw her sitting, Mrs. Settel realized that her husband had seen her long-dead grandmother, with whom she had lived as a child. Her husband had never seen a picture of her. Mr. Settel was in the textile business, and Mrs. Settel used to be a radio and television broadcaster.

I offered to visit the house, and did so the last week of February,

1965. The apartment on the fourth floor was done in modern style, and the Settels had made the most of the small area. There was a curious closet that suggested there had once been a door near the entrance to the bedroom. In the old days, the servants' quarters usually were located on the top floors, and this apartment undoubtedly was once just that.

I questioned Mr. Settel about the ghostly maid. Was there any light in the room at the time?

"Well, the sun was just coming up, and I could distinguish her outline quite clearly. She was a girl in her middle twenties, I'd say," he replied. "She was completely solid and real, not transparent or wavering. She had very long black hair, extremely white skin. I was terrified, stared at her for about thirty seconds, just lying there. Next thing, she was gone. We turned on the light, but, of course, there was nobody but us two in the apartment."

"What else have you observed here?" I asked.

"There was, and is, an oppressive heaviness in the atmosphere of this place, and a constant feeling of a presence other than our own," Mr. Settel replied. "Usually at night, between 9 and 3 A.M."

I turned again to Mrs. Settel.

"I almost committed suicide here once, something I would not normally think of," she confided. "Sometimes I seem to be almost possessed — I have the feeling if I allowed myself to leave my physical body, I would not be able to return."

The house had been built in 1897, and bought in 1910 from the builder by a Mrs. Gillen from Detroit. Before the house was built, the area had just been woods. From the time Mrs. Gillen bought the house, around 1910, Wall Streeters and such notables as Thomas Dewey had lived in the house. It had been a townhouse, subdivided by Mrs. Gillen into plush apartments.

There were five floors. The Settels had the fourth floor. A man named Alleyn had come to the house in 1925. From Panama, and

married to a West Indian woman, he died in the house in 1956 —
he dropped dead, it seems, on the second floor.

For twenty years, the Settel apartment had been owned by a
retired Army colonel named Villaflora and his wife. He was from
Panama and she was Polish.

The Settels were able to get a lot of information about the
building from one of the older tenants, a Mrs. Morgan. The superintendent's wife had committed suicide in the apartment downstairs.

The information thus obtained left a gap between 1897 when the
house was built, and 1910 when it was sold to Mrs. Gillen. Thirteen
years of mystery. Many interesting tenants coming and going!

I encouraged the Settels to use a Ouija board to see if their
combined psychic acumen would obtain anything evidential.

"Did you get anything worthwhile?" I asked. Ouija boards often
aren't reliable. It all depends on what checks out, of course.

"Yes indeed," Mr. Settel replied. "We got so much we stopped —
in a hurry. The communicator identified herself as Eudrice Fish. She
claimed to have come from Germany, and to have died in 1957 by
suicide. Much of it was garbled."

I took some photographs of the apartment, but none of them
showed anything unusual. I had decided there was nothing more I
could do in this case, when I received an urgent call from Mrs. Settel.

"Three nights after your visit, Mr. Holzer," she said, "I was lying
in bed. It was about 4 A.M., and I was not asleep, having just turned
out the lights. Suddenly, the bedsheet was pulled down from around
my neck to below my chest. I did not move or attempt to awaken my
husband, who was asleep beside me. A few minutes later, the corner
of the pillow beneath my head moved *as though it were being tugged*,
and I began to sense a presence. The air seemed heavy and expectant,
and briefly I felt myself floating again. To my surprise, nothing
further occurred, and I fell asleep in about five minutes after that.

"The night before — it was a Thursday; you were here on
Tuesday — I went into the bathroom to find the water running in

the sink. Neither of us had left it on. We are quite neat about such things. The bathroom also houses our cat, who seems to behave strangely at times lately. Last Christmas we went out and left the bathroom door open for her to go to her sandbox. On our return it was firmly closed — something the cat could not have done!"

I promised to come again, and this time bring Sybil Leek with me to see if contact with the ghost could be made.

Before I came, Mrs. Settel had a strange dream. She saw a male figure, and received the impression that she was very fond of this unknown man. She believed in him, but he was really quite evil. He seemed to be trying to talk her into something, and sway her. She was wondering if the ghost was trying to tell her something about her own life.

When I brought Sybil Leek to the apartment, a change took place in Sybil's face almost as soon as she set foot inside the door. The Victorian staircase and appointments outside had pleased my antique-loving friend, but when she had settled herself into the easy chair in the larger of the two rooms, she said immediately:

"It's not very pleasant here. I feel a person here who died very badly. It's a man. Something affecting his back. There is a younger person with him. They are dark, curly head, the man has a beard. European, Polish. About 1900. Something was lost here."

We adjourned to the bedroom, and Sybil went into trance. Soon she would be deeply "under."

A heavy male voice announced his presence.

"Oscar."

"Do you live here?" I asked.

"Yes."

"Your second name."

"Tratt. Oscar Tratt."

"Where are you from?"

"Efla. Near Cracow."

"What is your profession?"

"Make shoes. Out of wood. Wood shoes."

"Who lives here with you?"

"Mella. Woman. My *Gnaedige Frau*. My wife."

"Whom do you pay rent to?"

"Flynn. Sammy Flynn."

"What year is this?"

"1902."

"How old are you now?"

"Sixty-three."

"Are you well?"

"No. I'm waiting for Ernst to come back."

"Who is Ernst?"

"Mella's boy."

"Your son?"

"Who knows?"

"Why do you want him to come back?"

"Burn him."

"Why?"

"Took too much money from me." The ghost's voice rose in anger. "She let him take it!"

It wasn't clear whether he worked for Mella or whether she was his wife or both.

I continued the questioning.

"Did you get hurt here?"

"Yes, I broke my back. Ernst . . . his door by the steps, on this floor." Now the ghost broke into tears.

"I'm lost . . . find Ernst."

"Is there anyone else here? A woman perhaps?"

You could imagine the ghost shrugging, if ghosts can shrug.

"Common girl. They come and go. Looking for Ernst. Bad. Takes anybody's money . . . my back . . . bad boy."

"What is his family name?"

"Tratt . . . my son."

Schratt or Tratt — I couldn't be quite sure.

The son was about 35 and single, the ghost claimed. He belonged to the Jewish faith, and was somehow connected with a synagogue on Ninety-sixth Street. He also went to school on Ninety-sixth Street.

The ghostly voice began to falter and Oscar complained that he could not remember some things, and that his back hurt him.

"Did you go to the hospital?" I asked.

"No. Stayed here till they come for me."

"Why are you troubled?"

"Lost a lot of money here. Want to make some more shoes."

I began to send him away, gently, but firmly. After he had slipped out of Sybil's body, the medium's own personality reappeared, called back by me.

I asked Sybil, still entranced, to look around and report to me what she observed.

"There are lots of people at the top of the stairs . . . two men and two women. A man is falling down the stairs . . . and a little girl is crying."

"How old is the little girl?"

"Very pretty, like a little foreign girl. She's a servant. Perhaps 20 years old. She has a gray dress with a high neck. She's very unhappy because of what happened. She was upstairs, then she came down and hid in the cupboard . . . here. She was frightened of the young man that he might hurt her."

"Did she know him well?"

"Very well. He liked her."

"Was there anything between her and the young man?"

"Yes. She liked him, but she liked the old people, too. She used to listen to them quarrel."

"What were her duties in this house?"

"She had to look after a lot of gentlemen who lived in this house, but not really after these two here."

"What was her name?"

"Irene . . . Eurine . . . Erundite . . . Eireene." Sybil's voice expressed uncertainty.

"Why is she here?"

"No place to go."

"How did she die?"

"Very sick in her throat . . . died here. She never told anyone about the old man. My throat's bad . . ." Sybil was taking on the "passing symptoms" of the spectral maid.

"How long ago did she die?"

"1912."

Suddenly another person was speaking to us. A very agitated voice calling for "Mella!" Evidently, the servant girl had taken over. The throat seemed to hurt her still. Eventually she calmed down.

"What is your name?" I asked.

"Erundite." It could have been Erundice, or something like that.

"Where were you born?"

"Here . . . 27 London Place . . . down by the river."

I asked her to repeat her name. It now sounded like "Irene Dyke."

Her mother's name, she said, was Martha, and her father's Mostin Dyke. Or it could have been Austin Dyke. The voice was faint.

She did not know where her father came from. Only that it was far away where there were ships.

"What was your work here?"

"Servant. Laundry maid."

"Were there any pets in the house?"

"There was always something to fall over. Parrot. Ten cats."

"Any dogs in the house?"

"Oh, there was this big old monster . . . he was gray."

"Did you take him out?"

"He followed me."

"What sort of clothes did you wear when you served here?"

"Gray dress, and black apron . . . there is no water in the house, you know. Got to get some across the road. Dog fell into the river."

"What year is this?"

"1907-1908."

"Did you have an affair with Ernst?"

"I'm not going to say."

"Did you see him hurt his father?"

"Yes."

"What did you do after that?"

"I came in with Mella and I waited in the cupboard. I cried. Somebody came, that's why I stayed in the cupboard."

"Was Oscar gone then?"

"Think so. Never saw him again."

Everybody, it would seem, accused Ernst. He came back, and she saw him, but then her throat started to bother her.

"Why are you still here?"

"Mella said wait here in the cupboard."

She thought it was 1913. I coaxed her to leave the closet, and to forget about her bad throat.

"1913 I had my worst bad throat. It was very cold by the river. I went back to the cupboard."

"You're free now," I said. "You may leave this cupboard . . . this house . . . and join your loved ones."

Gradually, the tense body of the medium slackened as the servant girl left.

Soon, Sybil Leek was back to her old self.

"I feel fine," she said, and looked around. She remembered nothing of Oscar or the servant girl.

And there it is. How do you trace the name of a servant girl, even so unusual a name as Eurydice, or Irene Dyke, or whatever it was, in a rooming house in 1913? You can't. Telephones were still rare then, and the directories were far from complete.

Needless to say, Sybil knew nothing whatever about "Eurydice" or that a servant girl had been seen here by Mr. Settel. I had kept all that to myself.

Apparently, Oscar has made his peace with Ernst, and the pale young servant girl is forever out of the cupboard. The spot where Mr. Settel had seen her apparition was indeed where an old cupboard had been made into a walk-in closet. As for the big dog, why, there may be a place for him, too, on the other side. At any rate, the Settels have heard, seen, and felt nothing since Sybil's visit.

The Ghost Who Would Not Leave

Hardly had I finished investigating the rather colorful haunting in the New York State home of *Newsday* columnist Jack Altschul, which resulted in my name appearing in his column as a man who goes around chasing ghosts, than I heard from a gentleman, now deceased, who was the public relations director of the Sperry Company and a man not ordinarily connected with specters.

Ken Brigham wanted me to know that he had a resident ghost at his summer home in Maine, and what was I to do about it. He assured me that while the lady ghost he was reporting was not at all frightening to him and his family, he would, nevertheless, prefer she went elsewhere. This is a sentiment I have found pervasive with most owners of haunted property, and while it shows a certain lack of sentimentality, it is a sound point of view even from the ghost's perspective because being an earthbound spirit really has no future, so to speak.

All this happened in January of 1967. I was keenly interested. At the time, I was working closely with the late Ethel Johnson

Meyers, one of the finest trance mediums ever, and it occurred to me immediately that, if the case warranted it, I would get her involved in it.

I asked Mr. Brigham, as is my custom, to put his report in writing, so I could get a better idea as to the nature of the haunting. He did this with the precision expected from a public relations man representing a major instrument manufacturer. Here then is his initial report:

As a member of the public relation/advertising profession, I've always been considered a cynical, phlegmatic individual and so considered myself. I'm not superstitious, walk under ladders, have never thought about the "spirit world," am not a deeply religious person, etc., but . . .

Eight years ago, my wife and I purchased, for a summer home, a nonworking farm in South Waterford, Maine. The ten-room farmhouse had been unoccupied for two years prior to our acquisition. Its former owners were an elderly couple who left no direct heirs and who had been virtually recluses in their latter years. The house apparently was built in two stages; the front part about 1840, and the ell sometime around 1800. The ell contains the original kitchen and family bedroom; a loft overhead was used during the nineteenth century for farm help and children. The former owners for many years occupied only a sitting room, the kitchen, and a dining room; all other rooms being closed and shuttered. The so-called sitting room was the daily and nightly abode. We never met the Bells, both of whom died of old age in nursing homes in the area, several years before we purchased the farm. They left it to relatives; all the furniture was auctioned off.

The first summer my wife and I set about restoring the

farmhouse. The old kitchen became our livingroom; the Bell's sitting room became another bedroom; the old dining room, our kitchen. One bright noontime, I was painting in the new livingroom. All the doors were open in the house. Aware that someone was looking at me, I turned toward the bedroom door and there, standing in bright sunlight, was an elderly woman; she was staring at me. Dressed in a matronly housedress, her arms were folded in the stance common to many housewives. I was startled, thinking she must have entered the house via the open front door and had walked through the front sitting room to the now-bedroom. Behind her eyeglasses, she maintained a passive, inquisitive expression. For a moment or two, we stared at each other. I thought, What do you say to a native who has walked through your house, without sounding unneighborly? and was about to say something like What can I do for you? when she disappeared. She was there and then she wasn't. I hurried through the bedrooms and, of course, there was no one.

Once or twice that summer I was awakened by a sudden, chill draft passing through the second-floor room we used as a master bedroom. One early evening, while I was taking a shower, my wife called me from the livingroom with near-panic in her voice. I hurried downstairs as quickly as possible only to have her ask if I intended to remain downstairs.

Before closing the house up for the winter, I casually described the apparition to local friends without disclosing my reasons, excusing the inquiry from a standpoint I was interested in the previous owners. Apparently my description was accurate, for our friends wanted to know where I'd seen Mrs. Bell; I had difficulty passing it off.

My wife wasn't put off, however, and later that evening we compared notes for the first time. The night she called me, she explained, she had felt a cold draft pass behind her and had looked up toward the door of the former sitting room (which was well lighted). There, in the door, was the clear and full shadow of a small woman. My wife then cried out to me. The chill breeze went through the room and the shadow disappeared. My wife reported, however, that surprisingly enough she felt a sense of calm. No feeling of vindictiveness.

Over the years, we've both awakened spontaneously to the chill draft and on more than one occasion have watched a pinpoint light dance across the room. The house is isolated and on a private road, discounting any possible headlights, etc. After a moment or so, the chill vanishes.

A couple of times, guests have queried us on hearing the house creak or on hearing footsteps, but we pass these off.

The summer before last, however, our guests' reaction was different.

A couple with two small children stayed with us. The couple occupied the former sitting room, which now is furnished as a Victorian-style bedroom with a tremendous brass bed. Their daughter occupied another first-floor bedroom, and their son shared our son's bedroom on the second floor. A night light was left on in the latter bedroom and in the bathroom, thereby illuminating the upper hallway, and, dimly, the lower hallway. My wife and I occupied another bedroom on the second floor that is our custom.

During the early hours of the morning, we were awakened by footsteps coming down the upper hallway.

They passed our door, went into the master bedroom, paused, continued into our room and after a few minutes, passed on and down the staircase. My wife called out, thinking it was one of the boys, possibly ill. No answer. The chill breeze was present, and my wife again saw the woman's shadow against the bedroom wall. The children were sound asleep.

In the morning, our adult guests were quiet during breakfast, and it wasn't until later that the woman asked if we'd been up during the night and had come downstairs. She'd been awakened by the footsteps and by someone touching her arm and her hair. Thinking it was her husband, she found him soundly sleeping. In the moonlight, she glanced toward a rocking chair in the bedroom and said she was certain someone had moved it and the clothes left on it. She tried to return to sleep, but again was awakened, certain someone was in the room, and felt someone move the blanket and touch her arm.

My wife and I finally acknowledged our "ghost," but our woman guest assured us that she felt no fright, to her own surprise, and ordinarily wouldn't have believed such "nonsense," except that I, her host, was too "worldly" to be a spiritualist.

At least one other guest volunteered a similar experience.

Finally I admitted my story to our local friends, asking them not to divulge the story in case people thought we were "kooks." But I asked them if they would locate a photograph of the Bell family. Needless to say, the photograph they located was identical with my apparition. An enlargement now is given a prominent place in our livingroom.

Although this experience hasn't frightened us with the

house, it has left us puzzled. My wife and I both share the feeling that "whatever [it is] is more curious than unpleasant; more interested than destructive.

I was impressed and replied we would indeed venture Down East. It so happened that Catherine, whom I was married to at the time, and I were doing some traveling in upper New Hampshire that August, and Ethel Johnson Meyers was vacationing at Lake Sebago. All that needed to be done was coordinate our travel plans and set the date.

Mr. Brigham, who then lived in Great Neck, New York, was delighted and gave us explicit instructions on how to traverse New Hampshire from Pike, New Hampshire, where I was lecturing at the Lake Tarleton Club, to our intended rendezvous with Ethel in Bridgton, Maine, at the Cumberland Hotel. The date we picked was August 14, 1967. Ken and Doris Brigham then suggested we could stay over at the haunted house, if necessary, and I assured them that I doubted the need for it, being a bit cocksure of getting through to, and rid of, the ghost all in the same day.

* * *

Crossing the almost untouched forests from New Hampshire to Maine on a road called the Kancamagus Highway was quite an experience for us: we rode for a very, very long time without ever seeing a human habitation, or, for that matter, a gas station. But then the Indians whose land this was never worried about such amenities.

Before we left, we had received a brief note from Ken Brigham about the existence of this road cutting through the White Mountains. He also informed me that some of the witnesses to the phenomena at the house would be there for our visit, and I would have a chance to meet them, including Mrs. Mildred Haynes Noyes, a neighbor who was able to identify the ghostly apparition for the Brighams. Most of the phenomena had occurred in the livingroom, downstairs in the house, as well as in the long central hall, and in one upper-story front bedroom as well, Mr. Brigham added.

At the time I had thought of bringing a television documentary crew along to record the investigations, but it never worked out that way, and in the end I did some filming myself and sound recorded the interviews, and, of course, Ethel Meyers's trance.

When we finally arrived at the house in question in Waterford, Maine, Ethel had no idea where she was exactly or why. She never asked questions when I called on her skills. Directly on arrival she began pacing up and down in the grounds adjacent to the house as if to gather up her bearings. She often did that, and I followed her around with my tape recorder like a dog follows its master.

"I see a woman at the window, crying," she suddenly said and pointed to an upstairs window. "She wears a yellow hat and dress. There is a dog with her. Not from this period. Looking out, staring at something."

We then proceeded to enter the house and found ourselves in a very well appointed livingroom downstairs; a fire in the fireplace gave it warmth, even though this was the middle of August. The house and all its furnishings were kept as much as possible in the Federal period style, and one had the feeling of having suddenly stepped back into a living past.

When we entered the adjacent dining room, Ethel pointed at one of the tall windows and informed us that the lady was still standing there.

"Dark brown eyes, high cheekbones, smallish nose, now she has pushed back the bonnet hat, dark reddish-brown hair," Ethel intoned. I kept taking photographs pointing the camera toward the area where Ethel said the ghost was standing. The pictures did not show anything special, but then Ethel was not a photography medium, someone who has that particular phase of mediumship. I asked Ethel to assure the woman we had come in friendship and peace, to help her resolve whatever conflict might still keep her here.

I asked Ethel to try to get the woman's name. Ethel seemed to listen, then said, "I like to call her Isabelle, Isabelle . . . "

"How is she connected to the house?"

"Lived here."

I suggested that Ethel inform the woman we wanted to talk to her. Earnestly, Ethel then addressed the ghost, assuring her of no harm. Instead of being comforted, Ethel reported, the woman just kept on crying.

We asked the ghost to come with us as we continued the tour of the house; we would try and have her communicate through Ethel in trance somewhere in the house where she could be comfortable. Meanwhile Ethel gathered further psychic impressions as we went from room to room.

"Many layers here . . . three layers . . . men fighting and dying here . . . " she said. "Strong Indian influence also . . . then there is a small child here . . . later period . . . the men have guns, bleeding . . . no shoes . . . pretty far back . . . Adam . . . Joseph . . . Balthazar . . . war victims . . . house looks different . . . they're lying around on the floor, in pain . . . some kind of skirmish has gone on here."

I decided to chase the lady ghost again. We returned to the livingroom. Ethel picked a comfortable chair and prepared herself for the trance that would follow.

"I get the names Hattie . . . and Martin . . . not the woman at the window . . . early period . . . connected with the men fighting . . . not in house, outside . . . Golay? Go-something . . . it is their house. They are not disturbed but they give their energy to the other woman. Someone by the name of Luther comes around. Someone is called Marygold . . . Mary . . . someone says, the house is all different."

I decided to stop Ethel recounting what may well have been psychic impressions from the past rather than true ghosts, though one cannot always be sure of that distinction. But my experience has taught me that the kind of material she had picked up sounded more diffuse, more fractional than an earthbound spirit would be.

"Abraham . . . ," Ethel mumbled and slowly went into deep trance as we watched. The next voice we would hear might be her guide, Albert's, who usually introduces other entities to follow, or it might be a stranger — but it certainly would not be Ethel's.

"It's a man. Abram . . . Ibram . . ., " she said, breathing heavily. I requested her guide Albert's assistance in calming the atmosphere.

Ethel's normally placid face was now totally distorted as if in great pain and her hands were at her throat, indicating some sort of choking sensation; with this came unintelligible sounds of ah's and o's. I continued to try and calm the transition.

I kept asking who the communicator was, but the moaning continued, at the same time the entity now controlling Ethel indicated that the neck or throat had been injured as if by hanging or strangulation. Nevertheless, I kept up my request for identification, as I always do in such cases, using a quiet, gentle vocal approach and reassurances that the pain was of the past and only a memory now.

Finally, the entity said his name was Abraham and that he was in much pain.

"Abraham . . . Eben . . . my tongue!" the entity said, and indeed he sounded as if he could not use his tongue properly. Clearly, his tongue had been cut out, and I kept telling him that he was using the medium's now and therefore should be able to speak clearly. But he continued in a way that all I could make out was "my house."

"Is this your house?"

"Yes . . . why do you want to know . . . who are you?"

"I am a friend come to help you. Is this your house?"

"I live here . . ."

"How old are you?"

No answer.

"What year is this?"

"Seventy-eight . . . going on . . . seventy-nine . . ."

"How old are you?"

"Old man . . . fifty-two . . ."

"Where were you born?"

"Massachusetts . . . Lowell . . ."

"Who was it who hurt you?"

Immediately he became agitated again, and the voice became unintelligible, the symptoms of a cutout tongue returned. Once again, I calmed him down.

"What church did you go to?" I asked, changing the subject.

"Don't go to church much . . .," he replied.

"Where were you baptized?"

"St. Francis . . . Episcopal."

I suggested the entity should rest now, seeing that he was getting agitated again, and I also feared for the medium.

"I want justice . . . justice . . .," he said.

I assured him, in order to calm him down, that those who had done him wrong had been punished. But he would have none of it.

"They fight every night out there . . ."

Again, I began to exorcise him, but he was not quite ready.

"My daughter . . . Lisa . . . Elizabeth . . ."

"How old is she?"

"Thirteen . . . she cries for me, she cries for me, she weeps . . . all the blood . . . they take her, too . . ."

"Where is your wife?"

"She left us in misery. Johanna . . . don't mention her . . . she left us in misery."

"What year was that?"

"This year. NOW . . ."

"Why did she leave you?"

"I don't know."

"Where did she go?"

"I don't know."

And he added, "I will go to find her . . . I never see her . . ."

"What about your father and mother? Are they alive?"

"Oh no . . ."

"When did they die?"

"1776"

The voice showed a definite brogue now.

"Where are they buried?"

"Over the water . . . Atlantic Ocean . . . home . . ."

"Where did your people come from?"

"Wales . . . Greenough . . ."

Further questioning brought out he was a captain in the 5th regiment.

"Did you serve the king or the government of the colonies?" I asked. Proudly the answer came.

"The king."

When I asked him for the name of the commanding officer of the regiment he served in, he became agitated and hissed at me . . . "I am an American citizen . . . I'll have you know!"

"Are you a patriot or a Tory?"

"I will not have you use that word," he replied, meaning he was not a Tory.

I went on to explain that time had passed, but he called me mad; then I suggested I had come as a friend, which elicited a bitter reply.

"What are friends in time of war?"

I explained that the war had long been over.

"The war is not over . . . I am an American . . . don't tempt me again . . ."

Once again I pressed him for the name of his commanding

officer and this time we received a clear reply: Broderick. He was not infantry, but horse. We were finally getting some answers. I then asked him for the names of some of his fellow officers in the 5th regiment.

"All dead . . ., " he intoned, and when I insisted on some names, he added, Anthony . . . Murdoch . . . Surgeon . . . my head hurts!"

"Any officers you can remember?"

"Matthew . . . "

I asked, what battles was he involved in.

"Champlain . . . Saint Lawrence . . . it's bad, it's bad . . . "

He was showing signs of getting agitated again, and time was fleeting.

I decided to release the poor tortured soul, asking him whether he was ready to join his loved ones now. Once again he relived the wars.

"He won't come home again . . . Hatteras . . . fire . . . I'm weary."

I began to exorcise him, suggesting he leave the house where he had suffered so much.

"My house . . . my tongue . . . Indians," he kept repeating.

But finally with the help of Ethel's spirit guide (and first husband) Albert, I was able to help him across. Albert, in his crisp voice, explained that one of the female presences in the house, a daughter of the spirit we had just released, might be able to communicate now. But what I was wondering was whether a disturbed earthbound spirit was in the house also, not necessarily a relative of this man. Albert understood, and withdrew, and after a while, a faint, definitely female voice began to come from the medium's still entranced lips.

"Ella . . . " the voice said, faintly at first.

Then she added that she was very happy and had a baby with

her. The baby's name was Lily. She was Ella, she repeated. When I asked as to who she was in relation to the house, she said, "He always came . . . every day . . . William . . . my house . . . "

"Where is he? You know where he went?"

There was anxiety in her voice now. She said he left St. Valentine's Day, this year . . . and she had no idea what year that was.

Who was Willie? Was he her husband?

This caused her to panic.

"Don't tell them!" she implored me. The story began to look ominous. Willie, Ella, the baby . . . and not her husband?

She began to cry uncontrollably now. "Willie isn't coming anymore . . . where is he?"

What was she doing in the house?

"Wait for Willie . . . by the window . . . always by the window. I wait for him and take care of Lily, she is so sweet. What I can do to find Willie?"

I began to exorcise her, seeing she could not tell me anything further about herself. Her memory was evidently limited by the ancient grief. As I did so, she began to notice spirits. "There is my Papa . . . he will be very angry . . . don't tell anyone . . . take me now . . . my Papa thinks we are married . . . but we have no marriage . . . Willie must marry me . . . "

She cried even harder now.

"Andrew . . . my husband . . . "

Once again I asked Albert, the guide, to lead her outside, from the house. It wasn't easy. It was noisy. But it worked.

"She is out," Albert reported immediately following this emotional outburst, "but her father did find out."

"What period are we in now?"

"The eighteen-something."

"Is there anything in the way of a disturbance from the more recent past?"

"Yes, that is true. An older lady . . . she does not want to give up the home."

Albert then went on to explain that the woman at the window who had been seen had actually been used in her lifetime by the earlier entities to manifest through, which created confusion in her own mind as to who she was. Albert regretted that he could not have her speak to us directly. Andrew, he explained, was that more recent woman's father. Both women died in this house, and since the earlier woman would not let go, the later woman could not go on either, Albert explained.

"We have them both on our side, but they are closer to you because their thoughts are on the earth plane, you can reach them, as you are doing."

After assuring us and the owners of the house that all was peaceful now and that the disturbed entities had been released, Albert withdrew, and Ethel returned to herself as usual blissfully ignorant of what had come through her mediumship.

Two of the ladies mentioned earlier, who had been connected with the house and the phenomena therein, had meanwhile joined us. Mrs. Anthony Brooks, a lady who had been sleeping in one of the bedrooms with her husband two years prior to our visit had this to say.

"I had been asleep, when I was awakened by ruffling at the back of my head. I first thought it was my husband and turned over. But next thing I felt was pressure on my stomach, very annoying, and I turned and realized that my husband had been sound asleep. Next, my cover was being pulled from the bed, and there was a light, a very pale light for which there was no source. I was very frightened. I went upstairs to go to the bathroom and as I was on the stairs I felt I was being pushed and held on tightly to the banister."

I next talked to Mrs. Mildred Haynes Noyes, who had been

able to identify the ghostly lady at the window as being the former resident, Mrs. Bell. Everything she had told the Brighams was being reiterated. Then Ken Brigham himself spoke, and we went over his experiences once more in greater detail.

"I was standing in front of the fireplace, painting, and at that time there was a door to that bedroom over there which has since been closed up. It was a bright morning, about eleven o'clock, the doors were open, windows were open, my wife Doris was upstairs at the time, I was alone, and as I stood there painting, I glanced out and there, standing in the doorway, *was a woman*. As I was glancing at her I thought it peculiar that the neighbors would simply walk through my house without knocking.

"She stood there simply looking at me, with her arms folded, a woman who was rather short, not too heavy, dressed in a flower-print housedress, cotton, she had on glasses and wore flat-heel Oxford shoes, all of this in plain daylight. I did not know what to say to this woman who had walked into my house. I was about to say to her, What can I do for you? thinking of nothing more to say than that, and with that — she was gone. I raced back to the hall, thinking this little old lady had moved awfully fast, but needless to say, there was no one there. I said nothing to anyone, but several weeks later, during the summer, both my wife and I were awakened several times during the night by a very chilly breeze coming into the bedroom. That was one of the bedrooms upstairs. Neither of us said anything but we both sat up in bed and as we did so, we watched a little light dance across the wall! We are very isolated here, and there is no light from the outside whatsoever. This continued for the next year."

At this point it was decided that Mrs. Brigham would tell her part of the story.

"The first summer that we had the house," Mrs. Doris Brigham began, "I was sitting here, about five in the afternoon, my husband was upstairs, and my son was outside somewhere. I was alone and I was aware that someone was here, and on this white doorway, there was a solid black shadow. It was the profile of a woman from top to bottom, I could see the sharp features, the outline of the glasses, the pug in the back of her head, the long dress and shoes — all of a sudden, the shadow disappeared, and a cold breeze came toward me, and it came around and stood in back of my chair, and all of a sudden I had this feeling of peace and contentment, and all was right with the world. Then, all of a sudden, the cold air around my chair, I could feel it moving off. Then, practically every night in the room upstairs, I was awakened for several years in the middle of the night, by a feeling of someone coming into the room. But many times there would be the dancing lights. We moved into another bedroom, but even there we would be awakened by someone running their fingers up my hair! Someone was pressing against me, and the same night, a neighbor was in the house, and she told us the same story. Footsteps of someone coming up the stairs. A feeling of movement of air. A black shadow on the ceiling, and then it disappeared. Often when the children were sick, we felt her around. It was always strong when there were children in the house.''

I wondered whether she ever felt another presence in the house, apart from this woman.

Mrs. Brigham replied that one time, when she did not feel the woman around, she came into the house and felt very angry. That was someone else, she felt.

I decided it was time to verify, if possible, some of the material that had come through Mrs. Meyers in trance, and I turned to Ken Brigham for his comments.

"It has been one of the most astounding experiences I have ever had," he began. "There are several points which no one could know but my wife and myself. We did a considerable amount of research back through the deeds of the house. This only transpired a few weeks ago. I had been excavating up out front, preparing some drains, when I came across some foreign bricks, indicating that there had been an extension to the house. This is not the original house, the room we are in; there was a cottage here built for Continental soldiers, at the end of the revolutionary war.

These cottages were given to Massachusetts soldiers, in lieu of pay, and they got some acres up here. This house has been remodeled many times, the most recent around 1870. The town here was formed around 1775; the deeds we have are around 1800. Several things about the house are lost in legend. For example, down there is a brook called Mutiny Brook. There was a mutiny here, and there was bloodshed. There were Indians, yes, this was definitely Indian territory. At one time this was a very well settled area; as recently as 1900 there were houses around here."

I realized, of course, that this was no longer the case: the house we were in was totally isolated within the countryside now.

"The original town was built on this hill, but it has disappeared," Mr. Brigham continued, and then disclosed a strange coincidence (if there be such a thing!) of an actual ancestor of his having lived here generations ago, and then moving on to Canada.

"We only just discovered that at one time two brothers with their families decided to share the house and remodel it," Brigham continued his account. "But one of them died before they could move in. Much of what Mrs. Meyers spoke of in trance is known only locally."

"What about the two women Mrs. Meyers described?" I asked. "She mentioned a short, dark-haired woman."

"She was short, but had gray hair when I saw her," Mr. Brigham said. "A perfectly solid human being — I did not see her as something elusive. We only told our son about this recently, and he told us that he had heard footsteps of a man and a woman on the third floor."

"Anything else you care to comment on?"

"Well, we have the names of some of the owners over a period of time. There were many, and some of the names in the record match those given by Ethel Meyers, like Eben."

"When Mrs. Meyers mentioned the name Isabelle," Mrs. Brigham interjected, "I thought she meant to say Alice Bell, which of course was the former owner's name — the woman at the window."

"One thing I should tell you also, there seems to have been a link between the haunting and the presence of children. One of the former owners did have a child, although the neighbors never knew this," Ken Brigham said. "She had a miscarriage. Also, Lowell, Massachusetts, is where these Continental soldiers came from; that was the traditional origin at the time. Maine did not yet exist as a state; the area was still part of Massachusetts. One more thing: both Mr. and Mrs. Bell died without having any funerals performed. She died in a nursing home nearby, he in Florida. But neither had a funeral service."

"Well, they had one now," I remarked and they laughed. It was decided that the Brighams would search the records further regarding some of the other things that Ethel had said in trance, and then get back to me.

Mr. Brigham was as good as his word. On August 21, 1967, he sent me an accounting of what he had further discovered about the house, and the history of the area in which it stands. But it was not as exhaustive as I had hoped even though it confirmed many of the names and facts Ethel had given us in trance. I decided to wait until I myself could follow up on the material, when I had the chance.

Fortunately, as time passed, the Brighams came to visit my ex-wife Catherine and myself in August of the following year at our home in New York, and as a result Ken Brigham went back into the records with renewed vigor. Thus it was that on August 20, 1968, he sent me a lot of confirming material, which is presented here.

Ethel Meyers's mediumship had once again been proved right on target. The names she gave us, Bell, Eben, Murdoch, Blackguard, Willie, Abraham, why there they were in the historical records! Not ghostly fantasies, not guesswork . . . people from out of the past.

August 20, 1968

Dear Hans,

It was good hearing from Cathy and we did enjoy visiting with you. I presume that just about now you're again on one of your trips, but I promised to forward to you some additional information that we've gathered since last summer. Enclosed is a chronology of the history of the house as far as we've been able to trace back. Early this summer (the only time we made it up to Maine) we spent hours in the York, Maine, Registry of Deeds, but the trail is cold. Deeds are so vague that we can't be certain as to whether or not a particular deed refers to our property. We are, however, convinced by style of building, materials, etc., that the back part of our house is much older than thought originally — we suspect it goes back to the mid-1700s.

Although I haven't included reference to it, our reading of the town history (which is extremely garbled and not too accurate) indicates that one of the Willard boys, whose father had an adjoining farm, went off to the Civil War and never returned, although he is not listed as one of the wounded, dead, or missing. If memory serves me right, he was simply listed as W. Willard ("Willie"?). Now the "ghost" said her name was "Isabel"; unfortunately, we can find no records in the town history on the Bell family, although they owned the house from 1851 to 1959 and Eben Bell lived in the town from 1820–1900! This is peculiar in as much as nearly every other family is recounted in the Town History of 1874. Why? Could "Isabel" be a corruption of the Bell name, or perhaps there was an Isabel Bell. Checking backwards in a perpetual calendar it seems that during the mid-1800s Tuesday, St. Valentine's Day, occurred on February 14, 1865, 1860, and 1854; the first seems most logical since the others do not occur during the Civil War — which ended on [May] 26, 1865!*

Some of my other notes are self-explanatory.

Another question of course concerns the term "Black-guard" for our particular road and hill. An archaic term that connotes "rude" — note also that the map of 1850 does not show a family name beside our house . . . this could be because the property was between owners, or it could be that the owners were "rude" — which also could account for the lack of reference in Town History to the Bell family. It's an interesting sidelight.

Now, to more interesting pieces of information for you: 1) we've finally decided to sell the house and it's just like losing a child . . . I'm personally heartbroken, but I'm also a realist and it is ridiculous to try to keep it when we can't get up there often enough to maintain it. We have a couple of prospective buyers now but since we're not under pressure we want to make sure that any new owners would love it like we do and care for it.

2) And, then the strangest . . . Doris was going through some old photographs of the place and came across a color print from a slide taken by a guest we had there from Dublin, Ireland. And, it truly looks like an image in the

long view up the lane to the house. Three persons have noted this now. Then, on another slide it looks as though there were a house in the distance (also looking up the lane) which is only 1½ stories in height. We're having the company photographer blow them up to see what we will see. I'll certainly keep you posted on this!

Well, it all adds up to the fact that we did a lot more work and learned a lot more about the place . . . nearly all of which correlates with Ethel's comments. But as a Yankee realist, I'm just going to have to cast sentiment aside and let it go.

Drop us a line when you get a chance.

Sincerely yours,

*"Willie left on Tuesday, St. Valentine's Day."

Two points should be made here regarding this story. Ethel Johnson Meyers had many phases or forms of mediumship, but despite her fervent belief that she might also possess the ability to produce so-called extras, or supernormal photographs, she never did during my investigations. What she did produce at times on her own were so-called scotographs, similar to Rorschach effects used in psychiatry; they were the result of briefly exposing sensitive photographic paper to light and then interpreting the resulting shapes.

But genuine psychic photography shows clear cut images, faces, figures that need no special interpretation to be understood, and this, alas, did not occur in this case when I took the photographs with my camera in Mrs. Meyers's presence.

After the Brighams had sold the Maine property, they moved to Hampton, Virginia. Ken and Doris looked forward to many years of enjoying life in this gentler climate.

Unfortunately, exactly two years after our last contact, in August of 1970, Ken slipped and injured an ankle, which in turn led to complications and his untimely and sudden death.

As for the restless ones up in Maine, nothing further was heard, and they are presumed to be where they rightfully belong.

The following research material, supplied by the late Mr. Ken Brigham, is presented here to give the reader a better feel for the territory and times in which this took place.

Brigham's documentation:

1. Roberts, Kenneth, *March to Quebec,* Doubleday, 1938, p. 32. Listed in the King's Service: Thomas Murdock.

2. Carpenter, Allan, *Enchantment of America — Maine,* Children's Press, 1966, p. 27 — 85 years of Indian warfare, more than 1,000 Maine residents killed, hundreds captured; by year 1675, there were about 6,000 European settlers in what is now Maine.

3. Smith, Bradford, *Roger's Rangers & The French and Indian War,* Random House, 1956, p. 5 — Indians began to slaughter them when they marched out of Fort William Henry to surrender — women and children and men (1757); p. 6 — Robert Rogers of New York raised company of rangers in 1755, by 1758 had five companies. Ebenezer Webster came from his home in New Hampshire; p. 46 — mentioned Colonel Bradstreet; p. 176 — Ebenezer, 1761, returned east to Albany as Captain and then to New Hampshire where he married a girl named Mehitable Smith . . . pushed northward with men under Colonel Stevens and settled on 225 acres at northern edge of town of Salisbury. Later fought in revolutionary war.

Oxford County Registry of Deeds

(References: Book 14, p. 18; Bk. 25, p. 295; Bk. 49, p. 254; Bk.

Ghosts of New England

67, p. 264; Bk. 92, p. 158; Bk. 110, p. 149; Bk. 117, p. 268; Bk. 187, p. 197; Bk. 102, p. 135; Bk. 240, p. 477–478; Bk. 260, p. 381)

1805   Abraham (or Abram) Whitney sold to Nathan Jewell
1809   Nathan Jewell sold to William Monroe (part of land and the house) (1/9/09)
1823   Jonathan Stone bankrupt and sold to Peter Gerry (house), Thaddeus Brown and Josiah Shaw (5/19/23)
1836   Peter Gerry sold to Moses M. Mason (6/14/36)
1848   John Gerry sold to Daniel Billings (5/27/48)
1895   Semantha Bell sold to Caroline Bell (3/4/95)
1940   Edna Culhan (daughter of Caroline Bell) sold to Irving and Alice Bell (11/7/40)
1956   Alice Bell transferred to Archie and Ethel Bell (10/12/56)
1959   Archie and Ethel Bell sold to K. E. and D. M. Brigham (1/59)

Bk. 3, p. 484, Feb 7, 1799
Isaac Smith of Waterford for $800 sold to Nathaniel Geary of Harvard, Lot 2 in 6th Range (southerly half). Deed written February 7, 1799, but not recorded until September 24, 1808. (m. Unice Smith) (See notes 1 & 2)

Vol. 3, p. 99, Jan 6, 1800 (Fryeburg)
Nathaniel Geary and Betey Geary, his wife, sold to Peter Geary for $400 westerly end of southern half of Lot 2 in 6th Range. Notarized in York, January 6, 1800. On April 2, 1801 Betey Geary appeared and signed document which was registered on February 11, 1804.

Peter Gerry (or Geary) b. 1776 — d. 6/16/1847
m. Mary (b. 1782 — d. 3/16/1830)
m. Elizabeth (b. 1787 — d. 5/1/1858)
        c. Mary (b. 1834 or 1804 — d. 1844)

(see note 3) John C. (b. 1808)
   Roland (b. 1810 — d. 1842)
   m. Maria Farrar (b. 1811 — d. 1842)
   Abbie (b. 1812 — d. 1817)
   Elbridge (b. 1815 — m. Anna Jenness)

Bk. 92, p. 158, May 27, 1848
John Gerry sold for $100 (?) to Daniel Billings
Daniel Billings (b. 1780 Temple, Massachusetts)
. . . m. Sarah Kimball (b. 1786)
. . . c. Louise (m. William Hamlin)
   Caroline (b. 1810 — m. G. F. Wheeler — b. 1810)
   George C. (b. 1837 — d. 1919)
   . . . m. Rebecca Whitcomb, private F. Co., 9th Reg. — 3 years
      svc. Civil War)
   Maria (m. Calvin Houghton)
   James R. (m. Esther Clark)
   John D. (m. Esther Knowlton)
   Miranda

Bk. 102, p. 135, Oct 14, 1851
Daniel Billings sold to William F. Bell of Boston and Timothy Bell
   for $1,400

Bk. 117, p. 268, Dec 24, 1858
William Bell of Waterford paid his father, William F. Bell, $800 for
   Lot 2 in 6th Range

Bk. 187, p. 197, April 3, 1871
William Bell, "for support of self and wife," transferred to Timothy
   C. Bell "homestead farm" and its parts of lots.

Bk. 240, p. 24, 1894
Timothy Bell left property to his wife Semantha Bell

Bk. 240, p. 477–78, Mar 4, 1895

Ghosts of New England

Semantha Hamlin Bell transferred to Caroline Bell of Boston
    Caroline Bell (b. 4/4/1848 — d. 9/20/1926)
    . . . m. T. C. Bell (b. 10/10/1829 — d. 7/13/1894)
    . . . m. J. B. Bennett

1905
Caroline Bell (d. 1905??) left property to her son Irving Bell, "her
    sole heir."

Bk. 442, p. 133, Oct 30, 1940
Edna Bell Culhan (unmarried) of Cambridge, Mass. transferred to
    Irving and Alice Bell
Nov. 7, 1940
Irving Bell transferred to Edna Culhan "premises described in deed
    from Semantha to his mother Caroline Bell and he was her sole
    heir."

Bk. 560, p. 381, Oct 12, 1956
Archie and Ethel Bell inherited Lot 1 & 2 in the 5th Range and Lots
    1 & 2 in the 6th Range from Alice Bell
Jan 1959
Archie and Ethel Bell sold property to K. E. And D. M. Brigham

Notes

1. According to Bk. 2, pp. 445-46: On December 20, 1802,
   Nathaniel Gerry (wife Betey) for $800 sold to David Whitcomb
   of Boston, Mass., Lot 2 in 6th Range. Deed mentions road
   running thru land. Registered 1807 and notarized and signed by
   Justice of the Peace Eber Rice.
2. According to Bk. 9,. p. 467–68: On November 13, 1810, David
   Whitcomb for $150 sold to Peter Gerry Lot 2 in the 6th Range,
   including "Gerry Road." Apparently both these transactions
   (notes 1 & 2) were concerned with the westerly end of the
   northern half of Lot 2 in the 6th Range.

3. John C. Gerry (b. 1808): m. Nancy Farrar (b. 1810 — d. 1841), Nancy Sawin (b. 1819). He had an apothecary store in Fryeburg.

Interesting Notes

1. Local cemetery has gravestone of Hon. Lewis Brigham, b. 1816, d. 1866 (at Amherst, Mass.).
2. Eben Bell, (b. 8/5/1820 — d. 6/8/1900)
3. Richard and Samuel Brigham, and David Whitcomb, signed petition for incorporation on December 19, 1795.
4. Historical:

Waterford was in York County when it applied for incorporation (January 27, 1796).

Fryeburg (Pequawkett) was settled in 1763, Inc. 1777; in 1768 Fryeburg had population 300 plus.

November 17, 1796 — Isaac Smith petitioned, with others, Massachusetts for incorporation. Document stated there were fifty to sixty families in "said plantation."

History of Waterford, p. 25 — "and when the Indians attacked the growing settlements on the Androscoggin in 1781, and carried Lt. Segar* and others into Canadian captivity, Lt. Stephen Farrington led twenty-three men over this trail in hot, although vain pursuit of the savages."

(*Lt. Nathaniel Segar had cleared a few acres in 1774. A few townships, as Waterford and New Suncook [Lovell and Sweden] had been surveyed and awaited settlers. p. 22)

Waterford, settled 1775, incorporated 1797; population 1790 — 150; 1800 — 535

"Spirit of 76" (Commanger/Morris, p. 605) — General Burgoyne surrenders October 1777 . . . General John Stark agreed to work with Seth Warner because Warner was from New Hampshire or the Hampshire Grants (1777).

November 15, 1745 — First Massachusetts Regiment, under Sir

William Pepperrell — 8th company: Capt. Thomas Perkins, Lt. John Burbank, John Gerry (single).

Civil War: "Fifth Regiment commanded by Mark H. Dunnill of Portland. "Fifth was engaged in eleven pitched battles and eight skirmishes ere it entered on terrible campaign of the Wilderness which was an incessant battle. It captured 6 rebel flags and more prisoners than it had in its ranks."

5. Local Notes:

A) Androscoggin Trail was the main Indian route from the East Coast to Canada. Below our property, in the area of Lot 3 in the 4th Range, it follows a brook called "Mutiny Brook." The origin of the term used here is vague, but the natives say Indians mutinied there during the French and Indian Wars.

B) When the town was first settled, the pioneers built their homes on our hill rather than the flat land and the only road around Bear Lake was at the foot of Sweden and Blackguard roads.

C) Our road is called by the archaic word "Blackguard" which connotes villain. No one knows why.

D) The second floor of the house was constructed sometime after the first; timbers are hand hewn to the second floor and mill cut above. The house was rebuilt several times apparently; about 1890 or so two brothers and their families intended to live there but one died before taking residence. Also, foundations of an earlier building were uncovered near the back door.

The Ghost at Port Clyde

Port Clyde is a lovely little fishing village on the coast of Maine where a small number of native Yankees, who live there all year round, try to cope with a few summer residents, usually from New York or the Midwest. Their worlds do not really mesh, but the oldtimers realize that a little — not too much — tourism is really quite good for business, especially the few small hotels in and around Port Clyde and St. George, so they don't mind them too much. But the Down Easterners do keep to themselves, and it isn't always easy to get them to open up about their private lives or such things as, let us say, ghosts.

Carol Olivieri Schulte lived in Council Bluffs, Iowa, when she first contacted me in November of 1974. The wife of a lawyer, Mrs. Schulte is an inquisitive lady, a college graduate, and the mother of what was then a young son. Somehow Carol had gotten hold of some of my books and become intrigued by them, especially where ghosts were concerned, because she, too, had had a brush with the uncanny.

"It was the summer of 1972," she explained to me, "and I was sleeping in an upstairs bedroom," in the summer cottage her parents owned in Port Clyde, Maine.

"My girlfriend Marion and her boyfriend were sleeping in a bedroom across the hall with their animals, a Siamese cat and two dogs."

The cat had been restless and crept into Carol's room, touching her pillow and waking her. Carol sat up in bed, ready to turn on the light, when she saw standing beside her bed a female figure in a very white nightgown. The figure had small shoulders and long, flowing hair . . . and Carol could see right through her!

It became apparent, as she came closer, that she wanted to get Carol's attention, trying to talk with her hands.

"Her whole body suggested she was in desperate need of something. Her fingers were slender, and there was a diamond ring on her fourth finger, on the right hand. Her hands moved more desperately as I ducked under the covers."

Shortly after this, Carol had a dream contact with the same entity. This time she was abed in another room in the house, sleeping, when she saw the same young woman. She appeared to her at first in the air, smaller than life size. Her breasts were large, and there was a maternal feeling about her. With her was a small child, a boy of perhaps three years of age, also dressed in a white gown. While the child was with Carol on her bed, in the dream, the mother hovered at some distance in the corner. Carol, in the dream, had the feeling the mother had turned the child over to her, as if to protect it, and then she vanished. Immediately there followed the appearance of another woman, a black-hooded female, seeming very old, coming toward her and the child. Carol began to realize the dark-hooded woman wanted to take the child from her, and the child was afraid and clung to her. When the woman stood close to Carol's bed, still in the dream, Carol noticed her bright green eyes and crooked, large nose, and her dark complexion. She decided to fight her off, concentrating her thoughts on the white light she knew was an expression of psychic protection, and the dark-hooded woman disappeared. Carol was left with the impression that she had been connected with a school or institution of some kind. At this, the mother in her white nightgown returned and took the child back, looking at Carol with an expression of gratitude before disappearing again along with her child.

Carol woke up, but the dream was so vivid, it stayed with her for weeks, and even when she contacted me, it was still crystal clear in her mind. One more curious event transpired at the exact time Carol had overcome the evil figure in the dream. Her grandmother, whom she described as "a very reasoning, no-nonsense lively Yankee lady," had a cottage right in back of Carol's parents'. She was tending her stove, as she had done many times before, when it blew up right into her face, singing her eyebrows. There was nothing whatever wrong with the stove.

Carol had had psychic experiences before, and even her attorney husband was familiar with the world of spirits, so her contacting me for help with the house in Maine was by no means a family problem.

I was delighted to hear from her, not because a Maine ghost was so very different from the many other ghosts I had dealt with through the years, but because of the timing of Carol's request. It so happened that at that time I was in the middle of writing, producing and appearing in the NBC series called "In Search of . . ." and the ghost house in Maine would make a fine segment.

An agreement was arranged among all concerned, Carol, her husband, her parents, the broadcasting management, and me. I then set about to arrange a schedule for our visit. We had to fly into Rockland, Maine, and then drive down to Port Clyde. If I wanted to do it before Carol and her family were in residence, that, too, would be all right though she warned me about the cold climate up there during the winter months.

Ghosts of New England

In the end we decided on May, when the weather would be acceptable, and the water in the house would be turned back on.

I had requested that all witnesses of actual phenomena in the house be present to be questioned by me.

Carol then sent along pictures of the house and statements from some of the witnesses. I made arrangements to have her join us at the house for the investigation and filming for the period of May 13 to 15, 1976. The team — the crew, my psychic and me — would all stay over at a local hotel. The psychic was a young woman artist named Ingrid Beckman with whom I had been working and helping develop her gift.

And so it happened that we congregated at Port Clyde from different directions, but with one purpose in mind — to contact the lady ghost at the house. As soon as we had settled in at the local hotel, the New Ocean House, we drove over to the spanking white cottage that was to be the center of our efforts for the next three days. Carol's brother Robert had driven up from Providence, and her close friend Marion Going from her home, also in Rhode Island.

I asked Ingrid to stay at a little distance from the house and wait for me to bring her inside, while I spoke to some of the witnesses out of Ingrid's earshot. Ingrid understood and sat down on the lawn, taking in the beauty of the landscape.

Carol and I walked in the opposite direction, and once again we went over her experiences as she had reported them to me in her earlier statement. But was there anything beyond that, I wondered, and questioned Carol about it.

"Now since that encounter with the ghostly lady have you seen her again? Have you ever heard her again?"

"Well about three weeks ago before I was to come out here, I really wanted to communicate with her. I concentrated on it just before I went to sleep, you know. I was thinking about it, and I dreamed that she appeared to me the way she had in the dream that followed her apparition here in this house. And then I either dreamed that I woke up momentarily and saw her right there as I had actually seen her in this bedroom or I actually did wake up and see her. Now the sphere of consciousness I was in — I am doubtful as to where I was at that point. I mean it was nothing like the experience I experienced right here in this room. I was definitely awake, and *I definitely saw that ghost*. As to this other thing a couple of weeks ago — I wasn't quite sure."

"Was there any kind of message?"

"No, not this last time."

"Do you feel she was satisfied having made contact with you?"

"Yeah, I felt that she wanted to communicate with me in the same sense that I wanted to communicate with her. Like an old friend will want to get in touch with another old friend, and I get the feeling she was just saying, 'Yes, I'm still here.'"

I then turned to Carol's brother, Bob Olivieri, and questioned him about his own encounters with anything unusual in the house. He took me to the room he was occupying at the time of the experiences, years ago, but apparently the scene was still very fresh in his mind.

"Mr. Olivieri, what exactly happened to you in this room?"

"Well, one night I was sleeping on this bed and all of a sudden I woke up and heard footsteps — what I thought were footsteps — it sounded like slippers or baby's feet in pajamas — something like that. Well, I woke up and I came over, and I stepped in this spot, and I looked in the hallway and the sound stopped. I thought maybe I was imagining it. So I came back to the bed, got into bed again, and again I heard footsteps. Well, this time I got up and as soon as I came to the same spot again and looked into the hallway it stopped. I figured it was my nephew who was still awake. So I walked down the hallway and looked into the room where my sister and nephew were sleeping, and they were both sound asleep. I checked my parents' room, and they were also asleep. I just walked back. I didn't know what to do so I got into bed again, and I kept on hearing them. I kept on walking over, and they would still be going until I stepped in this spot where they would stop. As soon as I stepped here. And this happened for an hour. I kept getting up. Heard the footsteps, stepped in this spot and they stopped. So finally I got kind of tired of it and came over to my bed and lay down in bed and as soon as I lay down I heard the steps again, exactly what happened before — and they seemed to stop at the end of the hallway. A few minutes later I felt a pressure on my sheets, starting from my feet, and going up, up, up, going up further, further, slowly but surely . . . and finally something pulled my hair! Naturally I was just scared for the rest of the night. I couldn't get to sleep."

I thought it was time to get back to Ingrid and bring her into the house. This I did, with the camera and sound people following us every step of the way to record for NBC what might transpire in the house now. Just before we entered the house, Ingrid turned to me and said, "You know that window up there? When we first arrived, I noticed someone standing in it."

"What exactly did you see?"

"It was a woman . . . and she was looking out at us."

The house turned out to be a veritable jewel of Yankee authenticity, the kind of house a sea captain might be happy in, or perhaps only a modern antiquarian. The white exterior was matched by a spanking clean, and sometimes sparse interior, with every piece of furniture of the right period — the nineteenth and early twentieth centuries — and a feeling of being lived in by many people, for many years.

After we had entered the downstairs part where there was an ample kitchen and a nice day room, I asked Ingrid, as usual, to tell me whatever psychic impression she was gathering about the house, its people and its history. Naturally, I had made sure all along that

Ingrid knew nothing of the house or the quest we had come on to Maine, and there was absolutely no way she could have had access to specifics about the area, the people in the house — past and present — nor anything at all about the case.

Immediately Ingrid set to work, she seemed agitated.

"There is a story connected here with the 1820s or the 1840s," she began, and I turned on my tape recorder to catch the impressions she received as we went along. At first, they were conscious psychic readings, later Ingrid seemed in a slight state of trance and communication with spirit entities directly. Here is what followed.

"1820s and 1840s. Do you mean both or one or the other?"

"Well, it's in that time period. And I sense a woman with a great sense of remorse."

"Do you feel this is a presence here?"

"Definitely a presence here."

"What part of the house do you feel it's strongest in?"

"Well, I'm being told to go upstairs."

"Is it a force pulling you up?"

"No, I just have a feeling to go upstairs."

"Before you go upstairs, before you came here did you have any feeling that there was something to it?"

"Yes, several weeks ago I saw a house — actually it was a much older house than this one, and it was on this site — and it was a dark house and it was shingled and it was — as I say, could have been an eighteenth century house, the house that I saw. It looked almost like a salt box, it had that particular look. And I saw that it was right on the water and I sensed a woman in it and a story concerned with a man in the sea with this house."

"A man with the sea?"

"Yes."

"Do you feel that this entity is still in the house?"

"I do, and of course I don't feel this is the *original* house. I feel it was on this property, and this is why I sense that she is throughout the house. That she comes here because this is her reenactment."

I asked her to continue.

"I can see in my mind's eye the house that was on this property before, and in my mind I sense a field back in this direction, and there was land that went with this!"

"Now we are upstairs. I want you to look into every room and give me your impressions of it," I said.

"Well, the upstairs is the most active. I sense a woman who is waiting. This is in the same time period. There are several other periods that go with this house, but I will continue with this one. I also see that she has looked out — not from this very same window, but windows in this direction of the house — *waiting for somebody to come back.*"

"What about this room?"

"Well, this room is like the room where she conducted a vigil, waiting for someone. And I just got an impression where she said that, 'She' meaning a schooner, 'was built on the Kennebec River' . . . It seems to be a double-masted schooner, and it seems to be her husband who is on this. And I have an impression of novelties that he has brought her back. Could be from a foreign country. Perhaps the Orient or something like that."

"Now go to the corridor again and try some of the other rooms. What about this one?"

"I sense a young man in this room, but this is from a different time period. It's a young boy. It seems to be 1920s."

"Is that all you sense in this room?"

"That is basically what I sense in this room. The woman of the double-masted schooner story is throughout the house because as I have said, she doesn't really belong to this house. She is basically on the *property* — mainly she still goes through this whole house looking for the man to come home. And the front of the house is where the major activity is. She is always watching. But I have an impression now of a storm that she is very upset about. A gale of some kind. It seems to be November. I also feel she is saying something about . . . flocking sheep. There are sheep on this property."

"Where would you think is the most active room?"

"The most active room I think is upstairs and to the front, where we just were. I feel it most strongly there."

"Do you think we might be able to make contact with her?"

"Yes, I think so. Definitely I feel that she is watching *and I knew about her before I came.*"

"What does she look like?"

"I see a tall woman, who is rather thin and frail with dark hair and it appears to be a white gown. It could be a nightgown I see her in — it looks like a nightgown to me with a little embroidery on the front. Hand done."

"Let us see if she cares to make contact with us?"

"All right."

"If the entity is present, and wishes to talk to us, we have come as friends; she is welcome to use this instrument, Ingrid, to manifest."

"She is very unhappy here, Hans. She says her family hailed from England. I get her name as Margaret."

"Margaret what?"

"Something like H o g e n — it begins with an H. I don't think it is Hogan, Hayden, or something like that. I'm not getting the whole name."

"What period are you in now?"

"Now she says 1843. She is very unhappy because she wanted to settle in Kennebunk; she does not like it here. She doesn't like the responsibilities of the house. Her husband liked it in this fishing village. She is very unhappy about his choice."

"Is he from England?"

"Yes, their descendants are from England."

"You mean were they born here or in England?"

"That I'm not clear on. But they have told me that their descendants are English."

"Now is she here . . . ?"

"She calls Kennebunk the city. That to her is a center."

"What does she want? Why is she still here?"

"She's left with all this responsibility. Her husband went on a ship, to come back in two years."

"Did he?"

"No, she's still waiting for him."

"The name of the ship?"

"I think it's St. Catherine."

"Is it his ship? Is he a captain?"

"He is second in command. It's not a mate, but a second something or other."

"What is she looking for?"

"She's looking to be relieved."

"Of what?"

"Of the duties and the responsibilities."

"For what?"

"This house."

"Is she aware of her passing?"

"No, she's very concerned over the flocks. She says it's now come April, and it's time for shearing. She is very unhappy over this. In this direction, Hans, I can see what appears to be a barn, and it's very old fashioned. She had two cows."

"Is she aware of the people in the house now?"

"She wants to communicate."

"What does she want them to do for her?"

"She wants for them to help her with the farm. She says it's too much, and the soil is all rocky and she can't get labor from the town. She's having a terrible time. It's too sandy here."

"Are there any children? Is she alone?"

"They have gone off, she says."

"And she's alone now?"

"Yes, she is."

"Can you see her?"

"Yes, I do see her."

"Can she see you?"

"Yes."

"Tell her that this is 1976, and that much time has passed. Does she understand this?"

"She just keeps complaining; she has nobody to write letters to."

"Does she understand that her husband has passed on and that she herself is a spirit and that there is no need to stay if she doesn't wish to?"

"She needs to get some women from the town to help with the spinning."

"Tell her that the new people in the house are taking care of everything, and she is relieved and may go on. She's free to go."

"She said, 'to Kennebunk?'"

"Any place she wishes — to the city or to join her husband on the other side of life."

"She said, 'Oh, what I would do for a town house.'"

"Ask her to call out to her husband to take her away. He's waiting for her."

"What does Johnsbury mean? A Johnsbury."

"It's a place."

"She asking about Johnsbury."

"Does she wish to go there?"

"She feels someone may be there who could help her."

"Who?"

"It seems to be an uncle in Johnsbury."

"Then tell her to call out to her uncle in Johnsbury."

"She says he has not answered her letters."

"But if she speaks up now he will come for her. Tell her to do it now. Tell Margaret we are sending her to her uncle, with our love and compassion. That she need not stay here any longer. That she need not wait any longer for someone who cannot return. That she must go on to the greater world that awaits her outside, where she will rejoin her husband and she can see her uncle."

"She is wanting to turn on the lights. She is talking about the oil lamps. She wants them all lit."

"Tell her the people here will take good care of the house, of the lamps, and of the land."

"And she is saying, no tallow for the kitchen."

"Tell her not to worry."

"And the root cellar is empty."

"Tell her not to worry. We will take care of that for her. She is free to go — she is being awaited, she is being expected. Tell her to go on and go on from here in peace and with our love and compassion."

"She is looking for a lighthouse, or something about a lighthouse that disturbs her."

"What is the lighthouse?"

"She is very upset. She doesn't feel that it's been well kept; that this is one of the problems in this area. No one to tend things. I ought to be in Kennebunk, she says, where it is a city."

"Who lives in Kennebunk that she knows?"

"No one she knows. She wants to go there."

"What will she do there?"

"Have a town house."

"Very well, then let her go to Kennebunk."

"And go [to] the grocer," she says.

"Tell her she's free to go to Kennebunk. That we will send her there if she wishes. Does she wish to go to Kennebunk?"

"Yes, she does."

"Then tell her — tell her we are sending her now. With all our love . . . "

"In a carriage?"

"In a carriage."

"A black carriage with two horses."

"Very well. Is she ready to go?"

"Oh, I see her now in a fancy dress with a bonnet. But she's looking younger — she's looking much younger now. And I see a carriage out front with two dark horses and a man with a hat ready to take her."

"Did she get married in Kennebunk?"

"No."

"Where did she get married?"

"I don't get that."

"Is she ready to go?"

"Yes, she is."

"Tell her to get into the carriage and drive off."

"Yes, she's ready."

"Then go, Margaret — go."

"She says, many miles — three-day trip."

"All right. Go with our blessings. Do you see her in the carriage now?"

"Yes, the road goes this way. She is going down a winding road."

"Is she alone in the carriage?"

"Yes, she is, but there is a man driving."

"Who is the man who is driving?"

"A hired man."

"Is she in the carriage now?"

"Yes, she is."

"Is she on her way?"

"Yes."

"All right, then wave at her and tell her we send her away with our love."

"She looks to be about 22 now. Much younger."

"She's not to return to this house."

"She doesn't want to. She grew old in this house, she says."

"What was the house called then?"

"It was Point something."

"Did they build the house? She and her husband?"

"No, it was there."

"Who built it?"

"Samuel."

"And who was Samuel?"

"A farmer."

"They bought it from him?"

"Yes, they did. She says the deed is in the town hall."

"Of which town? Is it in this village?"

"Next town. Down the road."

"I understand. And in whose name is the deed?"

"Her husband's."

"First name."

"James."

"James what. Full name."

"It's something like Haydon."

"James Haydon from . . . ? What is Samuel's first name?"

"Samuels was the last name of the people who owned it."

"But the first name of the man who sold it. Does she remember that?"

"She never knew it."

"In what year was that?"

"1821."

"How much did they pay for the house?"

"Barter."

"What did they give them?"

"A sailing ship. A small sailing ship for fishing, and several horses. A year's supply of roots, and some paper — currency. Notes."

"But no money?"

"Just notes. Like promises, she says. Notes of promises."

"What was the full price of the house?"

"All in barter, all in exchange up here."

"But there was no sum mentioned for the house? No value?"

"She says, 'Ask my husband.'"

"Now did she and her husband live here alone?"

"Two children."

"What were their names?"

"Philip. But he went to sea."

"And the other one?"

"Francis."

"Did he go to sea too?"

"No."

"What happened to him?"

"I think Francis died."

"What did he die of?"

"Cholera. He was 17."

"Where did they get married? In what church?"

"Lutheran."

"Why Lutheran? Was she Lutheran?"

"She doesn't remember."

"Does she remember the name of the minister?"

"Thorpe."

"Thorpe?"

"Yes. Thorpe."

"What was his first name?"

"Thomas Thorpe."

"And when they were married, was that in this town?"

"No."

"What town was it in?"

"A long way away."

"What was the name of the town?"

"Something like Pickwick . . . a funny name like that . . . it's some kind of a province of a place. A Piccadilly — a province in the country she says."

"And they came right here after that? Or did they go anywhere else to live?"

"Saco. They went into Saco."

"That's the name of a place?"

"Yes."

"How long did they stay there?"

"Six months in Saco."

"And then?"

"Her husband had a commission."

"What kind of commission?"

"On a whaling ship."

"What was the name of the ship?"

"*St. Catherine.* I see *St. Catherine* or *St. Catherines.*"

"And then where did they move to?"

"Port Clyde."

" . . . and they stayed here for the rest of their lives?"

"Yes, until he went to sea and didn't come back one time."

"His ship didn't come back?"

"No."

"Does she feel better for having told us this?"

"Oh, yes."

"Tell her that she . . ."

"She says it's a long story."

"Tell her that she need not stay where so much unhappiness has transpired in her life. Tell her her husband is over there . . ."

"Yes."

"Does she understand?"

"Yes, she does."

"Does she want to see him again?"

"Yes."

"Then she must call out to him to come to her. Does she understand that?"

"Yes."

"Then tell her to call out to her husband James right now."

"He'll take her to Surrey or something like that, he says."

"Surrey."

"Surrey. Some funny name."

"Is it a place?"

"Yes, it is."

"Does she see him?"

"Yes."

"Are they going off together?"

"Yes, I see her leaving, slowly, but she's looking back."

"Tell her to go and not to return here. Tell her to go with love and happiness and in peace. Are they gone?"

"They are going. It's a reunion."

"We wish them well and we send them from this house, with our blessings, with our love and compassion, and in peace. Go on, go on. What do you see?"

"They are gone."

And with that, we left the house, having done enough for one day, a very full day. The camera crew packed up, so that we could continue shooting in the morning. As for me, the real work was yet to come: corroborating the material Ingrid Beckman had come up with.

I turned to Carol for verification, if possible, of some of the names and data Ingrid had come up with while in the house. Carol showed us a book containing maps of the area, and we started to check it out.

"Look," Carol said and pointed at the passage in the book, "this strip of land was owned by John Barter and it was right next to Samuel Gardner . . . and it says John Barter died in 1820 . . . the date mentioned by Ingrid! Ah, and there is also mention of the same Margaret Barter, and there is a date on the same page, November 23, 1882 . . . I guess that is when she died."

"Great," I said, pleased to get all this verification so relatively easily. "What exactly is this book?"

"It's a copy of the town's early records, the old hypothogue, of the town of St. George."

"Isn't that the town right next door?"

"Yes, it is."

"What about the name Hogden or Hayden or Samuel?"

"Samuel Hatton was a sailor and his wife was named Elmira," Carol said, pointing at the book. Ingrid had joined us now as I saw no further need to keep her in the dark regarding verifications — her part of the work was done.

"We must verify that," I said. "Also, was there ever a ship named *St. Catherine* and was it built on the Kennebec River as Ingrid claimed?"

But who would be able to do that? Happily, fate was kind; there was a great expert who knew both the area and history of the towns better than anyone around, and he agreed to receive us. That turned out to be a colorful ex-sailor by the name of Commander Albert Smalley, who received us in his house in St. George — a house, I might add, which was superbly furnished to suggest the bridge of a ship. After we had stopped admiring his mementos, and made some chitchat to establish the seriousness of our mission, I turned to the Commander and put the vital questions to him directly.

"Commander Albert Smalley, you've been a resident in this town for how long?"

"I was born in this town seventy-six years ago."

"I understand you know more about the history of Port Clyde than anybody else."

"Well, that's a moot question, but I will say, possibly, yes."

"Now, to the best of your knowledge, do the names Samuel and Hatton mean anything in connection with this area?"

"Yes, I know Hatton lived at Port Clyde prior to 1850. That I'm sure about."

"What profession did he have?"

"Sailor."

"Was there a ship named the *St. Catherine* in these parts?"

"Yes, there was."

"And would it have been built at the Kennebec River? Or connected with it in some way?"

"Well, as I recall it was, and I believe it was built in the Sewell Yard at the Kennebec River."

"Was there any farming in a small way in the Port Clyde area in the nineteenth century?"

"Oh yes, primarily that's what they came here for. But fishing, of course, was a prime industry."

"Now there's a lighthouse not far from Port Clyde which I believe was built in the early part of the nineteenth century. Could it have been there in the 1840s?"

"Yes. It was built in 1833."

"Now if somebody would have been alive in 1840, would they somehow be concerned about this comparatively new lighthouse?

Would it have worried them?"

"No, it would not. The residence is comparatively new. The old stone residence was destroyed by lightning. But the tower is the same one."

"Now you know the area of Port Clyde where the Leah Davis house now stands? Prior to this house, were there any houses in the immediate area?"

"I've always been told that there was a house there. The Davis that owned it told me that he built on an old cellar."

"And how far back would that go?"

"That would go back to probably 1870. The new house was built around 1870."

"And was there one before that?"

"Yes, there was one before that."

"Could that have been a farmhouse?"

"Yes, it could have been because there is a little farm in back of it. It's small."

"Now you of course have heard all kinds of stories — some of them true, some of them legendary. Have you ever heard any story of a great tragedy concerning the owners of the farmhouse on that point?"

"Whit Thompson used to tell some weird ghost stories. But everyone called him a damned liar. Whether it's true or not, I don't know, but I've heard them."

"About that area?"

"About that area."

"Was there, sir, any story about a female ghost — a woman?"

"I have heard of a female ghost. Yes, Whit used to tell that story."

"What did he tell you?"

"That was a long time ago, and I cannot recall just what he said about it—he said many things — but she used to appear, especially on foggy nights, and it was hard to distinguish her features — that was one of the things he used to tell about — and there was something about her ringing the bell at the lighthouse, when they used to ring the old fog bell there. I don't recall what it was."

"Now the story we found involved a woman wearing a kind of white gown, looking out to sea from the window as if she were expecting her sailor to return, and she apparently was quite faceless at first."

"I don't think Whitney ever told of her face being seen."

"Do you know of anybody in your recollection who has actually had an unusual experience in that particular area?"

"No, I don't."

"Commander, if you had the choice of spending the night in the house in question, would it worry you?"

"No, why should it?"

"You are not afraid of ghosts?"

"No. Why should I be?"

"They are people after all."

"Huh?"

"They are just people after all."

"Yes."

"Have you ever seen one?"

"No, I was brought up with mediums and spiritualists and as a kid I was frightened half to death, I didn't dare go out after dark, but I got over that."

"Thank you very much."

"The lighthouse and the gale . . . the ship in a gale . . . it all seems to fit . . . ," Ingrid mumbled as we got back into our cars and left the Commander's house.

And there you have it. A girl from the big city who knows nothing about the case I am investigating, nor where she might be taken, and still comes up with names and data she could not possibly know on her own. Ingrid Beckman was (and is, I suppose) a gifted psychic. Shortly after we finished taping the Port Clyde story, I left for Europe.

While I was away, Ingrid met a former disc jockey then getting interested in the kind of work she and I had been doing so successfully for a while. Somehow he persuaded her to give a newspaper interview about this case — which, of course, upset NBC a lot since this segment would not air for six months — not to mention myself. The newspaper story was rather colorful, making it appear that Ingrid had heard of this ghost and taken care of it . . . but then newspaper stories sometimes distort things, or perhaps the verification and research of a ghost story is less interesting to them than the story itself. But to a professional like myself, the evidence only becomes evidence when it is carefully verified. I haven't worked with Ingrid since.

As for the ghostly lady of Port Clyde, nothing further has been heard about her, either, and since we gently persuaded her not to hang on any longer, chances are indeed that she has long been joined by her man, sailing an ocean where neither gales nor nosy television crews can intrude.

Haunted Is the Trailer

Sometimes, one would think, the work of a psychic investigator must be downright drab. Little old ladies have nightmares, imaginative teenagers let off steam over frustrations in directions as yet unexplored, neurotics of uncertain sexuality fantasize about their special roles and talents. All this is grist for the investigator's mill, poor chap, and he has to listen and nod politely, for that's how he gets information. (The question Peter Lorre whispered across the screen, "Where is the information?" is the beacon toward which the psychic sleuth must be drawn.) And in fact it is perfectly possible for such people to have genuine ESP experiences. Anybody can play this game. All he or she needs is to be alive and kicking. ESP comes to just about everyone, and there's nothing anyone can do about it one way or the other. It is, therefore, necessary to have a completely open mind as to the kind of individual who might have a valid psychic experience. I can attest to this need much to my regret.

Several years ago, people approached me who had witnessed the amazing Ted Serios demonstrate his thought photography and who wanted me to work with the fellow. But my quasi-middle-class sense of propriety shied away from the midwestern bellhop when I realized that he drank and was not altogether of drawing room class. How wrong I was! A little later, Professor Jules Eisenbud of the University of Colorado showed better sense and less prejudice as to a person's private habits, and his work with Serios is not only a scientific breakthrough of the first order but was turned into a successful book for Eisenbud as well.

So it was with more than casual interest that I received a communication (via the U.S. mail) from a comely young lady named Rita Atlanta.

Her initial letter merely requested that I help her get rid of her ghost. Such requests are not unusual, but this one was — and I am not referring to the lady's occupation — exotic dancing in sundry nightclubs around the more or less civilized world. What made her case unusual was the fact that her ghost appeared in a thirty-year-old trailer near Boston.

"When I told my husband that we had a ghost," she wrote, "he laughed and said, 'Why should a respectable ghost move into a trailer? We have hardly room in it ourselves with three kids.'"

* * *

It seemed the whole business had started during the summer when the specter made its first sudden appearance. Although her husband could not see what she saw, Miss Atlanta's pet skunk evidently didn't like it and moved into another room. Three months later, her husband passed away, and Miss Atlanta was kept busy hopping the Atlantic (hence her stage name) in quest of nightclub work.

Since her first encounter with the figure of a man in her Massachusetts trailer, the dancer had kept the lights burning all night long. As someone once put it, "I don't believe in ghosts, but I'm scared of them."

Despite the lights, Miss Atlanta always felt a presence at the same time that her initial experience had taken place — between three and three-thirty in the morning. It would awaken her with such regularity that at last she decided to seek help.

At the time she contacted me, she was appearing nightly at the Imperial in Frankfurt, Germany, taking a bath onstage in an oversized champagne glass filled with under-quality champagne. The discriminating clientele that frequents the Imperial loved the French touch, and Rita Atlanta was and is a wow.

I discovered that her late husband was Colonel Frank Bane, an air force ace who had originally encouraged the Vienna-born girl to change from ballet to belly dancing, and eventually to what is termed exotic dancing, but which is better described as stripping.

I decided to talk to the "Champagne Bubble Girl" on my next overseas trip. She was working at that time in Stuttgart, but she came over to meet us at our Frankfurt hotel, and my wife was immediately taken with her pleasant charm and lack of show business phoniness. Then it was discovered that Rita was a Libra, like Catherine, and we repaired for lunch to the terrace of a nearby restaurant to discuss the ups and downs of a hectic life in a champagne glass, not forgetting the three kids in a house trailer.

* * *

In September of the previous year, she and her family had moved into a brand new trailer in Peabody, Massachusetts. After her encounter with the ghost, Rita made some inquiries about the nice grassy spot where she had chosen to park the trailer. Nothing had ever stood on the spot before. No ghost stories. Nothing. Just one little thing.

One of the neighbors in the trailer camp, which is at the outskirts of greater Boston, came to see her one evening. By this time Rita's heart was already filled with fear, fear of the unknown that had suddenly come into her life here. She freely confided in her neighbor, a girl by the name of Birdie Gleason. To her amazement, the neighbor nodded with understanding. She, too, had felt "something," an unseen presence in her house trailer next to Rita's.

"Sometimes I feel someone is touching me," she told Rita.

"What exactly did *you* see?" I asked Rita. Outside the street noises of Frankfurt belied the terrifying subject we were discussing.

"I saw a big man, almost seven foot tall, about three hundred fifty pounds, and he wore a long coat and a big hat."

But the ghost didn't just stand there glaring at her. Sometimes he made himself comfortable on her kitchen counter, with his ghostly legs dangling down from it. He was as solid as a man of flesh and blood, except that she could not see his face clearly since it was in the darkness of early morning.

Later, when I visited the house trailer with my highly sensitive camera, I took some pictures in the areas indicated by Miss Atlanta: the bedroom, the door to it, and the kitchen counter. In all three areas, strange phenomena manifested on my film. Some mirrorlike transparencies developed in normally opaque areas, which could not and cannot be explained.

When it happened the first time, she raced for the light and turned the switch, her heart beating wildly. The yellowish light of the electric lamp bathed the bedroom in a nightmarish twilight. But the spook had vanished. There was no possible way a real intruder could have come and gone so fast. No way out, no way in. Because this was during the time Boston was being terrorized by the infamous Boston Strangler, Rita had taken special care to double-lock the doors and secure all the windows. Nobody could have entered the trailer without making a great deal of noise. I have examined the locks and the windows — not even Houdini could have done it.

The ghost, having once established himself in Rita's bedroom, returned for additional visits — always in the early morning hours.

Sometimes he appeared three times a week, sometimes more often.

"He was staring in my direction all the time," Rita said with a slight Viennese accent. One could see that the terror had never really left her eyes. Even three thousand miles away, the spectral stranger had a hold on the woman.

Was he perhaps looking for something? No, he didn't seem to be. In the kitchen, he either stood by the table or sat down on the counter. Ghosts don't need food — so why the kitchen?

"Did he ever take his hat off?" I asked.

"No, never," she said and smiled. Imagine a ghost doffing his hat to the lady of the trailer!

What was particularly horrifying was the noiselessness of the apparition. She never heard any footfalls or rustling of his clothes as he silently passed by. There was no clearing of the throat as if he wanted to speak. Nothing. Just silent stares. When the visitations grew more frequent, Rita decided to leave the lights on all night. After that, she did not *see* him anymore. But he was still there, at the usual hour, standing behind the bed, staring at her. She knew he was. She could almost feel the sting of his gaze.

One night she decided she had been paying huge light bills long enough. She hopped out of bed, turned the light switch off and, as the room was plunged back into semidarkness, she lay down in bed again. Within a few minutes her eyes had gotten accustomed to the dark. Her senses were on the alert, for she was not at all sure what she might see. Finally, she forced herself to turn her head in the direction of the door. Was her mind playing tricks on her? There, in the doorway, stood the ghost — as big and brooding as ever.

With a scream, she dove under the covers. When she came up, eternities later, the shadow was gone from the door.

The next evening, the lights were burning again in the trailer, and every night thereafter, until it was time for her to fly to Germany for her season's nightclub work. Then she closed up the trailer, sent her children to stay with friends, and left with the faint hope that on her return in the winter, the trailer might be free of its ghost. But she wasn't at all certain.

It was getting dark outside now, and I knew Miss Atlanta soon had to fly back to Stuttgart for her evening's work. It was obvious to me that this exotic dancer was a medium, as only the psychic can see apparitions. I queried her about the past, and reluctantly she talked of her early years in Austria.

*   *   *

When she was a schoolgirl of eight, she suddenly felt herself compelled to draw a picture of a funeral. Her father was puzzled by the choice of so somber a subject by a little girl. But as she pointed out who the figures in her drawing were, ranging from her father to the more distant relatives, her father listened with lips tightly drawn. When the enumeration was over, he inquired in a voice of incredulity mixed with fear, "But who is being buried?"

"Mother," the little girl replied, without a moment's hesitation, and no more was said about it.

Three weeks later to the day, her mother was dead.

The war years were hard on the family. Her father, a postal employee, had a gift for playing the numbers, allegedly on advice from his deceased spouse. But Germany's invasion ended all that and eventually Rita found herself in the United States and married to an air force colonel.

She had forgotten her psychic experiences of the past, when the ghost in the trailer brought them all back only too vividly. She was frankly scared, knowing her abilities to receive messages from the beyond. But who was this man?

*   *   *

I visited Peabody with a medium to see what we could learn. Rita's oldest son greeted us at the door. It wasn't until the winter of the same year that Rita showed me around her trailer. It was a cold and moist afternoon.

Her son had seen nothing and neither believed nor disbelieved his mother. But he was willing to do some legwork for me to find out who the shadowy visitor might be.

It was thus that we learned that a few years before a man had been run over by a car very close by. Had the dead man, confused about his status, sought refuge in the trailer — the nearest house in his path? Was he trying to make contact with what he could sense was a medium, who would be able to receive his anxious pleas?

It was at this time that I took the unusual photographs of the areas Rita pointed out as being haunted. Several of these pictures show unusual mirrorlike areas, in which something must have been present in the atmosphere. But the ghost did not appear for me or, for that matter, Rita. And he has not reappeared since.

Perhaps our discovery of his problem and our long and passionate discussion of the situation reached his spectral consciousness, and he knew that he was out of his element in a trailer belonging to people not connected with his world.

Was this his way of finally, belatedly, doffing his hat to the lady of the house trailer, with an apology for his intrusions?

I haven't had any further word from Rita Atlanta, but the newspapers carry oversize ads now and then telling some city of the sensational performance of the girl in the champagne glass.

It is safe to assume that she can take her bath in the glass completely alone, something she had not been sure of before. For Rita, the eyes of a couple hundred visiting firemen in a Frankfurt nightclub are far less bothersome than one solitary pair of eyes staring from another world.

Ghosts around Boston

Sometime back, I often went to Boston to appear on radio or television, and as a result people kept telling me of their own psychic adventures — and problems. I tried to follow up on as many of these cases as I could, but there are limits even to my enthusiasm.

Since having a ghostly experience is not necessarily what people like to advertise — especially to the neighbors — some of these stories, which are all true, contain only the initials of the people involved. I, of course, know them but have promised not to divulge their full names, or heaven forbid, exact addresses.

* * *

Mrs. Geraldine W. is a graduate of Boston City Hospital and works as a registered nurse; her husband is a teacher, and they have four children. Neither Mr. nor Mrs. W. ever had the slightest interest in the occult; in fact, Mrs. W. remembers hearing some chilling stories about ghosts as a child and considering them just so many fairy tales.

One July, the W.'s decided to acquire a house about twenty

259

miles from Boston, as the conditions in the city seemed inappropriate for bringing up their four children. They chose a Victorian home sitting on a large rock overlooking a golf course in a small town.

Actually, there are two houses built next door to each other by two brothers. The one to the left had originally been used as a winter residence, while the other, their choice, was used as a summer home. It was a remarkable sight, high above the other houses in the area. The house so impressed the W.'s that they immediately expressed their interest in buying it. They were told that it had once formed part of the H. estate, and had remained in the same family until nine years prior to their visit. Originally built by a certain Ephraim Hamblin, it had been sold to the H. family and remained a family property until it passed into the hands of the P. family. It remained in the P.'s possession until the W.'s acquired it that spring.

Prior to obtaining possession of the house, Mrs. W. had a strange dream in which she saw herself standing in the driveway, looking up at the house. In the dream she had a terrible feeling of foreboding, as if something dreadful had happened in the house. On awakening the next morning, however, she thought no more about it and later put it out of her mind.

Shortly after they moved in on July 15, Mrs. W. awoke in the middle of the night for some reason. She looked up to the ceiling and saw what looked to her like a sparkler. It swirled about in a circular movement, then disappeared. On checking, Mrs. W. found that all the shades were drawn in the room, so it perplexed her how such a light could have appeared on the ceiling. But the matter quickly slipped from her mind.

Several days later, she happened to be sitting in the livingroom one evening with the television on very low since her husband was asleep on the couch. Everything was very quiet. On the arm of a wide-armed couch there were three packages of cigarettes side by side. As she looked at them, the middle package suddenly flipped over by itself and fell to the floor. Since Mrs. W. had no interest in psychic phenomena, she dismissed this as probably due to some natural cause. A short time thereafter, she happened to be sleeping in her daughter's room, facing directly alongside the front hall staircase. The large hall light was burning since the lamp near the children's rooms had burned out. As she lay in the room, she became aware of heavy, slow, plodding footsteps coming across the hallway.

Terrified, she kept her eyes closed tight because she thought there was a prowler in the house. Since everyone was accounted for, only a stranger could have made the noises. She started to pray over and over in order to calm herself, but the footsteps continued on the stairs, progressing down the staircase and around into the livingroom where they faded away. Mrs. W. was thankful that her prayers had been answered and that the prowler had left.

Just as she started to doze off again the footsteps returned. Although she was still scared, she decided to brave the intruder, whoever he might be. As she got up and approached the area where she heard the steps, they resounded directly in front of her — yet she could see absolutely no one. The next morning she checked all the doors and windows and found them securely locked, just as she had left them the night before. She mentioned the matter to her husband, who ascribed it to nerves. A few nights later, Mrs. W. was again awakened in the middle of the night, this time in her own bedroom. As she woke and sat up in bed, she heard a woman's voice from somewhere in the room. It tried to form words, but Mrs. W. could not make them out. The voice was hollow and sounded like something from an echo chamber. It seemed to her that the voice had come from an area near the ceiling over her husband's bureau. The incident did not prevent her from going back to sleep, perplexing though it was.

By now Mrs. W. was convinced that they had a ghost in the house. She was standing in her kitchen, contemplating where she could find a priest to have the house exorcised, when all of a sudden a trash bag, which had been resting quietly on the floor, burst open, spilling its contents all over the floor. The disturbances had become so frequent that Mrs. W. took every opportunity possible to leave the house early in the morning with her children, and not go home until she had to. She did not bring in a priest to exorcise the house, but managed to obtain a bottle of blessed water from Lourdes. She went through each room, sprinkling it and praying for the soul of whoever was haunting the house.

One evening, Mr. W. came home from work around six o'clock and went upstairs to change his clothes while Mrs. W. was busy setting the table for dinner. Suddenly Mr. W. called his wife and asked her to open and close the door to the back hall stairs. Puzzled by his request, she did so five times, each time more strenuously. Finally she asked her husband the purpose of this exercise. He admitted that he wanted to test the effect of the door being opened and closed in this manner because he had just observed the back gate to the stairs opening and closing by itself!

This was as good a time as any to have a discussion of what was going on in the house, so Mrs. W. went upstairs to join Mr. W. in the bedroom where he was standing. As she did so, her eye caught a dim, circular light that seemed to skip across the ceiling in two strokes; at the same time, the shade at the other end of the room suddenly snapped up, flipping over vigorously a number of times. Both Mr. and Mrs. W. started to run from the room; then, catching themselves, they returned to the bedroom.

On looking over these strange incidents, Mrs. W. admitted that there had been some occurrences that could not be explained by natural means. Shortly after they had moved to the house, Mr. W. had started to paint the interior, at the same time thinking about making some structural changes in the house because there were certain things in it he did not like. As he did so, two cans of paint were knocked out of his hands, flipping over and covering a good portion of the livingroom and hall floors.

Then there was that Saturday afternoon when Mr. W. had helped his wife vacuum the hall stairs. Again he started to talk about the bad shape the house was in, in his opinion, and as he condemned the house, the vacuum cleaner suddenly left the upper landing and traveled over the staircase all by itself, finally hitting him on the head with a solid thud!

But their discussion did not solve the matter; they had to brace themselves against further incidents, even though they did not know why they were happening or who caused them.

One evening Mrs. W. was feeding her baby in the livingroom near the fireplace, when she heard footsteps overhead and the dragging of something very heavy across the floor. This was followed by a crashing sound on the staircase, as if something very heavy had fallen against the railing. Her husband was asleep, but Mrs. W. woke him up and together they investigated, only to find the children asleep and no stranger in the house.

It was now virtually impossible to spend a quiet evening in the livingroom without hearing some uncanny noise. There was scratching along the tops of the doors inside the house, a rubbing sound along the door tops, and once in a while the front doorknob would turn by itself, as if an unseen hand were twisting it. No one could have done this physically because the enclosed porch leading to the door was locked and the locks were intact when Mrs. W. examined them.

The ghost, whoever he or she was, roamed the entire house. One night Mrs. W. was reading in her bedroom at around midnight when she heard a knocking sound halfway up the wall of her room. It seemed to move along the wall and then stop dead beside her night table. Needless to say, it did not contribute to a peaceful night. By now the older children were also aware of the disturbances. They, too, heard knocking on doors with no one outside, and twice Mrs. W.'s little girl, then seven years old, was awakened in the middle of the night because she heard someone walking about the house. Both her parents were fast asleep.

That year, coming home on Christmas night to an empty house, or what they *presumed* to be an empty house, the W.'s noticed that a Christmas light was on in the bedroom window. Under the circumstances, the family stayed outside while Mr. W. went upstairs to check the house. He found everything locked and no one inside. The rest of the family then moved into the lower hall, waiting for Mr. W. to come down from upstairs. As he reached the bottom of the stairs, coming from what he assured his family was an empty upper story, they all heard footsteps overhead from the area he had just examined.

On the eve of St. Valentine's Day, Mrs. W. was readying the house for a party the next evening. She had waxed the floors and spruced up the entire house, and it had gotten late. Just before going to bed, she decided to sit down for a while in her rocking chair. Suddenly she perceived a moaning and groaning sound coming across the livingroom from left to right. It lasted perhaps ten to fifteen seconds, then ended as abruptly as it had begun.

During the party the next evening, the conversation drifted to ghosts, and somehow Mrs. W. confided in her sister-in-law about what they had been through since moving to the house. It was only then that Mrs. W. found out from her sister-in-law that her husband's mother had had an experience in the house while staying over one night during the summer. She, too, had heard loud footsteps coming up the hall stairs; she had heard voices, and a crackling sound as if there had been a fire someplace. On investigating these strange noises, she had found nothing that could have caused them. However, she had decided not to tell Mrs. W. about it, in order not to frighten her.

Ghosts of New England

Because of her background and position, and since her husband was a respected teacher, Mrs. W. was reluctant to discuss their experiences with anyone who might construe them as imaginary, or think the family silly. Eventually, however, a sympathetic neighbor gave her one of my books, and Mrs. W. contacted me for advice. She realized, of course, that her letter would not be read immediately, and that in any event, I might not be able to do anything about it for some time. Frightening though the experiences had been, she was reconciled to living with them, hoping only that her children would not be hurt or frightened.

On March 3, she had put her three young boys to bed for a nap and decided to check if they were properly covered. As she went up the stairway, she thought she saw movement out of the corner of her eye. Her first thought was that her little boy, then four years old, had gotten up instead of taking his nap. But, on checking, she found him fast asleep.

Exactly one week later, Mrs. W. was in bed trying to go to sleep when she heard a progressively louder tapping on the wooden mantle at the foot of the bed. She turned over to see where the noise was coming from or what was causing it when it immediately stopped. She turned back to the side, trying to go back to sleep, when suddenly she felt something or someone shake her foot as though trying to get her attention. She looked down at her foot and saw absolutely nothing.

Finally, on March 26, she received my letter explaining some of the phenomena to her and advising her what to do. As she was reading my letter, she heard the sound of someone moving about upstairs, directly over her head. Since she knew that the children were sleeping soundly, Mrs. W. realized that her unseen visitor was not in the least bit put off by the advice dispensed her by the ghost hunter. Even a dog the W.'s had acquired around Christmas had its difficulty with the unseen forces loose in the house.

At first, he had slept upstairs on the rug beside Mrs. W.'s bed. But a short time after, he began to growl and bark at night, especially in the direction of the stairs. Eventually he took to sleeping on the enclosed porch and refused to enter the house, no matter how one would try to entice him. Mrs. W. decided to make some inquiries in the neighborhood, in order to find out who the ghost might be or what he might want.

She discovered that a paper-hanger who had come to do some work in the house just before they had purchased it had encountered considerable difficulties. He had been hired to do some paper hanging in the house, changing the decor from what it had been. He had papered a room in the house as he had been told to, but on returning the next day found that some of his papers were on upside down, as if moved around by unseen hands. He, too, heard strange noises and would have nothing further to do with the house. Mrs. W. then called upon the people who had preceded them in the house, the P. family, but the daughter of the late owner said that during their stay in the house they had not experienced anything unusual. Perhaps she did not care to discuss such matters. At any rate, Mrs. W. discovered that the former owner, Mr. P., had actually died in the house three years prior to their acquisition of it. Apparently, he had been working on the house, which he loved very much, and had sustained a fracture. He recovered from it, but sustained another fracture in the same area of his leg. During the recovery, he died of a heart attack in the livingroom.

It is conceivable that Mr. P. did not like the rearrangements made by the new owners and resented the need for repapering or repainting, having done so much of that himself while in the flesh. But if it is he who is walking up and down the stairs at night, turning doorknobs, and appearing as luminous balls of light — who, then, is the woman whose voice has also been heard?

So it appears that the house overlooking the golf course for the past hundred and twenty-two years has more than one spectral inhabitant in it. Perhaps Mr. P. is only a johnny-come-lately, joining the earlier shades staying on in what used to be their home. As far as the W.'s are concerned, the house is big enough for all of them, so long as they know their place!

* * *

Peter Q. comes from a devout Catholic family, part Scottish, part Irish. One June, Peter Q. was married, and his brother Tom, with whom he had always maintained a close and cordial relationship, came to the wedding. That was the last time the two brothers were happy together.

Two weeks later Tom and a friend spent a weekend on Cape Cod. During that weekend, Tom lost his prize possession, his collection of record albums worth several hundred dollars. Being somewhat superstitious, he feared that his luck had turned against him and, sure enough, his car was struck by a hit-and-run driver shortly afterwards.

Then in August of the same year, Tom and his father caught a very big fish on a fishing trip and won a prize consisting of a free trip during the season. As he was cleaning the fish to present it to the jury, the line broke and Tom lost the prize fish. But his streak of bad luck was to take on ominous proportions soon after. Two weeks later, Tom Q. died instantly, his friend David died the next day.

Even before the bad news was brought home to Peter Q. and the family, an extraordinary thing happened at their house. The clock in the bedroom stopped suddenly. When Peter checked it and wound it again, he found nothing wrong with it. By then, word of Tom's death had come, and on checking the time, Peter found that the clock had stopped at the very instant of his brother's death.

During the following days, drawers in what used to be their bedroom would open by themselves when there was no one about. This continued for about four weeks, then it stopped again. On the anniversary of Tom's death, Peter, who was then a junior at the university, was doing some studying and using a fountain pen to highlight certain parts in the books. Just then, his mother called him and asked him to help his father with his car. Peter placed the pen inside the book to mark the page and went to help his father. On returning an hour later, he discovered that a picture of his late brother and their family had been placed where Peter had left the pen, and the pen was lying outside the book next to it. No one had been in the house at the time since Peter's wife was out working.

Under the influence of Tom's untimely death and the phenomena taking place at his house, Peter Q. became very interested in life after death and read almost everything he could, talking with many of his friends about the subject, and becoming more and more convinced that man does in some mysterious way survive death. His wife disagreed with him and did not wish to discuss the matter.

One night, while her husband was away from the house, Peter's wife received a telepathic impression concerning continuance of life, and as she did so, a glowing object about the size of a softball appeared next to her in her bed. It was not a dream, for she could see the headlights from passing cars shining on the wall of the room, yet the shining object was still there next to her pillow, stationary and glowing. It eventually disappeared.

Many times since, Peter Q. has felt the presence of his brother, a warm, wonderful feeling; yet it gives him goose bumps all over. As for the real big send-off Tom had wanted from this life, he truly received it. The morning after his accident, a number of friends called the house without realizing that anything had happened to Tom. They had felt a strong urge to call, as if someone had communicated with them telepathically to do so.

Tom Q. was a collector of phonograph records and owned many, even though a large part of his collection had been stolen. The night before his fatal accident, he had played some of these records.

When Peter later checked the record player, he discovered that the last song his brother had played was entitled, "Just One More Day." Of the many Otis Redding recordings his brother owned, why had he chosen that one?

* * *

Mr. Harold B. is a professional horse trainer who travels a good deal of the time. When he does stay at home, he lives in an old house in a small town in Massachusetts. Prior to moving to New England, he and his wife lived in Ohio, but he was attracted by the Old World atmosphere of New England and decided to settle down in the East. They found a house that was more than two hundred years old, but unfortunately it was in dire need of repair. There was neither electricity nor central heating, and all the rooms were dirty, neglected, and badly in need of renovating. Nevertheless, they liked the general feeling of the house and decided to take it.

The house was in a sad state, mostly because it had been lived in for fifty-five years by a somewhat eccentric couple who had shut themselves off from the world. They would hardly admit anyone to their home, and it was known in town that three of their dogs had died of starvation. Mr. and Mrs. B. moved into the house on Walnut Road in October. Shortly after their arrival, Mrs. B. fractured a leg, which kept her housebound for a considerable amount of time. This was unfortunate since the house needed so much work. Nevertheless, they managed. With professional help, they did the house over from top to bottom, putting in a considerable amount of work and money to make it livable, until it became a truly beautiful house.

Although Mrs. B. is not particularly interested in the occult, she has had a number of psychic experiences in the past, especially of a precognitive nature, and has accepted her psychic powers as a matter of course. Shortly after the couple had moved into the house on Walnut Road, they noticed that there *was* something peculiar about their home.

One night, Mrs. B. was sleeping alone in a downstairs front room off the center entrance hall. Suddenly she was awakened by the sensation of a presence in the room, and as she looked up she saw the figure of a small woman before her bed, looking right at her. She could make out all the details of the woman's face and stature, and noticed that she was wearing a veil, as widows sometimes did in the past. When the apparition became aware of Mrs. B.'s attention, she lifted the veil and spoke to her, assuring her that she was not there to harm her but that she came as a friend. Mrs. B. was too overcome by it all to reply, and before she could gather her wits, the apparition drifted away.

Immediately, Mrs. B. made inquiries in town, and since she was able to give a detailed description of the apparition, it was not long until she knew who the ghost was. The description fit the former owner of the house, Mrs. C., to a tee. Mrs. C. died at age eighty-six, shortly before the B.'s moved into what was her former home. Armed with this information, Mrs. B. braced herself for the presence of an unwanted inhabitant in the house. A short time afterwards, she saw the shadowy outline of what appeared to be a heavy-set person moving along the hall from her bedroom. At first she thought it was her husband so she called out to him, but she soon discovered that her husband was actually upstairs. She then examined her room and discovered that the shades were drawn, so there was no possibility that light from traffic on the road outside could have cast a shadow into the adjoining hall. The shadowy figure she had seen did not, however, look like the outline of the ghost she had earlier encountered in the front bedroom.

While she was wondering about this, she heard the sound of a dog running across the floor. Yet there was no dog to be seen. Evidently her own dog also heard or sensed the ghostly dog's doings because he reacted with visible terror.

Mrs. B. was still wondering about the second apparition when her small grandson came and stayed overnight. He had never been to the house before and had not been told of the stories connected with it. As he was preparing to go to sleep, but still fully conscious, he saw a heavy-set man wearing a red shirt standing before him in his bedroom. This upset him greatly, especially when the man suddenly disappeared without benefit of a door. He described the apparition to his grandparents, who reassured him by telling him a white lie: namely, that he had been dreaming. To this the boy indignantly replied that he had not been dreaming, but, in fact, he had been fully awake. The description given by the boy not only fitted the shadowy outline of the figure Mrs. B. had seen along the corridor, but was a faithful description of the late Mr. C., the former owner of the house.

Although the ghost of Mrs. C. had originally assured the B.'s that she meant no harm and that she had come as a friend, Mrs. B. had her doubts. A number of small items of no particular value disappeared from time to time and were never found again. This was at times when intruders were completely out of the question.

Then Mrs. B. heard the pages of a wallpaper sampler lying on the dining room table being turned one day. Thinking her husband was doing it, she called out to him, only to find that the room was empty. When she located him in another part of the house, he reported having heard the pages being turned also, and this reassured Mrs. B. since she now had her husband's support in the matter of ghosts. It was clear to her that the late owners did not appreciate the many changes they had made in the house. But Mrs. B. also decided that she was not about to be put out of her home by a ghost. The changes had been made for the better, she decided, and the C.'s, even in their present ghostly state, should be grateful for what they had done for the house and not resent them. Perhaps these thoughts somehow reached the two ghosts telepathically; at any rate, the atmosphere in the house became quiet after that.

* * *

Barbara is a young woman with a good background who saw me on a Boston television program and volunteered her own experiences as a result. The following week, she wrote to me.

My family home, in Duxbury, Massachusetts, which is near Plymouth and the home of such notables as Myles Standish and John Alden, is one of the oldest houses in town although we do not know just how old it is.

Last February my brother Edward and his wife Doris and their family moved into the house. Before this my brother Carl and my father were there alone after my mother's death nearly a year ago.

The first occasion of odd happenings was on March 17, St. Patrick's Day. We are a very small part Irish — the name is about all that is left, O'Neil. A friend of mine and I went up to the farm to visit. Shortly after we arrived we heard a noise, which to me sounded like a baby whimpering as it awoke and to my sister-in-law as a woman moaning. I spoke to Doris, something about her baby being awake. She said no and let it pass until later when she told us that she had heard the same noise earlier in the morning and had gone upstairs to check on the baby. As she stood beside the crib, the baby sleeping soundly, she heard the noise again. She then called to the barn to see if all the dogs were accounted for — which they were.

Since this first noticed phenomenon the following things have occurred.

My sister-in-law is keeping a log — I may have omissions.

1. The upstairs door opened and closed (the latch type door) and a shadow filled the whole staircase. It was a calm,

272

Ghosts of New England

cloudy day, and the possibility of a draft is somewhat unlikely. Witnessed by Doris.

2. My brother Carl heard a voice saying, "Bring it back." This went on for several minutes but it was clear for the full time.

3. Footsteps upstairs heard by Doris.

4. Doris went into the front room to see the over-stuffed rocker rocking as though someone was in it. After she entered the chair began to stop as though someone got up.

5. July 4, Doris went upstairs and saw the outline of a man which just seemed to disappear.

Before Edward and Doris moved in, Carl and my father were living there alone (all are in the house now). There was no one in the house most of the time since my mother died nearly a year ago. During this time the girl who rents the other house on the farm twice saw the outline of a man over there — once sitting in a chair and another time she woke my brothers about this. She is very jittery about it and as a result does not know about the other things.

I suppose I could go on a bit about the family history. My grandmother traces her ancestry back to Myles Standish and John Alden; my grandfather from Nova Scotia of Scotch-Irish ancestry. I don't know who it was, but someone who lived in the house hanged himself in the barn.

Carl is a sensible, hard-working dairyman who graduated from the University of Massachusetts. Edward is a scoffer since he has observed nothing, recently discharged from the Navy as a lieutenant and is a graduate of Tufts University.

Doris is a very intelligent, levelheaded girl who, before these events, would have called herself a scoffer or disbeliever.

I graduated from Bridgewater Teachers College and at first tried to say that there was a logical explanation to these things but there have just been too many things.

My friend is an intelligent, clear thinking person.

I give you this background on the witnesses, not as a bragger or being vain, but to give you an idea of the type of witnesses. We are not the hysterical, imagining type.

The house has thirteen rooms (not all original) and the ghost seems to roam around at will."

* * *

It has been said that the people of Boston — proper Bostonians — are a breed all their own, polite, erudite, and very determined to have things their own way. I have found that these proper Bostonian ghosts are no different in the afterlife. Some of them may not be exactly erudite, but neither are they insolent or, heaven forbid, dumb.

The Possession of Mrs. F.

Possession for the sake of evil, or for the sake of continuing indefinitely a physical existence, is probably the most feared form of this phenomenon. But there exists a type of possession which is clearly confined in purpose and frequently also in time. In such cases, the possessor takes hold of an individual on the physical plane in order to finish some uncompleted task he or she was unable to accomplish while alive in the physical sense. Once that task has been accomplished, there is no further need for possession, and the possessor withdraws, continuing an existence in the proper dimension, that is, in the nonphysical world.

Nevertheless, there are aspects of this limited and quasi-intelligent possession that are not acceptable to the one to whom it occurs. In the desire to express a need of sorts or finish something that had been started and not ended, the possessor may overlook the desire of the individual not to be possessed, or to be free of such imposed power. Under such circumstances it is advisable to break the hold of the possessor in spite of any good intentions behind the action.

* * *

Virginia F. is an average person of full Irish descent. She describes herself as one of the Black Irish, those who think they are related to the Spanish Armada survivors who took refuge in Ireland in 1588 and later intermingled with the native population. Mrs. F. has five children and lives in a modest home in one of the largest cities in New England. The house was built in February of 1955 and sold to a Mr. and Mrs. J. S. Evidently the home was far from lucky for the first owner whose wife died of cancer in it after about four years. Then it was rented to a Captain M. for about a year. Apparently the good captain wasn't too happy there either for he left. The next owners were C. and E. B. Within a year of acquiring the house they filed for a divorce. A short time later, their oldest son was run over and killed by a truck. At that point, the house passed into the hands of Mrs. F. and her family. A little over two months after they had moved in, her father had a heart attack in the bathroom and died on the way to the hospital. For nine years Mrs. F. and her family managed to live in the house, but their marriage was not a happy one, and it ended in divorce in 1970. Whether or not the tragic atmosphere of the house has any bearing upon what transpired later is hard to tell, but Mrs. F. thought enough of it to advise me of it, and I'm inclined to think that the depressing atmosphere of a house may very well lead to psychic complications. It could very well be that an earlier dwelling stood on the same spot and that some of the older vibrations are clinging to the new house.

On May 25, 1970, Mrs. F.'s divorce was complete. In the fall of the same year she met another man. Francis and his sister Gloria had visited the house after a club meeting, and from that moment on, Mrs. F. and Francis were inseparable. It was love at first sight. For a few weeks, the two went everywhere together, and then the happiness came to a sudden end. Francis was ill with an incurable disease. He knew he did not have long to live. Instead of a wedding, she helped plan his funeral.

The night before he died, he told her he would never leave her and that nothing or no one could ever separate them. He also told her that he would come for her soon. That night he died. And when he died his electric clock stopped exactly at the moment he passed out of the body. For the last day of his life Francis had been attended day and night by Mrs. F. and her two sons, but nothing could have been done to save him.

When the man knew that his time was short, he started to talk with her about death and what he wanted to have done. She had promised him she would buy the lot in the cemetery next to his; faithful to his request, the day after she had buried him, February 14, 1972, she bought the lot next to his.

That day, strange things started to happen in her home. There was, first of all, a picture, which Francis had bought for her, showing the Minuteman on the Lexington Green. The picture would actually fly off the wall, no matter how many times she refastened it. This happened several times and the picture actually flung itself across the room, making a terrific noise. During the three days between Francis' death and his burial, a little valentine she had given him in the hospital would be moved by unseen hands. Someone took it from a ticket, to which it was fastened with a paper clip, and turned it around so that the side on which was written "Love G." was on top. But no one in the house had done it.

After the funeral, Mrs. F. fell asleep, exhausted from the emotional upset. At four o'clock in the morning she woke up to find that a piece of paper she had put in front of her, had been written upon while she was asleep. The words read, "Remember, I love you, Francis."

Realizing that this was a message somehow using her hands to write even though she might not be aware of it, she tried consciously to receive another message by automatic writing a week later. The first line consisted of scribbled letters that made no sense whatsoever.

But the second line became clearer. It was a love message written in the handwriting of the deceased. There was no mistaking it.

When she confided in her family doctor, he shook his head and prescribed sedatives. In her heartbroken state, Mrs. F. remembered how her fiance had promised her a pearl ring for Christmas but had been too sick then to buy it. The matter of the missing pearl ring had been a private joke between them. Two days after the last automatic message, she was putting some things away in the bedroom of her house. She carefully cleaned the top of her dresser and put everything in its proper place. A short time later her oldest daughter asked her to come up to the bedroom. There, on the dresser, was a pearl! How had it gotten there?

"Do these things truly happen, or am I on the verge of a breakdown?" Mrs. F. asked herself. She remembered how she had written to me some years ago concerning some ESP experiences she had had. Again she got in touch with me, this time for help. "Help me, please, to understand. And if you tell me that I'm losing my mind," she wrote, "then I'll go to the hospital." But I assured her that she was not insane. All she really wanted was to be with her Francis at this point.

Mrs. F. was indeed in a fix. There was nothing wrong with her love relationship, but Francis's promise to take her over to his side of life was another matter. I was convinced that those who were guiding him now would also instruct him accordingly. Gently I explained to Mrs. F. that love cannot fully bridge the gap between the two worlds of existence.

There is a time for them to be joined, but for the present she belonged to the world of the body and must continue to live in it as best she could. When she accepted her true position and also her renewed responsibility towards her children, the hold — which the deceased had had upon her for a while after his passing — lessened. It was as if Francis had understood that his business had indeed been finished. The knowledge of his continued existence in another dimension was all he wanted to convey to his one and only love. That done, he could await her coming in due time in the conviction that they would be together without the shadow of possession between them.

The Ghost at
Cap'n Grey's

Some of the best leads regarding a good ghost story come to me as the result of my having appeared on one of many television or radio programs, usually discussing a book dealing with the subject matter for which I am best known — psychic phenomena of one kind or another. So it happened that one of my many appearances on the Bob Kennedy television show in Boston drew unusually heavy mail from places as far away as other New England states and even New York.

Now if there is one thing ghosts don't really care much about it is time — to them everything is suspended in a timeless dimension where the intensity of their suffering or problem remains forever constant and alive. After all, they are unable to let go of what it is that ties them to a specific location, otherwise they would not be what we so commonly (and perhaps a little callously) call ghosts. I am mentioning this as a way of explaining why, sometimes, I cannot respond as quickly as I would like to when someone among the living reports a case of a haunting that needs to be looked into. Reasons were and are now mainly lack of time but more likely lack of funds to organize a team and go after the case. Still, by and large, I do manage to show up in time and usually manage to resolve the situation.

Thus it happened that I received a letter dated August 4, 1966, sent to me via station WBZ-TV in Boston, from the owner of Cap'n Grey's Smorgasbord, an inn located in Barnstable on Cape Cod. The owner, Mr. Lennart Svensson, had seen me on the show and asked me to get in touch.

"We have experienced many unusual happenings here. The building in which our restaurant and guest house is located was built in 1716 and was formerly a sea captain's residence," Svensson wrote.

I'm a sucker for sea captains haunting their old houses so I wrote back asking for details. Mr. Svensson replied a few weeks later, pleased to have aroused my interest. Both he and his wife had seen the apparition of a young woman, and their eldest son had also felt an unseen presence; guests in their rooms also mentioned unusual happenings. It appeared that when the house was first built the foundation had been meant as a fortification against Indian attacks. Rumor has it, Mr. Svensson informed me, that the late sea captain had been a slave trader and sold slaves on the premises.

Svensson and his wife, both of Swedish origin, had lived on the Cape in the early thirties, later moved back to Sweden, to return in 1947. After a stint working in various restaurants in New York, they acquired the inn on Cape Cod.

I decided a trip to the Cape was in order. I asked Sybil Leek to accompany me as the medium. Mr. Svensson explained that the inn would close in October for the winter, but he, and perhaps other witnesses to the phenomena, could be seen even after that date, should I wish to come up then. But it was not until June 1967, the following year, that I finally managed to get our act together, so to speak, and I contacted Mr. Svensson to set a date for our visit. Unfortunately, he had since sold the inn and, as he put it, the new owner was not as interested in the ghost as he was, so there was no way for him to arrange for our visit now.

But Mr. Svensson did not realize how stubborn a man I can be when I want to do something. I never gave up on this case, and decided to wait a little and then approach the new owners. Before I could do so, however, the new owner saw fit to get in touch with me instead. He referred to the correspondence between Mr. Svensson and myself, and explained that at the time I had wanted to come up, he had been in the process of redoing the inn for its opening. That having taken place several weeks ago, it would appear that "we have experienced evidence of the spirit on several occasions, and I now feel we should look into this matter as soon as possible." He invited us to come on up whenever it was convenient, preferably yesterday.

The new owner turned out to be an attorney named Jack Furman of Hyannis, and a very personable man at that. When I wrote we would indeed be pleased to meet him, and the ghost or ghosts, as the case might be, he sent us all sorts of information regarding flights and offered to pick us up at the airport. Mr. Furman was not shy in reporting his own experiences since he had taken over the house.

There has been on one occasion an umbrella mysteriously stuck into the stairwell in an open position. This was observed by my employee, Thaddeus B. Ozimek. On another occasion when the Inn was closed in the evening early, my manager returned to find the front door bolted from *the inside* which appeared strange since no one was in the building. At another time, my chef observed that the heating plant went off at 2:30, and the serviceman, whom I called the next day, found that a fuse was removed from the fuse box. At 2:30 in the morning, obviously, no one that we know of was up and around to do this. In addition, noises during the night have been heard by occupants of the Inn.

I suggested in my reply that our little team consisting, as it would, of medium (and writer) Sybil Leek, Catherine (my wife at the time), and myself, should spend the night at the Inn as good ghost hunters do. I also requested that the former owner, Mr. Svensson, be present for further questioning, as well as any direct witnesses to phenomena. On the other hand, I delicately suggested that no one not concerned with the case should be present, keeping in mind some occasions where my investigations had been turned into entertainment by my hosts to amuse and astound neighbors and friends.

In the end it turned out to be best to come by car as we had other projects to look into en route, such as Follins Pond, where we eventually discovered the possibility of a submerged Viking ship at the bottom of the pond. The date for our visit was to be August 17, 1967 — a year and two weeks after the case first came to my attention. But not much of a time lag, the way it is with ghosts.

When we arrived at the Inn, after a long and dusty journey, the sight that greeted us was well worth the trip. There, set back from a quiet country road amid tall, aged trees, sat an impeccable white colonial house, two stories high with an attic, nicely surrounded by a picket fence, and an old bronze and iron lamp at the corner. The windows all had their wooden shutters opened to the outside and the place presented such a picture of peace it was difficult to realize we had come here to confront a disturbance. The house was empty, as we soon realized, because the new owner had not yet allowed guests to return — considering what the problems were!

Quickly, we unburdened ourselves of our luggage, each taking a room upstairs, then returned to the front of the house to begin our usual inspection. Sybil Leek now let go of her conscious self the more to immerse herself in the atmosphere and potential presences of the place.

"There is something in the bedroom . . . in the attic," Sybil said immediately as we climbed the winding stairs. "I thought just now someone was pushing my hair up from the back," she then added.

Mr. Furman had, of course, come along for the investigation. At this point we all saw a flash of light in the middle of the room. None of us was frightened by it, not even the lawyer who by now had taken the presence of the supernatural in his house in his stride.

We then proceeded downstairs again, with Sybil assuring us that whatever it was that perturbed her up in the attic did not seem to be present downstairs. With that we came to a locked door, a door that Mr. Furman assured us that had not been opened in a long time. When we managed to get it open, it led us to the downstairs office or the room now used as such. Catherine, ever the alert artist and designer that she was, noticed that a door had been barred from the inside, almost as if someone had once been kept in that little room. Where did this particular door lead to, I asked Mr. Furman. It appeared it led to a narrow corridor and finally came out into the fireplace in the large main room.

"Someone told me if I ever dug up the fireplace," Mr. Furman intoned significantly, "I might find something."

What that something would be, was left to our imagination. Mr. Furman added that his informant had hinted at some sort of valuables, but Sybil immediately added, "bodies . . . you may find bodies."

She described, psychically, many people suffering in the house, and a secret way out of the house — possibly from the captain's slave trading days?

Like a doctor examining a patient, I then examined the walls both in the little room and the main room and found many hollow spots. A bookcase turned out to be a false front. Hidden passages seemed to suggest themselves. Quite obviously, Mr. Furman was not about to tear open the walls to find them. But Sybil was right: the house was honeycombed with areas not visible to the casual observer.

Sybil insisted we seat ourselves around the fireplace, and I insisted that the ghost, if any, should contact us there rather than our trying to chase the elusive phantom from room to room. "A way out of the house is very important," Sybil said, and I couldn't help visualizing the unfortunate slaves the good (or not so good) captain had held captive in this place way back.

But when nothing much happened, we went back to the office, where I discovered that the front portion of the wall seemed to block off another room beyond it, not accounted for when measuring the outside walls. When we managed to pry it open, we found a stairwell, narrow though it was, where apparently a flight of stairs had once been. I asked for a flashlight. Catherine shone it up the shaft: we found ourselves below a toilet in an upstairs bathroom! No ghost here.

We sat down again, and I invited the presence, whomever it was, to manifest. Immediately Sybil remarked she felt a young boy around the place, a hundred and fifty years ago. As she went more and more into a trance state, Sybil mentioned the name Chet . . . someone who wanted to be safe from an enemy . . . Carson . . .

"Let him speak," I said.

"Carson . . . 1858 . . . " Sybil replied, now almost totally entranced as I listened carefully for words coming from her in halting fashion.

"I will fight . . . Charles . . . the child is missing . . . "

"Whom will you fight? Who took the child?" I asked in return.

"Chicopee . . . child is dead."

"Whose house is this?"

"Fort . . . "

"Whose is it?"

"Carson . . ."

"Are you Carson?"

"Captain Carson."

"What regiment?"

"Belvedere . . . cavalry . . . 9th . . ."

"Where is the regiment stationed?"

There was no reply.

"Who commanded the regiment?" I insisted.

"Wainwright . . . Edward Wainwright . . . commander."

"How long have you been here?"

"Four years."

"Where were you born?"

"Montgomery . . . Massachusetts."

"How old are you now?"

There was no reply.

"Are you married?"

"My son . . . Tom . . . ten . . ."

"What year was he born in?"

"Forty . . . seven . . ."

"Your wife's name?"

"Gina . . ."

"What church do you go to?"

"I don't go."

"What church do you belong to?"

"She is . . . of Scottish background . . . Scottish kirk."

"Where is the kirk located?"

"Six miles . . ."

"What is the name of this village we are in now?"

"Chicopee . . ."

Further questioning gave us this information: that "the enemy" had taken his boy, and the enemy were the Iroquois. This was his fort and he was to defend it. I then began, as I usually do, when exorcism is called for, to speak of the passage of time and the need to realize that the entity communicating through the medium was aware of the true situation in this respect. Did Captain Carson realize that time had passed since the boy had disappeared?

"Oh yes," he replied. "Four years."

"No, a hundred and seven years," I replied.

Once again I established that he was Captain Carson, and there was a river nearby and Iroquois were the enemy. Was he aware that there were "others" here besides himself.

He did not understand this. Would he want me to help him find his son since they had both passed over and should be able to find each other there?

"I need permission . . . from Wainwright . . ."

As I often do in such cases, I pretended to speak for Wainwright and granted him the permission. A ghost, after all, is not a rational human being but an entity existing in a delusion where only emotions count.

"Are you now ready to look for your son?"

"I am ready."

"Then I will send a messenger to help you find him," I said, "but you must call out to your son . . . in a loud voice."

The need to reach out to a loved one is of cardinal importance in the release of a trapped spirit, commonly called a ghost.

"John Carson is dead . . . but not dead forever," he said in a faint voice.

"You lived here in 1858, but this is 1967," I reminded him.

"You are mad!"

"No, I'm not mad. Touch your forehead . . . you will see this is not the body you are accustomed to. We have lent you a body to communicate with us. But it is not yours."

Evidently touching a woman's head did jolt the entity from his beliefs. I decided to press on.

"Go from this house and join your loved ones who await you outside . . . "

A moment later Captain Carson had slipped away and a sleepy Sybil Leek opened her eyes.

I now turned to Mr. Furman, who had watched the proceedings with mounting fascination. Could he corroborate any of the information that had come to us through the entranced medium?

"This house was built on the foundations of an Indian fort," he confirmed, "to defend the settlers against the Indians."

"Were there any Indians here in 1858?"

"There are Indians here even now," Furman replied. "We have an Indian reservation at Mashpee, near here, and on Martha's Vineyard there is a tribal chief and quite a large Indian population."

He also confirmed having once seen a sign in the western part of Massachusetts that read "Montgomery" — the place Captain Carson had claimed as his birthplace. Also that a Wainwright family was known to have lived in an area not far from where we were now. However, Mr. Furman had no idea of any military personnel by that name.

"Sybil mentioned a river in connection with this house." Furman said, "And, yes, there is a river running through the house, it is still here."

Earlier Sybil had drawn a rough map of the house as it was in the past, from her psychic viewpoint, a house surrounded by a high fence. Mr. Furman pronounced the drawing amazingly accurate — especially as Sybil had not set foot on the property or known about it until our actual arrival.

"My former secretary, Carole E. Howes, and her family occupied this house," Mr. Furman explained when I turned my attention to the manifestations themselves. "They operated this house as an Inn twenty years ago, and often had unusual things happen here as she grew up, but it did not seem to bother them. Then the house passed into the hands of a Mrs. Nielson; then Mr. Svensson took over. But he did not speak of the phenomena until about a year and a half ago. The winter of 1965 he was shingling the roof, and he was just coming in from the roof on the second floor balcony on a cold day — he had left the window ajar and secured — when suddenly he heard the window sash come down. He turned around on the second floor platform and he saw the young girl, her hair windswept behind her. She was wearing white. He could not see anything below the waist, and he confronted her for a short period, but could not bring himself to talk — and she went away. His wife was in the kitchen sometime later, in the afternoon, when she felt the presence of someone in the room. She turned around and saw an older man dressed in black at the other end of the kitchen. She ran out of the kitchen and never went back in again.

"The accountant John Dillon's son was working in the kitchen one evening around ten. Now some of these heavy pots were hanging there on pegs from the ceiling. Young Dillon told his father two of them lifted themselves up from the ceiling, unhooked themselves from the pegs, and came down on the floor."

Did any guests staying at the Inn during Svensson's ownership complain of any unusual happenings?

"There was this young couple staying at what Mr. Svensson called the honeymoon suite," Mr. Furman replied. "At 6:30 in the morning, the couple heard three knocks at the door, three loud, distinct knocks, and when they opened the door, there was no one there. This sort of thing had happened before."

Another case involved a lone diner who complained to Svensson that "someone" was pushing him from his chair at the table in the dining room onto another chair, but since he did not see another person, how could this be? Svensson hastily had explained that the floor was a bit rickety and that was probably the cause.

Furman then recounted the matter of the lock: he and a young man who worked with him had left the Inn to bring the chef, who had become somewhat difficult that day, home to his own place. When Mr. Furman's assistant returned to the Inn at 2:30 in the morning, the door would not open, and the key would not work. After he had climbed into the house through an upstairs window, he found to his amazement that the door had been locked *from the inside*.

The story gave me a chill: that very day, after our arrival, nearly the same thing happened to us — except that we did not have to climb to the upper floor to get in but managed to enter through a rear door! Surely, someone did not exactly want us in the house.

The chef, by the way, had an experience of his own. The heating system is normally quite noisy, but one night it suddenly stopped and the heat went off. When the repair crew came the next day they discovered that a fuse had been physically removed from the fuse box, which in turn stopped the heating system from operating. The house was securely locked at that time so no one from the outside could have done this.

The famous case of an umbrella being stuck into the ceiling of the upstairs hall was confirmed by the brother of the young man, Mr. Bookstein, living in the house. He also pointed out to us that the Chicopee Indians were indeed in this area, so Sybil's trance utterances made a lot of sense.

"There was an Indian uprising in Massachusetts as late as the middle of the nineteenth century," he confirmed, giving more credence to the date, 1858, that had come through Sybil.

Was the restless spirit of the captain satisfied with our coming? Did he and his son meet up in the Great Beyond? Whatever came of our visit, nothing further has been heard of any disturbances at Cap'n Grey's Inn in Barnstable.

The Strange Case of Mrs. C.'s Late but Lively Husband

Death is not the end, no, definitely not. At least not for Mr. C. who lived the good life in a fair sized city in Rhode Island. But then he died, or so it would appear on the record. But Mrs. C. came to consult me about the very unusual complaint of her late husband's continuing attentions.

When someone dies unexpectedly, or in the prime of his physical life, and finds that he can no longer express his sexual appetite physically in the world into which he has been suddenly catapulted, he may indeed look around for someone through whom he can express this appetite on the earth plane. It is then merely a matter of searching out opportunities, regardless of personalities involved. It is quite conceivable that a large percentage of the unexplained or inexplicable sexual attacks by otherwise meek, timid, sexually defensive individuals upon members of the opposite sex — or even the same sex — may be due to sudden possession by an entity of this kind. This is even harder to prove objectively than are some of the murder cases involving individuals who do not recall what they have done and are for all practical purposes normal human beings before and after the crime. But I am convinced that the influence of discarnates can indeed be exercised upon susceptible individuals — that is to say, appropriately mediumistic individuals. It also appears from my studies that the most likely recipients of this doubtful honor are those who are sexually weak or inactive. Evidently the unused sexual energies are particularly useful to the discarnate entities for their own gains. There really doesn't seem to be any way in which one can foretell such attacks or prevent them, except, perhaps, by leading a sexually healthy and balanced life. *Those who are fulfilled in their natural drives on the earth plane are least likely to suffer from such invasions.*

On the other hand, there exist cases of sexual possession involving two partners who knew each other before on the earth plane. One partner was cut short by death, either violently or prematurely, and would now seek to continue a pleasurable relationship of the flesh from the new dimension. Deprived of a physical body to express such desires, however, the deceased partner would then find it rather difficult to express the physical desires to the partner remaining on the earth plane. With sex it certainly takes two, and if the remaining partner is not willing, then difficulties will have to be reckoned with. An interesting case came to my attention a few months ago. Mrs. Anna C. lives with her several children in a comparatively new house in the northeastern United States. She bought the house eighteen months after her husband had passed away. Thus there was no connection between the late husband and the new house. Nevertheless, her husband's passing was by no means the end of their relationship.

"My husband died five years ago this past September. Ever since then he has not let me have a peaceful day," she explained in desperation, seeking my help.

Two months after her husband had died, she saw him coming to her in a dream complaining that she had buried him alive. He explained that he wasn't really dead, and that it was all her fault and her family's fault that he died in the first place.

Mr. C. had lived a rather controversial life, drinking regularly and frequently staying away from home. Thus the relationship between himself and his wife was far from ideal. Nevertheless, there was a strong bond between them.

"In other dreams he would tell me that *he was going to have sex relations with me whether I wanted him to or not.* He would try to grab me and I would run all through the house with him chasing after me. I never let him get hold of me. He was like that when he was alive, too. The most important thing in life to him was sex, and he didn't care how or where he got it. Nothing else mattered to him," she complained, describing vividly how the supposedly dead husband had apparently still a great deal of life in him.

"He then started climbing on the bed and walking up and down on it and scaring me half to death. I didn't know what it was or what to do about it," she said, shaking like a leaf.

When Mr. C. could not get his wife to cooperate willingly, he apparently got mad. To express his displeasure, he caused all sorts of havoc around the household. He would tear a pair of stockings every day for a week, knock things over, and even go to the place where his mother-in-law worked as a cook, causing seemingly inexplicable phenomena to occur there as well. He appeared to an aunt in Indiana and told her to mind her own business and stay out of his personal relationship with Mrs. C. (It was the aunt who tried to get rid of him and his influences by performing a spiritualist ritual at the house.) Meanwhile, Mr. C. amused himself by setting alarm clocks to go off at the wrong times or stopping them altogether, moving objects from their accustomed places or making them disappear altogether, only to return them several days later to everyone's surprise. In general, he behaved like a good *poltergeist* should. But it didn't endear him any more to his erstwhile wife.

When Mrs. C. rejected his attentions, he started to try to possess his ten-year-old daughter. He came to her in dreams and told her that her mother wasn't really knowledgeable about anything. He tried everything in his power to drive a wedge between the little girl and her mother. As a result of this, the little girl turned more and more away from her mother, and no matter how Mrs. C. tried to explain things to her, she found the little girl's mind made up under the influence of her late father.

In a fit of destructiveness, the late Mr. C. then started to work on the other children, creating such a state of havoc in the household that Mrs. C. did not know where to turn any longer. Then the psychic aunt from Indiana came to New England to try to help matters. Sure enough, Mr. C. appeared to her and the two had a cozy talk. He explained that he was very unhappy where he was and was having trouble getting along with the people over there. To this, the aunt replied she would be very happy to help him get to a higher plane if that was what he wanted. But that wasn't it, he replied. He just wanted to stay where he was. The aunt left for home. Now the children, one by one, became unmanageable, and Mrs. C. assumed that her late husband was interfering with their proper education and discipline. "I am fighting an unseen force and cannot get through to the children," she explained.

Her late husband did everything to embarrass her. She was working as a clerk at St. Francis' rectory in her town, doing some typing. It happened to be December 24, 1971, Christmas Eve. All of a sudden she heard a thud in her immediate vicinity and looked down to the floor. A heavy dictionary was lying at her feet. The book had been on the shelf only a fraction of a second before. A co-worker wondered what was up. She was hard pressed to explain the presence of the dictionary on the floor since it had been on the shelf in back of them only a moment before. But she knew very well how the dictionary came to land at her feet.

Mr. C. prepared special Christmas surprises for his wife. She went to her parents' house to spend the holiday. During that time her nephew George was late for work since his alarm had not worked properly. On inspection it turned out that someone had stuck a pencil right through the clock. As soon as the pencil was removed, the clock started to work again. On investigation it turned out that no one had been near the clock, and when the family tried to place the pencil into the clock, as they had found it, no one could do it. The excitement made Mrs. C. so ill she went to bed. That was no way to escape Mr. C.'s attentions, however. The day before New Year's Eve, her late husband got to her, walking up and down on the bed itself. Finally she told him to leave her and the children alone, to go where he belonged. She didn't get an answer. But phenomena continued in the house, so she asked her aunt to come back once again. This time the aunt from Indiana brought oil with her and put it on each of the children and Mrs. C. herself. Apparently it worked, or so it seemed to Mrs. C. But her late husband was merely changing his tactics. A few days later she was sure that he was trying to get into one of the children to express himself further since he could no longer get at her. She felt she would be close to a nervous breakdown if someone would not help her get rid of the phenomenon and, above all, break her husband's hold on her. "I am anxious to have him sent on up where he can't bother anyone any more," she explained.

Since I could not go immediately, and the voice on the telephone sounded as if its owner could not hold out a single day more, I asked Ethel Johnson Meyers, my mediumistic friend, to go out and see what she could do. Mrs. C. had to go to Mrs. Meyers' house for a personal sitting first. A week later Ethel came down to Mrs. C.'s house to continue her work. What Mrs. Meyers discovered was somewhat of a surprise to Mrs. C. and to myself. It was Ethel's contention that the late husband, while still in the flesh, had himself been the victim of possession and had done the many unpleasant things (of which he was justly accused) during his lifetime, not of his own volition but under the direction of another entity. That the possessor was himself possessed seemed like a novel idea to me, one neither Mrs. Meyers nor I could prove. Far more important was the fact that Mrs. Meyers' prayers and commands to the unseen entity seemed to have worked, for he walks up and down Mrs. C.'s bed no more, and all is quiet. I believe the hold Mr. C. had upon his wife after his death was so strong because of an unconscious desire on her part to continue their relationship. Even though she abhorred him — and the idea of being sexually possessed by a man who had lost his physical body in the usual way — something within her, perhaps deeply buried within her, may have wanted the continuous sexual attention he had bestowed upon her while still in the body.

A Plymouth Ghost

I am not talking about *the* Plymouth where the Pilgrims landed but another Plymouth. This one is located in New Hampshire, in a part of the state that is rather lonely and sparsely settled even today. If you really want to get away from it all — whatever it may be — this is a pretty good bet. I am mentioning this because a person living in this rural area isn't likely to have much choice in the way of entertainment, unless of course you provide it yourself. But I am getting ahead of my story.

I was first contacted about this case in August 1966 when a young lady named Judith Elliott, who lived in Bridgeport, Connecticut, at the time, informed me of the goings-on in her cousin's country house located in New Hampshire. Judith asked if I would be interested in contacting Mrs. Chester Fuller regarding these matters? What intrigued me about the report was not the usual array of footfalls, presences, and the house cat staring at someone unseen — but the fact that Mrs. Fuller apparently had seen a ghost and identified him from a book commemorating the Plymouth town bicentennial.

When I wrote back rather enthusiastically, Miss Elliott forwarded my letter to her cousin, requesting more detailed and chronological information. But it was not until well into the following year that I finally got around to making plans for a visit. Ethel Johnson Meyers, the late medium, and my ex-wife Catherine, always interested in spooky houses since she used to illustrate some of my books, accompanied me. Mrs. Fuller, true to my request, supplied me with all that she knew of the phenomena themselves, who experienced them, and such information about former owners of the house and the house itself as she could garner. Here, in her own words, is that report, which of course I kept from the medium at all times so as not to influence her or give her prior knowledge of house and circumstances. Mrs. Fuller's report is as follows:

Location: The house is located at 38 Merrill Street in the town of Plymouth, New Hampshire. To reach the house, you leave Throughway 93 at the first exit for Plymouth. When you reach the set of lights on Main Street, turn right and proceed until you reach the blue Sunoco service station, then take a sharp left onto Merrill Street. The house is the only one with white picket snow fence out front. It has white siding with a red front door and a red window box and is on the right hand side of the street.

1. The first time was around the middle of June — about a month after moving in. It was the time of day when lights are needed inside, but it is still light outside. This instance was in the kitchen and bathroom. The bathroom and dining room are in an addition onto the kitchen. The doors to both rooms go out of the kitchen beside of each other, with just a small wall space between. At that time we had our kitchen table in that space. I was getting supper, trying to put the food on the table and keep two small

children (ages 2 and 5) off the table. As I put the potatoes on the table, I swung around from the sink toward the bathroom door. I thought I saw someone in the bathroom. I looked and saw a man. He was standing about half-way down the length of the room. He was wearing a brown plaid shirt, dark trousers with suspenders, and he [wore] glasses with the round metal frames. He was of medium height, a little on the short side, not fat and not thin but a good build, a roundish face, and he was smiling. Suddenly he was gone, no disappearing act or anything fancy, just gone, as he had come.

2. Footsteps. There are footsteps in other parts of the house. If I am upstairs, the footsteps are downstairs. If I am in the kitchen, they are in the livingroom, etc. These were scattered all through the year, in all seasons, and in the daytime. It was usually around 2 or 3 and always on a sunny day, as I recall.

3. Winter — late at night. Twice we (Seth and I) heard a door shutting upstairs. (Seth is an elderly man who stays with us now. When we first moved here he was not staying with us. His wife was a distant cousin to my father. I got acquainted with them when I was in high school. I spent a lot of time at their house and his wife and I became quite close. She died 11 years ago and since then Seth has stayed at his son's house, a rooming house, and now up here. He spent a lot of time visiting us before he moved in.) Only one door in the bedrooms upstairs works right, and that is the door to my bedroom. I checked the kids that night to see if they were up or awake, but they had not moved. My husband was also sound asleep. The door was already shut, as my husband had shut it tight when he went to bed to keep out the sound of the television. The sound of the door was very

distinct — the sound of when it first made contact, then the latch clicking in place, and then the thud as it came in contact with the casing. Everything was checked out — anything that was or could be loose and have blown and banged, or anything that could have fallen down. Nothing had moved. The door only shut once during that night, but did it again later on in the winter.

4. The next appearance was in the fall. I was pregnant at the time. I lost the baby on the first of November, and this happened around the first of October. Becky Sue, my youngest daughter, was 3 at the time. She was asleep in her crib as it was around midnight or later. I was asleep in my bedroom across the hall. I woke up and heard her saying, "Mommy, what are you doing in my bedroom?" She kept saying that until I thought I had better answer her or she would begin to be frightened. I started to say "I'm not in your room," and as I did I started to turn over and I saw what seemed to be a woman in a long white nightgown in front of my bedroom door. In a flash it was gone out into the hall. All this time Becky had been saying, "Mommy, what are you doing in my room?" As the image disappeared out in the hall, Becky changed her question to, "Mommy, what were you doing in my bedroom?" Then I thought that if I told her I wasn't in her room that she would really be scared. All this time I thought that it was Kimberly, my older daughter, getting up, and I kept waiting for her to speak to me. Becky was still sounding like a broken record with her questions. Finally I heard "It" take two steps down, turn a corner, and take three steps more. Then I went into Becky's room and told her that I had forgotten what I had gone into her room for and to lie down and go to sleep, which she did. All this time Kim had not moved. The next morning I was

telling Seth (who was living with us now) about it, and I remembered about the footsteps going downstairs. I wondered if Becky had heard them too, so I called her out into the kitchen and asked her where I went after I left her room. She looked at me as if I had lost my mind and said, "Downstairs!"

5. This was in the winter, around 2. Seth was helping me make the beds upstairs as they had been skipped for some reason. We heard footsteps coming in from the playroom across the kitchen and a short way into the hall. We both thought it was Becky Sue who was playing outdoors. She comes in quite frequently for little odds and ends. Still no one spoke. We waited for a while expecting her to call to me. Finally, when she did not call, I went downstairs to see what she wanted, and there was no one there. I thought that maybe she had gone back out, but there was no snow on the floor or tracks of any kind. This was also on a very sunny day.

6. This was also late at night in 1965, around 11. I was putting my husband's lunch up when there was a step right behind me. That scared me, although I do not know why; up until that time I had never had any fear. Maybe it was because it was right behind my back and the others had always been at a distance or at least in front of me.

I cannot remember anything happening since then. Lately there have been noises as if someone was in the kitchen or dining room while I was in the livingroom, but I cannot be sure of that. It sounds as if something was swishing, but I cannot *definitely* say that it is not the sounds of an old house.

History of House and Background of Previous Owners
The history of the house and its previous owners is

very hard to get. We bought the house from Mrs. Ora Jacques. Her husband had bought it from their son who had moved to Florida. The husband was going to do quite a bit of remodeling and then sell it. When he died, Mrs. Jacques rented it for a year and then sold it.

Mr. Jacques' son bought it from a man who used to have a doughnut shop and did his cooking in a back room, so I have been told. There was a fire in the back that was supposedly started from the fat. They bought the house from Mrs. Emma Thompson, who, with her husband, had received the house for caring for a Mr. Woodbury Langdon, and by also giving him a small sum of money. Mrs. Thompson always gave people the impression that she was really a countess and that she had a sister in Pennsylvania who would not have anything to do with her because of her odd ways.

Mrs. Thompson moved to Rumney where she contracted pneumonia about six months later and died.

Mr. and Mrs. Thompson moved in to take care of Mr. Woodbury Langdon after he kicked out Mr. and Mrs. Dinsmore. (Mr. Cushing gave me the following information. He lives next door, and has lived there since 1914 or 1918).

He was awakened by a bright flash very early in the morning. Soon he could see that the top room (tower room) was all afire. He got dressed, called the firemen, and ran over to help. He looked in the window of what is now our dining room but was then Mr. Langdon's bedroom. (Mr. Langdon was not able to go up and down stairs because of his age.) He pounded on the window trying to wake Mr. Langdon up. Through the window he could see Mr. and Mrs. Dinsmore standing in the doorway between the kitchen and the bedroom. They were laughing and Mr. Dinsmore had an oil can in his hand. All this time Mr. Langdon was sound asleep. Mr. Cushing got angry and began pounding harder and harder. Just as he began to open the window Mr. Langdon woke up and Mr. Cushing helped him out the window. He said that no one would believe his story, even the insurance company. Evidently Mr. Langdon did because soon after he kicked the Dinsmores out and that was when Mr. and Mrs. Thompson came to take care of him. Around 1927 he came down with pneumonia. He had that for two days and then he went outdoors without putting on any jacket or sweater. Mrs. Thompson ran out and brought him back in. She put him back in bed and warmed him up with coffee and wrapped him in wool blankets. He seemed better until around midnight. Then he began moaning. He kept it up until around 3, when he died.

Mr. Langdon was married twice. His first wife and his eighteen-year-old son died [of] typhoid fever. He had the wells examined and found that it came from them. He convinced his father to invest his money in putting in the first water works for the town of Plymouth. At that time he lived across town on Russell Street.

He later married a woman by the name of Donna. He worshipped her and did everything he could to please her. He remodeled the house. That was when he added on the bathroom and bedroom (dining room). He also built the tower room so that his wife could look out over the town. He also had a big estate over to Squam Lake that he poured out money on. All this time she was running around with anyone she could find. Mr. Cushing believes that he knew it deep down but refused to let himself believe it. She died,

Mr. Cushing said, from the things she got from the thing she did! He insists that it was called leprosy. In the medical encyclopedia it reads, under leprosy, "differential diag: tuberculosis and esp. syphilis are the two disease most likely to be considered." She died either in this house or at the estate on the lake. She was buried in the family plot in Trinity Cemetery in Holderness. She has a small headstone with just one name on it, Donna. There is a large spire shaped monument in the center of the lot, with the family's names on it and their relationship. The name of Woodbury Langdon's second wife is completely eliminated from the stone. There is nothing there to tell who she was or why she is buried there. This has puzzled me up to now, because, as she died around 1911, and he did not die until around 1927, he had plenty of time to have her name and relationship added to the family stone. Mr. Cushing thinks that, after her death, Mr. Langdon began to realize more and more what she was really like. He has the impression that Mr. Langdon was quite broke at the time of his death.

I cannot trace any more of the previous owners, as I cannot trace the house back any farther than around 1860. Mr. Langdon evidently bought and sold houses like other men bought and sold horses. If this is the house I believe it to be, it was on the road to Rumney and had to be moved in a backward position to where it is now. They had something like six months later to move the barn back. Then they had to put in a street going from the house up to the main road. They also had to put a fence up around the house. This property *did* have a barn, and there was a fence here. There is a small piece of it left. The deeds from there just go around in circles.

The man who I think the ghost is, is Mr. Woodbury

Langdon. I have asked people around here what Mr. Langdon looked like and they describe him VERY MUCH as the man I saw in the bathroom. The man in the bicentennial book was his father. There is something in his face that was in the face of the "ghost."

I have two children. They are: Kimberly Starr, age 9 years and Rebecca Sue, age 6 years. Kim's birthday is on April 2 and Becky's is on August 10.

I was born and brought up on a farm 4½ miles out in the country in the town of Plymouth. My father believes in spirits, sort of, but not really. My mother absolutely does not.

I carried the business course and the college preparatory course through my four years of high school. I had one year of nurses' training. I was married when I was 20, in June, and Kim was born the next April.

P.S. We have a black cat who has acted queer at times in the past.
1. He would go bounding up the stairs only to come to an abrupt halt at the head of the stairs. He would sit there staring at presumably empty space, and then take off as if he had never stopped.
2. Sometimes he stood at the bathroom door and absolutely refused to go in.
3. He had spells of sitting in the hallway and staring up the stairs, not moving a muscle. Then suddenly he would relax and go on his way.

* * *

We finally settled on August 12, a Saturday, in 1967, to have a go at Mr. Langdon or whoever it was that haunted the house, because Miss Elliott was getting married in July and Mrs. Fuller wanted very much to be present.

Eleanor Fuller greeted us as we arrived, and led us into the house. As usual Ethel began to sniff around, and I just followed her, tape recorder running and camera at the ready. We followed her up the stairs to the upper floor, where Ethel stopped at the bedroom on the right, which happened to be decorated in pink.

"I get an older woman wearing glasses," Ethel said cautiously as she was beginning to pick up psychic leads, "and a man wearing a funny hat."

I pressed Ethel to be more specific about the "funny hat" and what period hat. The man seemed to her to belong to the early 1800s. She assured me it was not this century. She then complained about a cold spot, and when I stepped into it I too felt it. Since neither doors nor windows could be held responsible for the strong cold draft we felt, we knew that its origin was of a psychic nature, as it often is when there are entities present.

I asked Ethel to describe the woman she felt present. "She is lying down . . . and I get a pain in the chest," she said, picking up the spirit's condition. "The eyes are closed!"

We left the room and went farther on. Ethel grabbed her left shoulder as if in pain.

"She is here with me, looking at me," Ethel said.

"She's been here."

"Why is she still here?" I asked.

"I get a sudden chill when you asked that," Ethel replied.

"She tells me to go left . . . I am having difficulty walking . . . I think this woman had that difficulty."

We were walking down the stairs, when Ethel suddenly became a crone and had difficulty managing them. The real Ethel was as spry and fast as the chipmunks that used to roam around her house in Connecticut.

"I think she fell down these stairs," Ethel said and began to cough. Obviously, she was being impressed by a very sick person.

We had barely got Ethel to a chair when she slipped into full trance and the transition took place. Her face became distorted as in suffering, and a feeble voice tried to manifest through her, prodded by me to be clearer.

"Lander . . . or something . . ." she mumbled.

What followed was an absolutely frightening realization by an alien entity inside Ethel's body that the illness she was familiar with no longer existed now. At the same time, the excitement of this discovery made it difficult for the spirit to speak clearly, and we were confronted with a series of grunts and sighs.

Finally, I managed to calm the entity down by insisting she needed to relax in order to be heard.

"Calm . . . calm . . ." she said and cried, "good . . . he knows . . . he did that . . . for fifty years . . . the woman!"

She had seized Mr. Fuller's hand so forcefully I felt embarrassed for her, and tried to persuade the spirit within Ethel to let go, at the same time explaining her true condition to her, gently, but firmly.

After I had explained how she was able to communicate with us, and that the body of the medium was merely a temporary arrangement, the entity calmed down, asking only if he loved her, meaning the other spirit in the house. I assured her that this was so, and then called on Albert, Ethel's spirit guide, to help me ease the troubled one from Ethel's body and thus free her at the same time from the house.

And then the man came into Ethel's body, very emotionally, calling out for Sylvia.

Again I explained how he was able to communicate.

"You see me, don't you." he finally said as he calmed down. "I loved everyone . . . I'll go, I won't bother you . . ."

I called again for Albert, and in a moment his crisp voice replaced the spirit's outcries.

"The man is a Henry MacLellan . . . there stood in this vicinity another house . . . around 1810, 1812 . . . to 1820 . . . a woman connected with this house lies buried here somewhere, and he is looking for her. His daughter . . . Macy? . . . Maisie? About 1798 . . . 16 or 18 years old . . . has been done wrong . . . had to do with a feud of two families . . . McDern . . . "

Albert then suggested letting the man speak to us directly, and so he did in a little while. I offered my help.

"It is futile," he said. "My problem is my own."

"Who are you?"

"Henry. I lived right here. I was born here."

"What year? What year are we in now as I speak with you?"

"I speak to you in the year 1813."

"Are you a gentleman of some age?"

"I would have forty-seven years."

"Did you serve in any governmental force or agency?"

"My son . . . John Stuart Mc . . . "

"McDermot? Your son was John Stuart McDermot?"

"You have it from my own lips."

"Where did he serve?"

"Ticonderoga."

And then he added, "My daughter, missing, but I found the bones, buried not too far from here. I am satisfied. I have her with me."

He admitted he knew he was no longer "on the earth plane," but was drawn to the place from time to time.

"But if you ask me as a gentleman to go, I shall go," he added. Under these circumstances — rare ones, indeed, when dealing with hauntings — I suggested he not disturb those in the present house, especially the children. Also, would he not be happier in the world into which he had long passed.

"I shall consider that," he acknowledged, "You speak well, sir.

I have no intention of frightening."

"Are you aware that much time has passed . . . that this is not 1813 any more?" I said.

"I am not aware of this, sir . . . it is always the same time here."

Again I asked if he served in any regiment, but he replied his leg was no good. Was it his land and house? Yes, he replied, he owned it and built the house. But when I pressed him as to where he might be buried, he balked.

"My bones are here with me . . . I am sufficient unto myself."

I then asked about his church affiliation, and he informed me his church was "northeast of here, on Beacon Road." The minister's name was Rooney, but he could not tell me the denomination. His head was not all it used to be.

"A hundred and fifty years have passed," I said, and began the ritual of exorcism. "Go from this house in peace, and with our love."

And so he did.

Albert, Ethel's guide, returned briefly to assure us that all was as it should be and Mr. McDermot was gone from the house; also, that he was being reunited with his mother, Sarah Ann McDermot. And then Albert too withdrew and Ethel returned to her own self again.

I turned to Mrs. Fuller and her cousin, Miss Elliott, for possible comments and corroboration of the information received through Mrs. Meyers in trance.

* * *

It appears the house that the Fullers were able to trace back as far as about 1860 was moved to make room for a road, and then set down again not far from that road. Unfortunately going further back proved difficult. I heard again from Mrs. Fuller in December of that year. The footsteps were continuing, it seemed, and her seven-year-old daughter Becky was being frightened by them. She had not yet been able to find any record of Mr. McDermot, but vowed to continue her search.

That was twenty years ago, and nothing further turned up, and I really do not know if the footsteps continued or Mr. McDermot finally gave up his restless quest for a world of which he no longer was a part.

As for Mr. Langdon, whom Ethel Meyers had also identified by name as a presence in the house, he must by now be reunited with his wife Donna, and I hope he has forgiven her her trespasses, as a good Christian might: over there, even her sins do not matter any longer.

A New Hampshire Artist
and Her Ghosts

Elizabeth Nealon Weistrop is a renowned sculptress who lives far away from the mainstream of city life in rural New Hampshire. I talked to her the other day when I had occasion to admire a particularly striking bronze medallion she had created for the Society of Medallists. It was a squirrel such as abound in her New England woods.

Mrs. Weistrop's experiences have given her a sense of living with the uncanny, far from being afraid of it or worried.

"What were the most striking examples of your brush with the uncanny — that is of yourself or your family?" I queried her.

"There are many," Mrs. Weistrop replied, "but I'll try to give you the most evidential incidents. For example, in 1954 when our Debby was six years old, the doctor decided she should be taken out of the first grade and remain at home to recover from nervousness that resulted from a serious infection she had recently recovered from. She missed going to school with her sister Betsy, two years older, but played every day with five-year-old Donna Esdale, a neighbor's little girl.

"Our family, my husband, our two girls, and I, were living in a cottage in West Dennis on Cape Cod at the time and located a better place in Yarmouthport — a warmer house with a studio I could use for sculpture. Donna's father owned a truck, so we paid him to move us to the new house.

"Three weeks later (we had seen no one from West Dennis), Betsy, Debby, and I were eating breakfast and Debby said, 'What happened to Donna?' I said, 'What do you mean?' Debby said, 'Why was Donna's face all covered with blood?' Then Betsy and I explained to Debby that she had just had a bad dream and that Donna was all right, but Debby insisted with questions. 'Did a truck hit her?' 'Did someone hit her in the face?' 'Why was her face all covered with blood?' And no matter how Betsy and I explained about dreams, Debby refused to understand and asked the same questions.

"Finally, the school bus came. Betsy went to school and Debby looked after her wistfully, wanting to go to school too.

"During the day Debby played with her new black puppy, and I was busy working at sculpture, and the breakfast session left my mind.

"About nine o'clock that evening, Donna's father, Ralph, came to the studio and asked how everyone was. I said we were all fine and automatically asked [after] his family. He said, 'All right, except that last night my wife and I were up all night. Donna had nose bleeds all night and her face was just covered with blood!'

"Debby was asleep but Betsy was standing near me, and we turned and stared at each other in wonder.

"While living on Cape Cod in 1956, we rented a house from a Mrs. Ridley in West Hyannisport. The house she rented to us had belonged to her mother, a woman in her eighties who had recently died. Mrs. Ridley lived next door with her husband and a daughter, Rodella. I found them pleasant people, proud of their American Indian ancestry and sadly missing the grandmother fondly referred to as 'Gunny.' They spoke of her so often and of her constant activity making repairs on the home she loved that I almost felt I knew her. When they told me of their own supernatural experiences, they did not find a skeptic in me, as my own mother whom I had loved dearly had been gifted with ESP. My mother had been the old child born with a caul {veil} in an Irish family of eleven children, and as I grew up I became very familiar with my mother's amazing and correct predictions. My own experiences with the unknown had been limited to a strong feeling of a force or power leading and directing me in my work as a sculptor.

"One sunny fall afternoon, I was alone concentrating on a sculpture of St. Francis. My husband, Harry, was away for the day and our two girls were in school, when I heard a loud thump from the bedroom which our girls shared. This room had been the large sunny bedroom of 'Gunny' and within easy view of where I was working. I stopped work to investigate, expecting to see that a large piece of furniture had collapsed or been overturned. As I searched the room and looked out of the window, I could discover nothing that could have made such a sound. Still puzzled, I walked into the next room, the kitchen, and noted that our highly nervous dog was sleeping soundly — a dog who was always on her feet barking at the slightest sound. The clock in the kitchen said 2:30 and that would give me one half hour more to concentrate on St. Francis, so I went back to work, still wondering.

"That evening after the girls were asleep I walked outside in back of the house, and Mrs. Ridley, who was sitting on her back porch, invited me into her house to have coffee with her, her daughter, and her daughter's fiance.

"While we chatted around the table, Mrs. Ridley told of sitting by her kitchen window that afternoon and having *seen her mother,* 'Gunny,' *just as clear as day, walk up the path from the woods* to our house and go over and knock on her own bedroom window at our house.

"I asked, 'What time was that?' and Mrs. Ridley answered, 'At 2:30.' "

John, up in Vermont

This isn't exactly a ghost story, if ghosts are troubled individuals unaware of their passing and status, with some sort of compulsion unresolved. But then again, it is, if you consider the afterlife full of fine distinctions as to who is a ghost and who is simply a troubled spirit.

Not far from Stowe, Vermont, in what I have long thought of as the most beautiful part of New England, there is a country house that once belonged to the late lyricist John LaTouche. He and a friend, who shall remain nameless, co-owned the place, I believe, and for all I know, the friend still does. But John hasn't really left entirely either. He is buried up there in Vermont in a flower bed, amid his favorite trees and hills. That is, his body is. As for the rest, well now, that is another matter entirely.

I first met John LaTouche through the late medium and psychic investigator Eileen Garrett over lunch at the Hotel St. Regis in New York. She thought, and rightly so, that we would become friends since we had in common not only our professional pursuits — I, too, am a lyricist, among other professional aspects — but also our intense involvement with the paranormal. Soon after this initial meeting, John invited me to a private dinner party at his home on East 55th Street, right across from an ancient firehouse, where he occupied the magnificent penthouse — at the time he was doing well financially (which was not always the case) because his "Ballad for Americans" and the musical *The Legend of Baby Doe* were paying him handsomely.

With the party was also my late friend and medium Ethel Johnson Meyers and the actress Future Fulton, who was very psychic, and the four of us held a seance after dinner.

Picture my surprise when it was John who went under first, showing he had trance abilities also. Regrettably, I do not have an exact transcript of what came through him at that time, but it seemed that a distant ancestor of his, a Breton lady, wanted to manifest and reassure him in his work and quest for success. No sooner had he returned to his normal state, than Ethel described in great detail what the spirit looked like, and considering that Ethel would not have known the details of an eighteenth century Breton woman's costume, this seemed rather interesting to me at the time.

Sometimes, when people with psychic gifts link up, the mediumship goes back and forth as the case may require. Several months after this initial get-together, I was in rehearsal with a musical revue, my first theatrical involvement, in which Future Fulton had a singing role. I had made an appointment with John to see him the Friday of that week. "Are you fry Freeday?" I asked, "I mean, are you free Friday?" We set a meeting for three o'clock. Unfortunately, it slipped my mind in the heat of rehearsals until about 2 on Friday. It became impossible for me to break away from the goings-on and get to a phone, and I had visions of John never wanting to speak to me again for having stood him up. When Future noticed my distress, she inquired as to its cause, and when I told her, she said, "Oh well, that's nothing. I will get through to John."

With that she sat down on a bench, leaned back, closed her eyes for a moment, and then said cheerfully, "It is done. Don't worry about it."

Being forever the scientific investigator, I was not really relieved. As soon as I could, at around seven o'clock. I rushed to the nearest telephone and called John. Before he could say a word, I began to apologize profusely for the missed appointment, and my inability to notify him.

"What are you babbling about?" John interjected, when I caught my breath for a moment. "Of course you called me."

"I did not."

"No? Then why is there a message on my tape machine from you telling me you could not make it?"

"There is?"

"Yes . . . must have been around two or so because I got back in time for our meeting a little after that, and it was on the tape."

I did not know what to say. Later, I told John, who just shook his head and smiled.

Time went on, and we met now and again, usually at his house. On one occasion, we were invited for a run-through of a new work he and his friend with whom he shared the house in Vermont had written. John seemed in the best of health and creative activity.

It was in August of 1956, and I had just come home from the opening night of my play *Hotel Excelsior,* a less than brilliant piece of mine at the Provincetown Theatre in Greenwich Village, and I checked my answering service as was my custom.

"Only one message," the operator said laconically. "John LaTouche has died."

I was in a state of shock. But as I found out, John had gone to his Vermont retreat that weekend and nothing had been wrong. Now John was overweight, and he liked to eat well. Apparently too well, for after a heavy meal he had had a heart attack and died. Or rather, his body gave out.

For it was not the end of our friendship by a long shot. I did not attend the funeral up in Vermont, which was for close family only. His mother Effy did, and Effy and I were friendly for a while after, until she too passed into the Great Beyond.

Maybe three or four months passed.

Ethel Meyers and I were doing a routine investigation of a haunted house somewhere in Connecticut. Picture my surprise when she suddenly went into trance, and the next voice I heard was not some obscure ghostly person stuck in that particular house for whatever personal reasons, but my old friend John LaTouche!

"Greetings, Hans," he said in almost his usual voice, and then went on to explain how touched he was by his funeral amid the flowers up in Vermont. But he was not there. Not John.

Since that time, John has communicated with me now and again, telling me that he has adjusted to his sudden departure from the physical world — he was only 39 at the time of his death — and that he was still creating works of art for the stage, Over There.

Then, too, he became sort of an adviser to me, especially in matters theatrical, and he began to use not only Ethel Meyers as his channel, but also others.

I don't know when the celestial Board of Directors will want to send John back to earth in his next incarnation, but for the moment at least, he seems to be a free spirit doing his thing, communicating hither and yon, apparently able to drop in, so to speak, at seances and investigations, at will. The only place I am sure he is not at, is up in Vermont under the flowers.

The Ghosts of Stamford Hill

"**M**r. Holzer," the voice on the phone said pleasantly, "I've read your book and that's why I'm calling. We've got a ghost in our house."

Far from astonished, I took paper and pencil and, not unlike a grocery-store clerk taking down a telephone order, started to put down the details of the report.

Robert Cowan is a gentleman with a very balanced approach to life. He is an artist who works for one of the leading advertising agencies in New York City and his interests range widely from art to music, theater, history, and what have you. But not to ghosts, at least not until he and his actress-wife, Dorothy, moved into the 1780 House on Stamford Hill. The house is thus named for the simplest of all reasons: it was built in that year.

Mr. Cowan explained that he thought I'd be glad to have a look at his house, although the Cowans were not unduly worried about the presence of a nonrent-paying guest at their house. Although it was a bit disconcerting at times, it was curiosity as to what the ghost wanted and who the specter was that had prompted Bob Cowan to seek the help of The Ghost Hunter.

I said, "Mr. Cowan, would you mind putting your experiences

in writing, so I can have them for my files?" I like to have written reports (in the first person, if possible) so that later I can refer back to them if similar cases should pop up, as they often do.

"Not at all," Bob Cowan said. "I'll be glad to write it down for you."

The next morning I received his report, along with a brief history of the 1780 House.

Here is a brief account of the experiences my wife and I have had while living in this house during the past nine and a half years. I'll start with myself because my experiences are quite simple.

From time to time (once a week or so) during most of the time we've lived here I have noticed unidentifiable movements out of the corner of my eye . . . day or night. Most often, I've noticed this while sitting in our parlor and what I see moving seems to be in the livingroom. At other times, and only late at night when I am the only one awake, I hear beautiful but unidentified music seemingly played by a full orchestra, as though a radio were on in another part of the house.

The only place I recall hearing this is in an upstairs bedroom and just after I've gone to bed. Once I actually got up, opened the bedroom door to ascertain if it was perhaps music from a radio accidentally left on, but it wasn't.

Finally, quite often I've heard a variety of knocks and crashes that do not have any logical source within the structural setup of the house. A very loud smash occurred two weeks ago. You'd have thought a door had fallen off its hinges upstairs but, as usual, there was nothing out of order.

My wife, Dorothy, had two very vivid experiences about five years ago. One was in the kitchen, or rather outside of a kitchen window. She was standing at the sink in the evening and happened to glance out the window when she saw a face glaring in at her. It was a dark face but not a Negro, perhaps Indian; it was very hateful and fierce.

At first she thought it was a distorted reflection in the glass but in looking closer, it was a face glaring directly at her. All she could make out was a face only and as she recalls it, *it seemed translucent*. It didn't disappear, *she did!*

On a summer afternoon my wife was taking a nap in a back bedroom and was between being awake and being asleep when she heard the sounds of men's voices and the sound of working on the grounds — rakes, and garden tools — right outside of the window. She tried to arouse herself to see who they could be, but she couldn't get up.

At that time, and up to that time we had only hired a single man to come in and work on the lawn and flower beds. It wasn't until at least a year later that we hired a crew that came in and worked once a week, and we've often wondered if this was an experience of precognition. My wife has always had an uneasy feeling about the outside of the back of the house and still sometimes hears men's voices outside and will look out all windows without seeing anyone.

She also has shared my experiences of seeing "things" out of the corner of her eye and also hearing quite lovely music at night. She hasn't paid attention to household noises because a long time ago I told her "all old houses have odd structural noises" . . . which is true enough.

Prior to our living here the house was lived in for about 25 years by the Clayton Rich family, a family of five. Mr. Rich died towards the end of their stay here. By the time we bought it, the three children were all married and had moved away.

For perhaps one year prior to that a Mrs. David Cowles lived here. She's responsible for most of the restoration along with a Mr. Frederick Kinble.

Up until 1927 or 1928 the house was in the Weed family ever since 1780. The last of the line were two sisters who hated each other and only communicated with each other through the husband of one of the sisters. They had divided the house and used two different doors. One used the regular front door into the stair hall and the other used the "coffin door" into the parlor.

Mr. Cowan added that they were selling the house — not because of ghosts but because they wanted to move to the city again. I assured him that we'd be coming up as soon as possible.

Before we could make arrangements to do so, I had another note from the Cowans. On February 9, 1964, Bob Cowan wrote that they heard a singing voice quite clearly downstairs, and music again.

It wasn't until the following week, however, that my wife and I went to Stamford Hill. The Cowans offered to have supper ready for us that Sunday evening and to pick us up at the station since nobody could find the house at night who did not know the way.

It was around six o'clock in the evening when our New Haven train pulled in. Bob Cowan wore the Scottish beret he had said he would wear in order to be recognized by us at once. The house stands at the end of a winding road that runs for about ten minutes through woodland and past shady lanes. An American eagle over the door, and the date 1780, stood out quite clearly despite the dusk that had started to settle on the land. The house has three levels, and the Cowans used the large room next to the kitchen in what might be called the cellar or ground level for their dining room.

They had adorned it with eighteenth-century American antiques in a most winning manner, and the fireplace added a warmth to the room, making it seem miles removed from bustling New York.

On the next level were the livingroom and next to that a kind of sitting room. The fireplace in each of these rooms connected one to the other. Beyond the corridor there was the master bedroom and Bob's colorful den. Upstairs were two guest rooms, and there was a small attic accessible only through a hole in the ceiling and by ladder. Built during the American Revolution, the house stands on a wooded slope, which is responsible for its original name of Woodpecker Ridge Farm.

Many years ago, after the restoration of the house was completed, Harold Donaldson Eberlin, an English furniture and garden expert, wrote about it:

> With its rock-ribbed ridges, it boulder-strewn pastures and its sharply broken contours like the choppy surface of a wind-blown sea, the topographical conditions have inevitably affected the domestic architecture. To mention only two particulars, the dwellings of the region have had to accommodate themselves to many an abrupt hillside site and the employment of some of the omnipresent granite boulders. Part of the individuality of the house at Woodpecker Ridge Farm lies in the way it satisfies these conditions without being a type house.
>
> Before communal existence, the country all thereabouts bore the pleasantly descriptive name of Woodpecker Ridge, and Woodpecker Ridge Farm was so called in order to keep alive the memory of this early name. Tradition says that the acres now comprised within the boundaries of Woodpecker Ridge Farm once formed part of the private hunting ground of *the old Indian chief Ponus.*

Old Ponus may, perhaps, appear a trifle mythical and shadowy, as such long-gone chieftains are wont to be. Very substantial and real, however, was Augustus Weed, who built the house in 1780. And the said Augustus was something of a personage.

War clouds were still hanging thick over the face of the land when he had the foundation laid and the structure framed. Nevertheless, confident and forward-looking, he not only reared a staunch and tidy abode, indicative of the spirit of the countryside, but he seems to have put into it some of his own robust and independent personality as well.

It is said that Augustus was such a notable farmer and took such justifiable pride in the condition of his fields that he was not afraid to make a standing offer of one dollar reward for every daisy that anyone could find in his hay.

About 1825 the house experienced a measure of remodeling in accordance with the notions prevalent at the time. Nothing very extensive or ostentatious was attempted, but visible traces of the work then undertaken remain in the neo-Greek details that occur both outside and indoors.

It is not at all unlikely that the "lie-on-your-stomach" windows of the attic story date from this time and point to either a raising of the original roof or else some alteration of its pitch. These "lie-on-your-stomach" windows — so called because they were low down in the wall and had their sills very near the level of the floor so that you had almost to lie on your stomach to look out of them — were a favorite device of the *neo-Grec* era for lighting attic rooms. And it is remarkable how much light they actually do give, and what a pleasant light it is.

The recent remodeling that brought Woodpecker

Farmhouse to its present state of comeliness and comfort impaired none of the individual character the place had acquired through the generations that had passed since hardy Augustus Weed first took up his abode there. It needs no searching scrutiny to discern the eighteenth-century features impressed on the structure at the beginning — the stout timbers of the framing, the sturdy beams and joists, the wide floor boards, and the generous fireplaces. Neither is close examination required to discover the marks of the 1825 rejuvenation.

The fashions of columns, pilasters, mantelpieces, and other features speak plainly and proclaim their origin.

The aspect of the garden, too, discloses the same sympathetic understanding of the environment peculiarly suitable to the sort of house for which it affords the natural setting. The ancient well cover, the lilac bushes, the sweet-briers, the August lilies, and the other denizens of an old farmhouse dooryard have been allowed to keep their long-accustomed places.

In return for this recognition of their prescriptive rights, they lend no small part to the air of self-possessed assurance and mellow contentment that pervades the whole place.

After a most pleasant dinner downstairs, Catherine and I joined the Cowans in the large livingroom upstairs. We sat down quietly and hoped we would hear something along musical lines.

As the quietness of the countryside slowly settled over us, I could indeed distinguish faraway, indistinct musical sounds, as if someone were playing a radio underwater or at great distance. A check revealed no nearby house or parked car whose radio could be responsible for this.

After a while we got up and looked about the room itself. We were standing about quietly admiring the furniture when both my wife and I and, of course, the Cowans, clearly heard footsteps overhead.

They were firm and strong and could not be mistaken for anything else, such as a squirrel in the attic or other innocuous noises. Nor was it an old house settling.

"Did you hear that?" I said, almost superfluously.

"We all heard it," my wife said and looked at me.

"What am I waiting for?" I replied, and faster than you can say Ghost Hunter, I was up the stairs and into the room above our heads where the steps had been heard. The room lay in total darkness. I turned the switch. There was no one about. Nobody else was in the house at the time, and all windows were closed. We decided to assemble upstairs in the smaller room next to the one in which I had heard the steps. The reason was that Mrs. Cowan had experienced a most unusual phenomenon in that particular room.

"It was like lightning," she said, "a bright light suddenly come and gone."

I looked the room over carefully. The windows were arranged in such a manner that a reflection from passing cars was out of the question. Both windows, far apart and on different walls, opened into the dark countryside away from the only road.

Catherine and I sat down on the couch, and the Cowans took chairs. We sat quietly for perhaps twenty minutes without lights, except a small amount of light filtering in from the stairwell. It was very dark, certainly dark enough for sleep, and there was not light enough to write by.

As I was gazing toward the back wall of the little room and wondering about the footsteps I had just heard so clearly, I saw a blinding flash of light, white light, in the corner facing me. It came on and disappeared very quickly, so quickly in fact that my wife, whose head had been turned in another direction at the moment, missed it. But Dorothy Cowan saw it and exclaimed, "There it is again. Exactly as I saw it."

Despite its brevity I was able to observe that the light cast a shadow on the opposite wall, so it could not very well have been a hallucination.

I decided it would be best to bring Mrs. Meyers to the house, and we went back to New York soon after. While we were preparing our return visit with Mrs. Meyers as our medium, I received an urgent call from Bob Cowan.

"Since seeing you and Cathy at our house, we've had some additional activity that you'll be interested in. Dottie and I have both heard knocking about the house but none of it in direct answer to questions that we've tried to ask. On Saturday, the twenty-ninth of February, I was taking a nap back in my studio when I was awakened by the sound of footsteps in the room above me . . . the same room we all sat in on the previous Sunday.

"The most interesting event was on the evening of Thursday, February 27. I was driving home from the railroad station alone. Dottie was still in New York. As I approached the house, I noticed that there was a light on in the main floor bedroom and also a light on up in the sewing room on the top floor, a room Dottie also uses for rehearsal. I thought Dottie had left the lights on. I drove past the house and down to the garage, put the car away and then walked back to the house and noticed that the light in the top floor was now off.

"I entered the house and noticed that the dogs were calm (wild enough at seeing me, but in no way indicating that there was anyone else in the house). I went upstairs and found that the light in the bedroom was also off. I checked the entire house and there was absolutely no sign that anyone had been there . . . and there hadn't been, I'm sure."

On Sunday, March 15, we arrived at the 1780 House, again at dusk. A delicious meal awaited us downstairs, then we repaired to the upstairs part of the house.

We seated ourselves in the large livingroom where the music had been heard, and where we had been standing at the time we heard the uncanny footsteps overhead.

"I sense a woman in a white dress," Ethel said suddenly. "She's got dark hair and a high forehead. Rather a small woman."

"I was looking through the attic earlier," Bob Cowan said thoughtfully, "and look what I found — a waistcoat that would fit a rather smallish woman or girl."

The piece of clothing he showed us seemed rather musty. There were a number of articles up there in the attic that must have belonged to an earlier owner of the house — much earlier.

A moment later, Ethel Meyers showed the characteristic signs of onsetting trance. We doused the lights until only one back light was on.

At first, only inarticulate sounds came from the medium's lips. "You can speak," I said, to encourage her. "You're among friends." The sounds now turned into crying.

"What is your name?" I asked, as I always do on such occasions. There was laughter — whether girlish or mad was hard to tell.

Suddenly, she started to sing in a high-pitched voice.

"You can speak, you can speak," I kept assuring the entity. Finally she seemed to have settled down somewhat in control of the medium.

"Happy to speak with you," she mumbled faintly.

"What is your name?"

I had to ask it several times before I could catch the answer clearly.

"Lucy."

"Tell me, Lucy, do you live here?"

"God be with you."

"Do you live in this house?"

"My house."

"What year is this?"

The entity hesitated a moment, then turned toward Dorothy and said, "I like you."

I continued to question her.

"How old are you?"

"Old lady."

"How old?"

"God be with you."

The conversation had been friendly until I asked her, "What is your husband's name?" The ghost drew back as if I had spoken a horrible word.

"What did you say?" she almost shouted, her voice trembling with emotion. "I have no husband — God bless you — what were you saying?" she repeated, then started to cry again. "Husband, husband," she kept saying as if it was a thought she could not bear.

"You did not have a husband, then?"

"Yes, I did."

"Your name again?"

"Lucy . . . fair day . . . where is he? The fair day . . . the pretty one, he said to me look in the pool, and you will see my face."

"Who is he?" I asked.

But the ghost paid no heed to me. She was evidently caught up in her own memories.

"I heard a voice, Lucy, Lucy . . . fair one . . . alack . . . they took him out . . . they laid him cold in the ground . . . ."

"What year was that?" I wanted to know.

"Year, year?" she repeated. "Now, *now!*"

"Who rules this country now?"

Ghosts of New England

"Why, he who seized it."

"Who rules?"

"They carried him out . . . the Savior of our country. General Washington."

"When did he die?"

"Just now."

I tried to question her further, but she returned to the thoughts of her husband.

"I want to stay here . . . I wait at the pool . . . look, he is there!" She was growing excited again.

"I want to stay here now, always, forever . . . rest in peace . . . he is there always with me."

"How long ago did you die?" I asked, almost casually. The reaction was somewhat hostile.

"I have not died . . . never . . . All Saints!"

I asked her to join her loved one by calling for him and thus be set free of this house. But the ghost would have none of it.

"Gainsay what I have spoke . . ."

"How did you come to this house?" I now asked.

"Father . . . I am born here."

"Was it your father's house?"

"Yes."

"What was his name?" I asked, but the restless spirit of Lucy was slipping away now, and Albert, the medium's control, took over. His crisp, clear voice told us that the time had come to release Ethel.

"What about this woman, Lucy?" I inquired. Sometimes the control will give additional details.

"He was not her husband . . . he was killed before she married him," Albert said.

No wonder my question about a husband threw Lucy into an uproar of emotions.

In a little while, Ethel Meyers was back to her old self, and as usual, did not remember anything of what had come through her entranced lips.

Shortly after this episode my wife and I went to Europe.

* * *

As soon as we returned, I called Bob Cowan. How were things up in Stamford Hill? Quiet? Not very.

"Last June," Bob recalled, "Dottie and I were at home with a friend, a lady hair dresser, who happens to be psychic. We were playing around with the Ouija board, more in amusement than seriously. Suddenly, the Sunday afternoon quiet was disrupted by heavy footsteps coming up the steps outside the house. Quickly, we hid the Ouija board, for we did not want a potential buyer of the house to see us in this unusual pursuit. We were sure someone was coming up to see the house. But the steps stopped abruptly when they reached the front door. I opened [it], and there was no one outside."

"Hard to sell a house that way," I commented. "Anything else?"

"Yes, in July we had a house guest, a very balanced person, not given to imagining things. There was a sudden crash upstairs, and when I rushed up the stairs to the sewing room, there was this bolt of material that had been standing in a corner, lying in the middle of the room as if thrown there by unseen hands! Margaret, our house guest, also heard someone humming a tune in the bathroom, although there was no one in there at the time. Then in November, when just the two of us were in the house, someone knocked at the door downstairs. Again we looked, but there was nobody outside. One evening when I was in the 'ship' room and Dottie in the bedroom, we heard footfalls coming down the staircase.

"Since neither of us was causing them and the door was closed, only a ghost could have been walking down those stairs."

"But the most frightening experience of all," Dorothy Cowan

broke in, "was when I was sleeping downstairs and, waking up, wanted to go to the bathroom without turning on the lights, so as not to wake Bob. Groping my way back to bed, I suddenly found myself up on the next floor in the blue room, which is pretty tricky walking in the dark. I had the feeling someone was forcing me to follow them into that particular room."

I had heard enough, and on December 15, we took Ethel Johnson Meyers to the house for another go at the restless ones within its confines. Soon we were all seated in the ship room on the first floor, and Ethel started to drift into a trance.

"There is a baby's coffin here," she murmured. "Like a newborn infant's."

The old grandfather clock in back of us kept ticking away loudly.

"I hear someone call Maggie," Ethel said. "Margaret."

"Do you see anyone?"

"A woman, about five foot two, in a long dress, with a big bustle in the back. Hair down, parted in the middle, and braided on both sides. There is another young woman . . . Laurie . . . very pretty face, but so sad . . . she's looking at you, Hans . . . "

"What is it she wants?" I asked quietly.

"A youngish man with brown hair, curly, wearing a white blouse, taken in at the wrists, and over it a tan waistcoat, but no coat over it . . . "

I asked what he wanted and why he was here. This seemed to agitate the medium somewhat.

"Bottom of the well," she mumbled, "stone at bottom of the well."

Bob Cowan changed seats, moving away from the coffin door to the opposite side of the room. He complained of feeling cold at the former spot, although neither door nor window was open to cause such a sensation.

"Somebody had a stick over his shoulder," the medium said now, "older man wearing dark trousers, heavy stockings. His hair is gray and kind of longish; he's got that stick."

I asked her to find out why.

"Take him away," Ethel replied. "He says, 'Take him away!'"

"But he was innocent, he went to the well. Who is down in the well? Him who I drove into the well, him . . . I mistook . . ."

Ethel was now fully entranced, and the old man seemed to be speaking through her.

"What is your name?" I asked.

"She was agrievin'," the voice replied, "she were grievin' I did that."

"What is your name?"

"Ain't no business to you."

"How can I help you?"

"They're all here . . . accusin' me . . . I see her always by the well."

"Did someone die in this well?" Outside, barely twenty yards away, was the well, now cold and silent in the night air.

"Him who I mistook. I find peace, I find him, I put him together again."

"What year was that?"

"No matter to you now . . . I do not forgive myself . . . I wronged, I wronged . . . I see always her face look on me."

"Are you in this house now?" I asked.

"Where else can I be and talk with thee?" the ghost shot back.

"This isn't your house anymore," I said quietly.

"Oh, yes it is," the ghost replied firmly. "The young man stays here only to look upon me and mock me. It will not be other than mine. I care only for that flesh that I could put again on the bone, and I will restore him to the bloom of life and the rich love of her who suffered through my own misdemeanor."

"Is your daughter buried here?" I asked, to change the subject. Quietly, the ghostly voice said, "Yes."

But he refused to say where he himself was laid to final — or not so final — rest.

At this point the ghost realized that he was not in his own body, and as I explained the procedure to him, he gradually became calmer. At first, he thought he was in his own body and could use it to restore to life the one he had slain. I kept asking him who he was. Finally, in a soft whisper, came the reply, "Samuel."

"And Laurie?"

"My daughter . . . oh, he is here, the man I wronged . . . Margaret, Margaret!" He seemed greatly agitated with fear now.

The big clock started to strike. The ghost somehow felt it meant him.

"The judgment, the judgment . . . Laurie . . . they smile at me. I have killed. He has taken my hand! He whom I have hurt."

But the excitement proved too much for Samuel. Suddenly, he was gone, and after a brief interval, an entirely different personality inhabited Ethel's body. It was Laurie.

"Please forgive him," she pleaded. "I have forgiven him."

The voice was sweet and girlish.

"Who is Samuel?"

"My grandfather."

"What is your family name"

"Laurie Ho-Ho- . . . if I could only get that name."

But she couldn't.

Neither could she give me the name of her beloved, killed by her grandfather. It was a name she was not allowed to mention around the house, so she had difficulty remembering now, she explained.

"What is your mother's name?" I asked.

"Margaret."

"What year were you born?"

Hesitatingly, the voice said, "Seventeen-fifty-six."

"What year is this now?"

"Seventeen seventy-four. We laid him to rest in seventeen seventy-four."

"In the church?"

"No, Grandfather could not bear it. We laid him to rest on the hill to the north. We dug with our fingers all night. Didn't tell Grandpa where we put it."

"How far from here is it?"

"No more than a straight fly of the lark."

"Is the grave marked?"

"Oh, no."

"What happened to your father?"

"No longer home, gone."

I explained to Laurie that the house would soon change hands, and that she must not interfere with this. The Cowans had the feeling that their ghosts were somehow keeping all buyers away, fantastic though this may be at first thought. But then all of psychic research is pretty unusual and who is to say what cannot be?

Laurie promised not to interfere and to accept a new owner of "their" house. She left, asking again that her grandfather be forgiven his sins.

I then asked Albert, Ethel's control, to take over the medium. That done, I queried him regarding the whole matter.

"The father is buried far from here, but most of the others are buried around here," he said. "During the year seventeen seventy-seven . . . Grandfather was not brought here until later when there was forgiveness. The body was removed and put in Christian burial."

"Where is the tombstone?" I asked.

"Lying to the west of a white structure," Albert replied in his precise slightly accented speech, "on these grounds. The tombstone is broken off, close to the earth. The top has been mishandled by vandals. The old man is gone, the young man has taken him by the hand."

"What was the young man's name?"

"She called him Benjamin."

"He was killed in the well?"

"That is right. He has no grave except on the hill."

"Is the old man the one who disturbs this house?"

"He is the main one who brings in his rabble, looking for the young man."

"Who is Lucy?" I asked, referring back to the girl who had spoken to us at the last seance in the late spring.

"That is the girl you were talking about, Laurie. Her name is really Lucy. One and the same person."

"She was not actually married to the young man?"

"In her own way, she was. But they would not recognize it. There were differences in religious ideas. . . . But we had better release the medium for now."

I nodded, and within a moment or two, Ethel was back to herself, very much bewildered as to what went on while she was in trance.

"How do you reconcile these dates with the tradition that this house was built in seventeen eighty?" I asked Bob Cowan.

He shook his head.

"It is only a tradition. We have no proof of the actual date."

We went to the upstairs sewing room where the latest manifestations had taken place, and grouped ourselves around the heavy wooden table. Ethel almost immediately fell into trance again. She rarely does twice in one sitting.

The voice reverberating in the near darkness now was clearly that of a man, and a very dominating voice it was.

"Who are you?" I demanded.

"Sergeant-major . . . . " No name followed. I asked why was he here in this house.

"One has pleasant memories."

"Your name?"

"Sergeant-major Harm."

"First name?"

Instead of giving it, he explained that he once owned the house and was "friend, not foe." I looked at Bob Cowan, who knows all the owners of the property in the old records, and Bob shook his head. No Harm.

"When I please, I come. I do not disturb willingly. But I will go," the new visitor offered. "I will take him with me; you will see him no more. I am at peace with him now. He is at peace with me."

"How did you pass over?" I inquired.

"On the field of battle. On the banks of the Potomac . . . seventeen seventy-six."

"What regiment were you in?" I continued.

"York . . . Eight . . . I was foot soldier . . . eighteenth regiment . . . "

"What army?"

"Wayne . . . Wayne . . . "

"Who was your commanding general?"

"Broderick."

"Who was the colonel of your regiment?"

"Wayne, Wayne."

"You were a sergeant-major?"

"Sergeant-major, eighteenth regiment, foot infantry."

"Where were you stationed?"

"New York."

"Where in New York?"

"Champlain."

"Your regimental commander again?"

"Broderick." Then he added, not without emotion, "I died under fire, first battle of Potomac."

"Where are you buried?"

"Fort Ticonderoga, New York."

I wondered how a soldier fighting on the banks of the Potomac could be buried in upstate New York. But I must confess that the word "Potomac" had come so softly that I could have been mistaken.

"The date of your death?"

"Seventeen seventy-six."

Then he added, as the voice became more and more indistinct, "I will leave now, but I will protect you from those who . . . who are hungry to . . . " The voice trailed off into silence.

A few moments later, Ethel emerged from the trance with a slight headache, but otherwise her old self. As usual, she did not recall anything that had come through her entranced lips.

* * *

We returned to New York soon after, hoping that all would remain quiet in the Cowan house, and, more important, that there would soon be a new laird of the manor at the 1780 House.

I, too, heard the ghostly music, although I am sure it does not connect with the colonial ghosts we were able to evoke. The music I heard sounded like a far-off radio, which it wasn't since there are no houses near enough to be heard from. What I heard for a few moments in the livingroom sounded like a full symphony orchestra playing the music popular around the turn of this century.

Old houses impregnated with layers upon layers of people's emotions frequently also absorb music and other sounds as part of the atmosphere.

What about the sergeant-major?

I checked the regimental records. No soldier named Harm, but a number of officers (and men) named Harmon. I rechecked my tapes. The name "Harm" had been given by the ghost very quietly. He could have said Harmon. Or perhaps he was disguising his identity as they sometimes will.

But then I discovered something very interesting. In the Connecticut state papers there is mention of a certain Benjamin Harmon, Jr., Lt., who was with a local regiment in 1776. The murdered young man had been identified as "Benjamin." Suddenly we have another ghost named Harm or Harmon, evidently an older personality. Was he the father of the murdered young man?

The 1780 House is, of course, recorded as dating back to 1780 only. But could not another building have occupied the area? Was the 1780 House an adaptation of a smaller dwelling of which there is no written record?

We can neither prove nor disprove this.

It is true, however, that General "Mad" Anthony Wayne was in charge of the revolutionary troops in the New York area at the time under discussion.

At any rate, all this is knowledge not usually possessed by a lady voice teacher, which is what Ethel Meyers was when not being a medium.

Two years after our visit, the local archaeological society asked for permission to dig around the property since some interesting artifacts had been found on the grounds of the house next door. Picture their — and everyone's — surprise when they found, near a dried up well on the Cowan property, two partly damaged tombstones inscribed "Samuel" and "Benjamin." The stones and the inscriptions were of the late eighteenth century.

The house later changed hands and the Cowans moved to Georgia. I have not heard anything further about any disturbances at the 1780 House, nor do I frankly expect any: Over There Samuel and Benjamin must have made up long ago, and perhaps even have had a go at it again for another round of incarnation, somewhere, some place, some time.

Ghosts of New England

The Haunted Organ at Yale

Yale University in New Haven, Connecticut, is an austere and respectable institution, which does not take such matters as ghostly manifestations very lightly. I must, therefore, keep the identity of my informant a secret, but anyone who wishes to visit Yale and admire its magnificent, historical organ is, of course, at liberty to do so, provided he or she gets clearance from the proper authorities. I would suggest, however, that the matter of ghostly goings-on not be mentioned at such a time. If you happen to experience something out of the ordinary while visiting the organ, well and good, but let it not be given as the reason to the university authorities for your intended visit.

I first heard about this unusual organ in 1969 when a gentleman who was then employed as an assistant organist at Yale had been asked to look after the condition and possible repairs of the huge organ, a very large instrument located in Woolsey Hall. This is the fifth largest organ in the world and has a most interesting history.

Woolsey Hall was built as part of a complex of three buildings for Yale's two-hundredth anniversary in 1901 by the celebrated architects, Carere and Hastings. Shortly after its completion the then university organist, Mr. Harry B. Jepson, succeeded in getting the Newberry family, of the famous department store clan, to contribute a large sum of money for a truly noble organ to be built for the hall.

Even in 1903 it was considered to be an outstanding instrument because of its size and range. By 1915, certain advances in the technology of pipe organs made the 1903 instruments somewhat old fashioned. Again Jepson contacted the Newberry family about the possibility of updating their gift so that the organ could be rebuilt and the hall enlarged. This new instrument was then dedicated in 1916 or thereabouts.

By 1926 musical tastes had again shifted toward romantic music, and it became necessary to make certain additions to the stops as well as the basic building blocks of the classical ensemble. Once again the Newberry family contributed toward the updating of the instrument. The alterations were undertaken by the Skinner Organ Company of Boston, in conjunction with an English expert by the name of G. Donald Harrison. Skinner and Harrison did not get on well together and much tension was present when they restored and brought the venerable old organ up-to-date.

Professor Harry Jepson was forced to retire in the 1940s, against his wishes, and though he lived down the street only two blocks from Woolsey Hall, he never again set foot into it to play the famous organ that he had caused to be built. He died a bitter and disappointed man sometime in 1952.

The last university organist, Frank Bozyan, retired in the 1970s, with great misgivings. He confided to someone employed by the hall that he felt he was making a mistake; within six months after his retirement he was dead. As time went on, Woolsey Hall, once a temple of beauty for the fine arts, was being used for rock and roll groups and mechanically amplified music. Undoubtedly, those connected with the building of the hall and the organ would have been horrified at the goings-on had they been able to witness them.

The gentleman who brought all of this to my attention, and who shall remain nameless, had occasion to be in the hall and involved with the organ itself frequently. He became aware of a menacing and melancholic sensation in the entire building, particularly in the basement and the organ chambers. While working there at odd hours late at night, he became acutely aware of some sort of unpleasant sensation just lurking around the next corner or even standing behind him! On many occasions he found it necessary to look behind him in order to make sure he was alone. The feeling of a presence became so strong he refused to be there by himself, especially in the evenings. Allegedly, the wife of one of the curators advised him to bring a crucifix whenever he had occasion to go down to the organ chambers. She also claimed to have felt someone standing at the entrance door to the basement, as if to keep strangers out.

I visited Yale and the organ one fine summer evening in the company of my informant, who has since found employment elsewhere. I, too, felt the oppressive air in the organ chambers, the sense of a presence whenever I moved about. Whether we are dealing here with the ghost of the unhappy man who was forced to retire and who never set foot again into his beloved organ chamber, or whether we are dealing with an earlier influence, is hard to say. Not for a minute do I suggest that Yale University is haunted or that there are any evil influences concerning the university itself. But it is just possible that sensitive individuals visiting the magnificent organ at Woolsey Hall might pick up some remnant of an unresolved past.

The Terror on the Farm

North Woodstock, Connecticut, is New England at its best and quietest: rolling farmland seldom interrupted by the incursions of factories and modern city life.

The village itself seems to have weathered the passage of time rather well and with a minimum of change. Except for the inevitable store signs and other expressions of contemporary American bad taste, the village is as quiet today as it must have been, say, two hundred years ago, when America was young.

On Brickyard Road, going toward the outer edges of the village and standing somewhat apart from the inhabited areas, is an old farmhouse. At the time this incident takes place, it had obviously seen better days; it was totally dilapidated and practically beyond repair. Still, it was a house of some size and quite obviously different from the ordinary small farmhouses of the surrounding countryside.

For the past fifty years, the sixteen-room house, had been the property of the Duprey family. The house itself was built in pre-revolutionary times by the Lyons family, who used it as a tavern. The place was a busy spot on the Boston-Hartford road, and a tavern here did well indeed in the days when railroads had not yet come into existence.

After the Lyons Tavern changed hands, it belonged successfully to the Potters, Redheads, Ides, and then the Dupreys. But it finally became a private dwelling, the center of the surrounding farm, and no longer a public house.

Very little is known about its early history beyond what I've told here at least that is what Mrs. Florence Viner discovered when she considered buying the house. She did learn, however, that Mrs. Emery Duprey, a previous owner, had suffered great tragedy in the house. One morning she had taken a group of neighbor children to school. The school was in a one-room house, less than a mile distant. Her fourteen-year-old daughter Laura was left behind at the house because she had not been feeling well that day. When Mrs. Duprey returned home a short time later, she found the girl gone. Despite every effort made, the girl was never seen again nor was any trace found of her disappearance.

Mr. and Mrs. Charles Viner decided to buy the house in 1951 despite its deplorable condition. They wanted a large country house and did not mind putting it in good condition; in fact, they rather looked forward to the challenging task.

It was on Good Friday of that year that they moved in. Although they started the restoration immediately, they stayed at the house and made do, like the pioneers they felt they had now become.

The farm itself was still a working farm, and they retained a number of farm workers from the surrounding area to work it for them. The only people staying at the house at all times were the Viners, their daughter Sandra, and the help.

Two months after their arrival, one evening Mrs. Viner and her daughter, then eleven years old, were alone in the house, sitting in the kitchen downstairs, reading.

"Who is upstairs?" the girl suddenly inquired.

Mrs. Viner had heard furtive footsteps also, but had decided to ignore them. Surely, the old house was settling or the weather was causing all sorts of strange noises.

But the footsteps became clearer. This was no house settling. This was someone walking around upstairs. For several minutes, they sat in the kitchen, listening as the steps walked all over the upper floor. Then Mrs. Viner rose resolutely, went to her bedroom on the same floor and returned with a .22 revolver she had in the drawer of her night table just in case prowlers showed up. The moment she re-entered the kitchen, she clearly heard two heavy thumps upstairs. It sounded as if a couple of heavy objects had fallen suddenly and hit the floor. Abruptly, the walking ceased as if the thumps were the end of a scene being re-enacted upstairs.

Too frightened to go up and look into what she *knew* to be an empty room, Mrs. Viner went to bed. When her husband returned a little later, however, they investigated upstairs together. There was nothing out of place nor indeed any sign that anyone had been up there.

But a few days later, the same phenomenon recurred. First, there were the footsteps of someone walking up and down upstairs, as if in great agitation. Then two heavy thumps and the sound of a falling object and abrupt silence. The whole thing was so exactly the same each time it almost became part of the house routine, and the Viners heard it so many times they no longer became panicky because of it.

When the house regained its former splendor, they began to have overnight guests. But whenever anyone stayed at the house, inevitably, the next morning they would complain about the constant walking about in the corridor upstairs. Mrs. Ida Benoit, Mrs. Viner's mother, came downstairs the morning after her first night in the house and assured her daughter, "I'll never sleep in *this* house again. Why, it's haunted. Someone kept walking through my bedroom."

Her daughter could only shrug and smile wanly. She knew very well what her mother meant. Naturally, the number of unhappy guests grew, but she never discussed the phenomena with anyone beforehand. After all, it was just possible that *nothing* would happen. But in ten years of occupancy, there wasn't a single instance where a person using a bedroom upstairs was not disturbed.

A year after they had moved in, Mrs. Viner decided to begin to renovate a large upstairs bedroom. It was one of those often used as a guest room. This was on a very warm day in September, and despite the great heat, Mrs. Viner liked her work and felt in good spirits. She was painting the window sash and singing to herself with nothing particular on her mind. She was quite alone upstairs at the time and for the moment the ghostly phenomena of the past were far from her thoughts.

Suddenly, she felt the room grow ice cold. The chill became so intense she began to shudder and pulled her arms around herself as if she were in mid-winter on an icy road. She stopped singing abruptly and at the same time she felt the strong presence of another person in the room with her.

"Someone's resenting very much what I'm doing," she heard herself think.

Such a strong wave of hatred came over her she could not continue. Terrified, she nevertheless knew she had to turn around and see who was in the room with her. It seemed to take her an eternity to muster sufficient strength to move a single muscle.

Suddenly, she felt a cold hand at her shoulder. Someone was standing behind her and evidently trying to get her attention. She literally froze with fear. When she finally moved to see who it was the hand just melted away.

With a final effort, she jerked herself around and stared back into the room. There was no one there. She ran to the door, screaming, "I don't know who you are or what you are, but you won't drive me out of this house."

Still screaming, she ran down the stairs and onto the porch. There she caught her breath and quieted down. When her daughter came home from school, she felt relieved. The evil in that room had been overpowering, and she avoided going up there as much as possible after that experience.

"I'll never forget that hand, as long as I live," she explained to her husband.

In the years that followed, they came to terms with the unseen forces in the house. Perhaps her determined effort not to be driven out of her home had somehow gotten through to the specter. At any rate, the Viners were staying and making the house as livable as they could. Mrs. Viner gave birth to two more children, both sons, and as Sandra grew up, the phenomena seemed to subside. In 1958, a second daughter was born, and Sandra left for college. But three weeks later the trouble started anew.

One night in September, she was sitting in the downstairs livingroom watching television with James Latham, their farm worker. The two boys and the baby had been in bed for hours. Suddenly, there was a terrific explosion in the general direction of the baby's room. She ran into the room and found it ice cold — cold as an icebox. From the baby's room another door leads out into the hall, which was usually closed for obvious reasons. But now it stood wide open, evidently thrust open with considerable force. The lock was badly bent from the impact and the radiator, which the door had hit in opening, was still reverberating from it. The baby was not harmed in any way, but Mrs. Viner wondered if perhaps the oil burner had blown up.

She went down into the basement to check but found everything normal. As she returned to the baby's room she suddenly had the distinct impression that the phenomenon was somehow connected with the presence of a *young girl*.

She tried to reason this away since no young girl was present in the household, nor was there any indication that this tied in in any way with the tragic disappearance of Mrs. Duprey's girl, of which she, of course, knew about. Try as she might, she could not shake this feeling that a young girl was the focal point of the disturbances at the house.

One night her sister had joined her in the livingroom downstairs. Suddenly there was a loud crash overhead in what they knew was an empty bedroom. Mrs. Viner left her worried sister downstairs and went up alone. A table in the bedroom had been knocked over. No natural force short of a heavy earthquake could have caused this. The windows were closed, and there was no other way in which the table could topple over by itself. She was so sure that this could not have been caused by anything but human intruders, she called the state police.

The police came and searched the house from top to bottom but found no trace of any intruder.

Mrs. Viner then began to wonder about the goings-on. If these unseen forces had the power to overturn heavy tables, surely they might also harm people. The thought frightened her. She had until then considered living with a ghost or ghosts rather on the chic side; now it took on distinctly threatening overtones. She discussed it with her husband but they had put so much work and money into the house that the thought of leaving again just did not appeal to them.

It was inevitable that she should be alone in the house, except for the children, at various times. Her husband was away on business, and the farm help were out where they belonged. Often Mrs. Viner found herself walking through the rooms hoping against rational reasoning that she would come face to face with the intruder. Then she could address her or him — she was not sure how many there were — and say, "Look, this is my house now, we've bought it and rebuilt it, and we don't intend to leave it. Go away and don't hang around; it's no use." She often rehearsed her little speech for just such a confrontation. But the ghost never appeared when she was ready.

Meanwhile the footsteps followed by the heavy thumps kept recurring regularly, often as many as four times in a single week. It was usually around the same time of the evening, which led her to believe that it represented some sort of tragedy that was being re-enacted upstairs by the ghostly visitors. Or was she merely tuning in on a past tragedy and what she and the others were hearing was in fact only an echo of the distant past? She could not believe this, especially as she still remembered vividly the ice cold hand that grabbed her shoulder in the bedroom upstairs on that hot September day. And a memory would not cause a heavy door to swing open by itself with such violence that it burst the lock.

No, these were not memory impressions they were hearing. These were actual entities with minds of their own, somehow trapped between two states of being and condemned by their own violence to live forever in the place where their tragedy had first occurred. What a horrible fate, Mrs. Viner thought, and for a moment she felt great compassion for the unfortunate ones.

But then her own involvement reminded her that it was, after all, her house and her life that was being disrupted. She had a better right to be here than they had, even if they had been here before.

Defiantly, she continued to polish and refine the appointments in the house until it looked almost as if it had never been a dilapidated, almost hopelessly derelict, house. She decided to repaper one of the bedrooms upstairs, so that her guests would sleep in somewhat more cheerful surroundings. The paper in this particular room was faded and very old and deserved to be replaced. As she removed the dirty wallpaper, the boards underneath became visible again. They were wide and smooth and obviously part of the original boards of the house.

After she had pulled down all the paper from the wall facing away from the window, she glanced up at it. The wall, exposed to light after goodness knows how many years, was spattered with some sort of paint.

"This won't do at all," she decided, and went downstairs to fetch some rags and water. Returning to the room, she started to remove what she took for some very old paint. When she put water on the stains, the spots turned a bright red!

Try as she might, she could not remove the red stains. Finally she applied some bleach, but it only turned the spots a dark brown. It finally dawned on her that this wasn't paint but blood. On closer investigation, her suspicion was confirmed. She had stumbled upon a blood-spattered wall — but what had taken place up here that had caused this horrible reminder?

Somehow she felt that she had gotten a lead in her quest for the solution to the phenomena plaguing the house. Surely, someone had been killed up there, but who and why?

She went into the village and started to talk to the local people. At first, she did not get much help. New Englanders are notoriously shy about family matters. But eventually Mrs. Viner managed to get some information from some of the older, local people who had known about the house on Brickyard Road for a long time.

When the house was still a public tavern, that is somewhere around the turn of the nineteenth century or the very end of the eighteenth, there had been two men at the tavern who stayed overnight as guests. Their names are shrouded in mystery, and perhaps they were very unimportant as history goes.

But there was also a young girl at the tavern, the kind innkeepers used to hire as servant girls in those days. If the girl wanted to be just that, well and good; if she wanted to get involved with some of the men that passed through on their way to the cities, that was her own business. Tavern keepers in those days were not moral keepers and the hotel detective had not yet been conceived by a Puritan age. So the servant girls often went in and out of the guests' rooms, and nobody cared much.

It appears that one such young girl was particularly attractive to two men at the same time. There were arguments and jealousy. Finally the two men retired to a room upstairs and a fight to the finish followed. As it was upstairs, most likely it was in the girl's own room, with one suitor discovering the other obtaining favors he had sought in vain, perhaps. At any rate, as the horrified girl looked on, the two men killed each other with their rapiers, and their blood, intermingled in death, spattered upon the wall of the room.

As she walked back from the village with this newly gained knowledge, Mrs. Viner understood clearly for the first time, why her house was indeed haunted. The restless footsteps in the room upstairs were the hurried steps of the unhappy suitor. The scuffling noises that followed and the sudden heavy thumps would be the fight and the two falling bodies — perhaps locked in death. The total silence that always ensued after the two heavy falls clearly indicated to her that the stillness of death following the struggle was being re-enacted along with the tragedy itself.

And how right she had been about a girl being the central force in all this!

But why the hostility towards her? Why the icy hand on the shoulder? Did the girl resent her, another woman, in this house? Was she still hoping her suitor would come for her, and did she perhaps take Mrs. Viner for competition? A demented mind, especially when it has been out of the body for a hundred and fifty years, can conjure up some strange ideas.

But her fighting energies were somehow spent, and when an opportunity arose to sell the house, Mrs. Viner agreed readily to do so. The house then passed into the hands of Samuel Beno after the

Viners had lived in it from 1951 to 1961. For five years, Mr. Beno owned the house but never lived in it. It remained unoccupied, standing quietly on the road.

Only once was there a flurry of excitement about it in recent years. In 1966 someone made off with $5,000 worth of plumbing and copper piping. The owner naturally entrusted the matter to the state police, hoping the thieves would eventually return for more. The authorities even placed tape recorders in the house in case the thieves did return.

Since then not much has been heard about the house and one can only presume that the tragic story of the servant girl and her two suitors has had its final run. But one can't be entirely sure until the next tenant moves into the old Lyons Tavern. After all, blood does not come off easily, either from walls or from men's memories.

The Old Merchant's House Ghost

When New York was still young and growing, a neighborhood that is now given over to derelicts and slums was an elegant, quiet area of homes and gardens. The world was right and peaceful in the young republic circa 1820. Gradually, however, the in people, as we call them nowadays, moved farther uptown, for such is the nature of a city confined to a small island. It can only move up, never down or out. Greenwich Village was still pretty far uptown, although the city had already spread beyond its limits, and the center of New York was somewhere around the city hall district (now considered way downtown).

Real estate developers envisioned the east side of Fifth Avenue as the place to put up elegant homes for the well-to-do. One of the more fashionable architects of that time was John McComb, who had plans for a kind of terrace of houses extending from Lafayette Street to the Bowery, with the back windows of the houses looking out on John Jacob Astor's property nearby. Now Mr. Astor was considered somewhat uncouth socially by some of his contemporaries (on one occasion he mistook a lady's voluminous sleeve for a dinner napkin), but nobody had any second thoughts about his prosperity or position in the commercial world. Thus, any house looking out upon such a desirable neighborhood would naturally attract a buyer, the builders reasoned, and they proved to be right.

Called brownstones because of the dark brick material of their facades, the houses were well-appointed and solid. Only one of them is still left in that area, while garages, factories, and ugly modern structures have replaced all the others.

The house in question was completed in 1830 and attracted the eagle eye of a merchant named Seabury Tredwell, who was looking for a proper home commensurate with his increasing financial status in the city. He bought it and moved in with his family.

Mr. Tredwell's business was hardware, and he was one of the proud partners in Kissam & Tredwell, with offices on nearby Dey Street. A portly man of fifty, Mr. Tredwell was what we would today call a conservative. One of his direct ancestors had been the first Episcopal bishop of New York, and though a merchant, Tredwell evinced all the outward signs of an emerging mercantile aristocracy. The house he acquired certainly looked the part: seven levels, consisting of three stories, an attic and two cellars, large, Federal style windows facing Fourth Street, a lovely garden around the house, and an imposing columned entrance door that one reached after ascending a flight of six marble stairs flanked by wrought-iron gate lanterns — altogether the nearest a merchant prince could come to a real nobleman in his choice of domicile.

Inside, too, the appointments are lavish and in keeping with the traditions of the times: a Duncan Phyfe banister ensconces a fine staircase leading to the three upper stories and originates in an elegant hall worthy of any caller.

As one steps into this hall, one first notices a huge, high-ceilinged parlor to the left. At the end of this parlor are mahogany double doors separating the room from the dining room, equally as large and impressive as the front room. The Duncan Phyfe table was at one time set with Haviland china and Waterford crystal, underlining the Tredwell family's European heritage. Each room has a large fireplace and long mirrors adding to the cavernous appearance of the two rooms. Large, floor-to-ceiling windows on each end shed light into the rooms, and when the mahogany doors are opened, the entire area looks like a ballroom in one of those manor houses Mr. Tredwell's forebears lived in in Europe.

The furniture — all of which is still in the house — was carefully chosen. Prominent in a corner of the parlor is a large, rectangular piano. Without a piano, no Victorian drawing room was worth its salt. A music box is on top for the delight of those unable to tinkle the ivories yet desirous of musical charms. The box plays "Home Sweet Home," and a sweet home it is indeed.

Farther back along the corridor one comes upon a small family room and a dark, ugly kitchen, almost L-shaped and utterly without charm or practical arrangements, as these things are nowadays understood. But in Victorian New York, this was a proper place to cook. Maidservants and cooks were not to be made cheerful, after all; theirs was to cook and serve, and not to enjoy.

On the first floor — or second floor, if you prefer, in today's usage — two large bedrooms are separated from each other by a kind of storage area, or perhaps a dressing room, full of drawers and cabinets. Off the front bedroom there is a small bedroom in which a four-poster bed takes up almost all the available space. The bed came over from England with one of Mrs. Tredwell's ancestors.

Leading to the third floor, the stairs narrow, and one is well advised to hold on to the banister lest he fall and break his neck. The third floor now serves as the curator's apartment. The Old Merchant's House is kept up as a private museum and is no longer at the mercy of the greedy wrecker. But when Seabury Tredwell lived in the house, the servants' rooms were on the third floor. Beyond that, a low-ceilinged attic provided additional space, and still another apartment fills part of the basement, also suitable for servants' usage.

All in all, it is the kind of house that inspires confidence in its owner. Mr. Tredwell's acquisition of the house helped establish him in New York society as a force to be reckoned with, for that, too, was good for his expanding business. He was eminently aided in this quest by the fact that his wife Eliza, whom he had married while still on his way up, had given him six daughters. Three of the girls made good marriages, left the parental homestead, and apparently made out very well, for not much was heard about them one way or another. Of the remaining three girls, however, plenty is recorded, and lots more is not, though it's undoubtedly true.

The three bachelor girls were named Phoebe, Sarah, and Gertrude. Phoebe's main interest was the Carl Fischer piano in the parlor, and she and her sister Sarah would often play together. Gertrude, the last of the Tredwell children, born in 1840, was different from the rest of them and kept herself apart. There were also two boys, but somehow they did not amount to very much, it is said, for it became necessary later, when of all the children only they and Gertrude were left, to appoint a cousin, Judge Seabury, to supervise the management of the estate. Brother Horace, in particular, was much more interested in tending the four magnolia trees that dominated the view from the tearoom.

To this day, nobody knows the real reason for a secret passage from a trap door near the bedrooms to the East River, a considerable distance. Recently, it was walled up to prevent rats from coming through it, but it is still there, holding on to its strange mystery — that is, to those who do not *know*.

Some of the things that transpired behind the thick walls of the Old Merchant's House would never have been brought to light were it not for the sensitive who walked its corridors a century later and piece for piece helped reconstruct what went on when the house was young. Only then did the various pieces of the jigsaw puzzle slowly sink into place, pieces that otherwise might never have found a common denominator.

When the house finally gave up its murky secrets, a strange calm settled over it, as if the story had wanted to be told after all those years to free it from the need of further hiding from the light.

* * *

Seabury Tredwell's stern Victorian ways did not sit well with all members of his family. The spinster girls in particular were both afraid of and respectful toward their father, and found it difficult to live up to his rigid standards. They wanted to marry but since no suitable person came along they were just as happy to wait. Underneath this resignation, however, a rebellious spirit boiled up in Sarah. Five years older than Gertrude, she could not or would not wait to find happiness in an age where the word scarcely had any personal meaning.

Tredwell ruled the family with an iron hand, demanding and getting blind submission to his orders. Thus it was with considerable misgivings that Sarah encouraged a budding friendship with a young man her father did not know, or know of, whom she had met accidentally at a tearoom. That in itself would have been sufficient reason for her father to disallow such a friendship. He was a man who considered anyone who referred to chicken *limbs* as legs, indecent. He ordered the legs of his chairs and tables covered, so they might not incite male visitors to unsavory ideas!

It took a great deal of ingenuity for Sarah to have a liaison with a strange man and not get caught. But her mother, perhaps out of rebellion against Tredwell, perhaps out of compassion for her neglected daughter, looked the other way, if not encouraged the relationship. And ingenious Sarah also found another ally in her quest for love. There was a Negro servant who had known and cared for her since her birth, and he acted as a go-between for her and the young man. For a few weeks, Sarah managed to sneak down to meet her paramour. Accidentally, she had discovered the secret passageway to the river and used it well. At the other end it led to what was then pretty rough ground and an even rougher neighborhood, but the young man was always there waiting with a carriage, and she felt far safer with him than in the cold embrace of her father's fanatical stare. Although Tredwell boasted to his friends that his house had "seven hundred locks and seven hundred keys," this was one door he had forgotten about.

Why an architect in 1830 would want to include a secret passageway is a mystery on the surface of it. But there were still riots in New York in those years, and the British invasion of 1812 was perhaps still fresh in some people's memories. A secret escape route was no more a luxury in a patrician American home than a priest hole was in a Catholic house in England. One never knew how things might turn. There had been many instances of slave rebellions, and the underground railroad, bringing the escapees up from the South, was in full swing then in New York.

One meeting with the young man, who shall remain nameless here, led to another, and before long, nature took its course. Sarah was definitely pregnant. Could she tell her father? Certainly not. Should they run off and marry? That seemed the logical thing to do, but Sarah feared the long arm of her family. Judge Seabury, her father's distinguished cousin, might very well stop them. Then too, there was the question of scandal. To bring scandal upon her family was no way to start a happy marriage.

Distraught, Sarah stopped seeing the young man. Nights she would walk the hallways of the house, sleepless from worry, fearful of discovery. Finally, she had to tell someone, and that someone was her sister Gertrude. Surprisingly, Gertrude did understand and comforted her as best she could. Now that they shared her secret, things were a little easier to bear. But unfortunately, things did not improve. It was not long before her father discovered her condition and all hell broke loose.

With the terror of the heavy he was, Tredwell got the story out of his daughter, except for the young man's name. This was especially hard to keep back, but Sarah felt that betraying her lover would not lead to a union with him. Quite rightfully, she felt her father would have him killed or jailed. When the old merchant discovered that there had been a go-between, and what was more, a man in his employ, the old Negro man was hauled over the coals. Only the fact that he had been with them for so many years and that his work was useful to the family prevented Tredwell from firing him immediately. But he abused the poor man and threatened him until the sheer shock of his master's anger changed his character: where he had been a pleasant and helpful servant, there was now only a shiftless, nervous individual, eager to avoid the light and all questions.

This went on for some weeks or months. Then the time came for the baby to be born and the master of the house had another stroke of genius. He summoned the black servant and talked with him at length. Nobody could hear what was said behind the heavy doors, but when the servant emerged his face was grim and his eyes glassy. Nevertheless, the old relationship between master and servant seemed to have been restored, for Tredwell no longer abused the man after this meeting.

What happened then we know only from the pieces of memory resurrected by the keen insight of a psychic: no court of law would ever uphold the facts as true in the sense the law requires, unfortunately, even if they are, in fact, true. One night there was a whimpering heard from the trapdoor between the two bedrooms upstairs, where there is now a chest of drawers and the walled-off passageway down to the river. Before the other servants in the house could investigate the strange noises in the night, it was all over and the house was silent again. Tredwell himself came from his room and calmed them.

"It is nothing," he said in stentorian tones, "just the wind in the chimney."

Nobody questioned the words of the master, so the house soon fell silent again.

But below stairs, in the dank, dark corridor leading to the river, a dark man carried the limp body of a newborn baby that had just taken its first, and last, breath.

Several days later, there was another confrontation. The evil doer wanted his pay. He had been promised a certain sum for the unspeakable deed. The master shrugged. The man threatened. The master turned his back. Who would believe a former slave, a runaway slave wanted down South? Truly, he didn't have to pay such a person. Evil has its own reward, too, and the dark man went back to his little room. But the imprint of the crime stuck to the small passage near the trap door and was picked up a century later by a psychic. Nobody saw the crime. Nobody may rightfully claim the arrangement between master and servant ever took place. But the house knows and its silence speaks louder than mere facts that will stand up in court.

When Sarah awoke from a stupor, days later, and found her infant gone, she went stark raving mad. For a time, she had to be restrained. Somehow, word leaked out into the streets of the city below, but no one ever dared say anything publicly. Sarah was simply indisposed to her friends. Weeks went by and her pain subsided. Gradually a certain relief filled the void inside her. She had lost everything, but at least her lover was safe from her father's clutches. Although she never knew for sure, whenever she glanced at the colored manservant, she shrank back: his eyes avoided her and her heart froze. Somehow, with the illogical knowledge of a mother, she *knew*. Then too, she avoided the passage near the trap door. Nothing could get her to walk through it. But as her health returned, her determination to leave also received new impetus. She could not go on living in this house where so much had happened. One day, she managed to get out of the door. It was a windy fall night, and she was badly dressed for it. Half-mad with fear of being followed, she roamed the streets for hours. Darkness and her mental condition took their toll. Eventually she found herself by the water. When she was found, she was still alive, but expired before she could be brought back to the house.

Her death — by her own hands — was a blow to the family. Word was given out that Sarah had died in a carriage accident. It sounded much more elegant, and though no one ever found out what carriage, as she had been in bed for so long, and just learned to walk about the house again, it was accepted because of the unspoken code among the Victorians: one man's tragedy is never another's gossip. Then, too, the question of suicide was a thorny one to resolve in an age that had not yet freed the human personality even in the flesh: it had to be an accident.

Thus Sarah was laid to rest along with the others of her family in the Christ Churchyard in Manhasset, Long Island, properly sanctified as behooves the daughter of an important citizen whose ancestor was a bishop.

What had happened to Sarah did not pass without making a deep and lasting impression on the youngest girl, Gertrude, who was called Gitty when she was young. She tried not to talk about it, of course, but it made her more serious and less frivolous in her daily contacts.

She was now of the age where love can so easily come, yet no one had held her hand with the slightest effect on her blood pressure. True, her father had introduced a number of carefully screened young men, and some not so young ones, in the hope that she might choose one from among them. But Gertrude would not marry just to please her father, yet she would not marry against his wishes. There had to be someone she could love and whom her father could also accept, she reasoned, and she was willing to wait for him.

While she was playing a game with time, spring came around again, and the air beckoned her to come out into the garden for a walk. While there, she managed to catch the eye of a young man on his way past the house. Words were exchanged despite Victorian propriety, and she felt gay and giddy.

She decided she would not make the mistake her sister had made in secretly seeing a young man. Instead, she encouraged the shy young man, whose name was Louis, to seek entry into her house openly and with her father's knowledge, if not yet blessings. This he did, not without difficulties, and Seabury Tredwell had him investigated immediately. He learned that the young man was a penniless student of medicine.

"But he'll make a fine doctor someday," Gertrude pleaded with her father.

"Someday," the old man snorted. "And what is he going to live on until then? I tell you what. *My* money."

Tredwell assumed, and perhaps not without reason, that everybody in New York knew that his daughters were heiresses and would have considerable dowries as well. This idea so established itself in his mind, he suspected every gentleman caller of being a fortune hunter. The young man was, of course, he argued, not after his daughter's love, but merely her money and that would never do.

Gertrude was no raving beauty although she possessed a certain charm and independence. She was petite, with a tiny waistline, blue eyes and dark hair, and she greatly resembled Britain's Princess Margaret when the latter was in her late twenties.

Tredwell refused to accept the young medical student as a

serious suitor. Not only was the young man financially unacceptable, but worse, he was a Catholic. Tredwell did not believe in encouraging marriages out of the faith and even if Louis had offered to change religions, it is doubtful the father would have changed his mind. In all this he paid absolutely no heed to his daughter's feelings or desires, and with true Victorian rigidity, forbade her to see the young man further.

There was finally a showdown between father and daughter. Tredwell, no longer so young, and afflicted with the pains and aches of advancing age, pleaded with her not to disappoint him in his last remaining years. He wanted a good provider for her, and Louis was not the right man. Despite her feelings, Gertrude finally succumbed to her father's pleading and sent the young man away. When the doors closed on him for the last time, it was as if the gates of Gertrude's heart had also permanently closed on the outside world: hence she lived only for her father and his well-being and no young man ever got to see her again.

Seabury Tredwell proved a difficult and thankless patient as progressive illness forced him to bed permanently. When he finally passed away in 1865, the two remaining sisters, Gertrude and Phoebe, continued to live in the house. But it was Gertrude who ran it. They only went out after dark and only when absolutely necessary to buy food. The windows were always shuttered and even small leaks covered with felt or other material to keep out the light and cold.

As the two sisters cut themselves off from the outside world, all kinds of legends sprang up about them. But after Phoebe died and left Gertrude all alone in the big house, even the legends stopped and gradually the house and its owner sank into the oblivion afforded yesterday's sensation by a relentless, everchanging humanity.

Finally, at age ninety-three, Gertrude passed on. The year was 1933, and America had bigger headaches than what to do about New

York's last authentic brownstone. The two servants who had shared the house with Gertrude to her death, and who had found her peacefully asleep, soon left, leaving the house to either wreckers or new owners, or just neglect. There was neither electricity nor telephone in it, but the original furniture and all the fine works of art Seabury Tredwell had put into the house were still there. The only heat came from fireplaces with which the house was filled. The garden had long gone, and only the house remained, wedged in between a garage and nondescript modern building. Whatever elegance there had been was now present only inside the house or perhaps in the aura of its former glories.

The neighborhood was no longer safe, and the house itself was in urgent need of repairs. Eventually, responsible city officials realized the place should be made into a museum, for it presented one of the few houses in America with everything — from furniture to personal belongings and clothes — still intact as it was when people lived in it in the middle of the nineteenth century. There were legal problems of clearing title, but eventually this was done and the Old Merchant's House became a museum.

*　*　*

When the first caretaker arrived to live in the house, it was discovered that thieves had already broken in and made off with a pair of Sheffield candelabra, a first edition of Charlotte Bronte, and the Tredwell family Bible. But the remainder was still intact, and a lot of cleaning up had to be done immediately.

One of the women helping in this work found herself alone in the house one afternoon. She had been busy carrying some of Miss Gertrude's clothing downstairs so that it could be properly displayed in special glass cases. When she rested from her work for a moment, she looked up and saw herself being watched intently by a woman on the stairs. At first glance, she looked just like Princess Margaret of England, but then she noticed the strange old-fashioned clothes the woman wore and realized she belonged to another age. The tight fitting bodice had a row of small buttons and the long, straight skirt reached to the floor. As the volunteer stared in amazement at the stranger, wondering who it could be, the girl on the stairs vanished.

At first the lady did not want to talk about her experience, but when it happened several times, and always when she was alone in the house, she began to wonder whether she wasn't taking leave of her senses. But soon another volunteer moved into the picture, a lady writer who had passed the house on her way to the library to do some research. Intrigued by the stately appearance of the house, she looked into it further and before long was in love with the house.

There was a certain restlessness that permeated the building after dark, but she blamed it on her imagination and the strange neighborhood. She did not believe in ghosts nor was she given to fancies, and the noises didn't really disturb her.

She decided that there was a lot of work to be done if the museum were to take its proper place among other showplaces, and she decided to give the tourists and other visitors a good run for their money — all fifty cents' worth of it.

The next few weeks were spent in trying to make sense out of the masses of personal effects, dresses, gowns, shoes, hats. The Tredwells had left everything behind them intact — as if they had intended to return to their earthly possessions one of these days and to resume life as it was.

Nothing had been given away or destroyed and Mrs. R., writer that she was, immediately realized how important it was that the residence be kept intact for future research of that period. She went to work at once and as she applied herself to the job at hand, she began to get the *feel* of the house as if she had herself lived in it for many years.

She started her job by taking an inventory of the late Gertrude Tredwell's wardrobe once again. This time the job had to be done properly, for the visitors to the museum were entitled to see a good display of period costumes. As she picked through Gertrude's vast wardrobe one article at a time, she had the uncanny feeling of being followed step for step. The house was surrounded by slums and the danger of real break-ins very great, but this was different: no flesh and blood intruders followed her around on her rounds from the third floor down to the basement and back again for more clothes.

Often a chilly feeling touched her as she walked through the halls, but she attributed that to the moist atmosphere in the old house.

One day when she entered the front bedroom that used to be Gertrude's, from the hall bedroom, she had the distinct impression of another presence close to her. Something was brushing by her to reach the other door that opened into the front bedroom before she did!

When this happened again sometime later, she began to wonder if the stories about the house being haunted, which circulated freely in the neighborhood, did not have some basis in fact. Certainly there was a presence, and the sound of another person brushing past her was quite unmistakable.

While she was still deliberating whether or not to discuss this with any of her friends, an event took place that brought home the suspicion that she was never quite alone in the house.

It was on a morning several months after her arrival, that she walked into the kitchen carrying some things to be put into the display cases ranged along the wall opposite the fireplace. Out of the corner of her eye she caught sight of what looked like the figure of a small, elegant woman standing in front of this huge fireplace. While Mrs. R. was able to observe the brown taffeta gown she was wearing, her head was turned away, so she could not see her features. But there were masses of brown hair. The whole thing was in very soft focus, rather misty without being insubstantial. Her hands, however, holding a cup and saucer, were very beautiful and quite sharply defined against her dark gown.

Mrs. R. was paralyzed, afraid to turn her head to look directly at her. Suddenly, however, without any conscious volition, she spun around and quickly walked out of the room into the hall. By the time she got to the stairs she was covered with cold perspiration, and her hands were shaking so violently she had to put down the things she was carrying.

Now she knew that Gertrude Tredwell was still around, but not the way she looked when she died. Rather, she had turned back her memory clock to that period of her life when she was gayest and her young man had not yet been sent away by a cruel and unyielding father.

When the realization came to Mrs. R. as to who her ghostly friend was, her fears went away. After all, who would have a better right to be in this house than the one who had sacrificed her love and youth to it and what it stood for in her father's view. This change of her attitude must have somehow gotten through to the ghostly lady as well, by some as yet undefinable telegraph connecting all things, living and dead.

Sometime thereafter, Mrs. R. was arranging flowers for the table in the front parlor. The door was open to the hallway and she was quite alone in the house. She was so preoccupied with the flower arrangement, she failed to notice that she was no longer alone.

Finally, a strange sound caught her attention, and she looked up from the table. The sound was that of a taffeta gown swishing by in rapid movement. As her eyes followed the sound, she saw a woman going up the stairs. It was the same, petite figure she had originally seen at the fireplace sometime before. Again she wore the brown taffeta gown. As she rounded the stairs and disappeared from view, the sound of the gown persisted for a moment or two after the figure herself had gotten out of sight.

This time Mrs. R. did not experience any paralysis or fear. Instead, a warm feeling of friendship between her and the ghost sprang up within her, and contentedly, as if nothing had happened, she continued with her flower arrangement.

During this time, the curator of the Old Merchant's House was a professional antiquarian named Janet Hutchinson who shared the appointments with her friend Emeline Paige, editor of *The Villager,* a neighborhood newspaper, and Mrs. Hutchinson's son, Jefferson, aged fourteen. In addition, there was a cat named Eloise who turned out to be a real fraidicat for probably good and valid reasons.

Although Mrs. Hutchinson did not encounter anything ghostly during her tenure, the lady editor did feel very uneasy in the back bedroom, where much of the tragedy had taken place.

Another person who felt the oppressive atmosphere of the place, without being able to rationalize it away for any good reasons, was Elizabeth Byrd, the novelist, and her friend, whom I must call Mrs. B., for she shies away from the uncanny in public. Mrs. B. visited the house one evening in 1964. As she stood in what had once been Gertrude's bedroom, she noticed that the bedspread of Gertrude's bed was indented *as if someone had just gotten up from it*. Clearly, the rough outline of a body could be made out.

As she stared in disbelief at the bed, she noticed a strange perfume, in the air. Those with her remarked on the scent, but before anyone could look for its sources, it had evaporated. None of the ladies with Mrs. B. had on any such perfume, and the house had been sterile and quiet for days.

Since that time, no further reports of any unusual experiences have come to mind. On one occasion in 1965, photographs of the fireplace near which Mrs. R. had seen the ghost of Gertrude Tredwell were taken simultaneously by two noted photographers with equipment previously tested for proper functioning. This was done to look into the popular legend that this fireplace could not be photographed and that whenever anyone attempted it, that person would have blank film as a result. Perhaps the legend was started by a bad photographer, or it was just that, a legend, for both gentlemen produced almost identical images of the renowned fireplace with their cameras. However, Gertrude Tredwell was not standing in front of it.

This is as it should be. Mrs. R., the untiring spirit behind the Historical Landmarks Society that keeps the building going and out of the wreckers' hands, feels certain that Gertrude need not make another appearance now that everything is secure. And to a Victorian lady, that matters a great deal.

The Old Merchant's House, forever threatened by the wrecker's ball, receives visitors Sundays from 1 to 4. I saw it last about a year ago, as I write these lines in 1988, with a psychic lady named Kathleen Roach. Directly she stepped inside Gertrude's parlor, she turned around and asked me to get her out of the house; the jealousy and anger of the old girl evidently never left the house. So if you happen to run into her, be kind.

The Ghosts at the
Morris-Jumel Mansion

We had hardly returned to our home in New York, when my friend Elizabeth Byrd telephoned to inquire if I had gotten that grave opened yet. I hadn't, but I should really let you in at the beginning.

You see, it all started with an article in the *New York Journal-American* on January 11, 1964, by Joan Hanauer, in which the ghostly goings-on at Jumel Mansion in New York City were brought to public attention. Youngsters on a field trip from P.S. 164, Edgecombe Avenue and 164th Street, said a tall, gray-haired, elderly woman stepped out onto the balcony and told them to be quiet.

The description fit Mme. Jumel.

Could it have happened?

Mrs. Emma Bingay Campbell, curator of the Mansion at 160th Street and Edgecombe, said no.

"I don't believe in ghosts," she said, "but it was very strange. The house was locked and empty. We know that. There could not have been a woman there. But several of the children insist they saw and heard her.

"It was shortly before 11, opening time for the house, which dates back to 1765.

"When I came over to the children to explain they must wait for John Duffy, the second gardener, to unlock the doors at 11," Mrs. Campbell said, "one of the girls wanted to know why the tall woman who had come out on the balcony to reprimand them for boisterousness couldn't let them in. There couldn't have been any such woman — or anyone else — in the house.

"The woman the children described resembled Mme. Jumel, who some thought murdered her husband in the house in 1832, then married Aaron Burr the following year.

"But the children couldn't know that, or what she looked like.

"They also couldn't know that the balcony on which the apparition appeared separated Mme. Jumel's and Burr's bedrooms."

Elizabeth Byrd was then working on a story about Manhattan ghosts for a magazine, so we decided to follow up this case together. First we contacted the public school authorities and obtained permission to talk to the children. The teacher assembled the entire group she had originally taken to the Jumel Mansion, and we questioned them, separately and together. Their story was unchanged. The woman appeared on the balcony, suddenly, and she told them to be quiet.

"How did she disappear?" I wanted to know.

One youngster thought for a moment, then said hesitantly, "She sort of glided back into the house."

"Did you see the balcony doors open?" I asked the girl.

"No, sir," she replied firmly.

"Then did she glide through the door?"

"She did."

The dress they described the ghost as wearing does exist — but it is put away carefully upstairs in the mansion and was not on display, nor is this common knowledge, especially among eleven-year-old schoolgirls.

There was a cooking class in progress when we arrived, and the girls cheerfully offered us samples of their art. We declined for the moment and went on to see the curator of the mansion, Mrs. Campbell. This energetic lady takes care of the mansion for the Daughters of the American Revolution in whose charge the City of New York had placed the museum.

"Is this the first report of a haunting here?" I wanted to know.

Mrs. Campbell shook her head. "Here," she said, and took down from one of the shelves in her office a heavy book. "William Henry Shelton's work, *The Jumel Mansion,* pages two hundred and seven and two hundred and eight report earlier ghosts observed here."

"Have you ever seen or heard anything?"

"No, not yet, but others have. There was that German nurse who lived here in eighteen sixty-five — she heard strange noises even then. Footsteps have been heard by many visitors here when there was no one about. The ghost of Mme. Jumel appeared to a retired guard at the door of this room."

"How would you like me to investigate the matter?" I offered. A date was set immediately.

First, I thought it wise to familiarize myself with the physical layout of the historic house. I was immediately struck by its imposing appearance. Historian John Kent Tilton wrote:

> Located on the highest elevation of Manhattan is one of the most famous old historic houses in the nation, the Morris-Jumel Mansion. The locality was originally called Harlem Heights by the Dutch in the days of New Amsterdam and was then changed to Mount Morris during the English ownership, before receiving the present name of Washington Heights.

The plot of land upon which the old mansion is situated was originally deeded in 1700 to a Dutch farmer named Jan Kiersen, from part of the "half morgen of land of the common woods" of New Haarlem.

Lieutenant Colonel Roger Morris purchased the estate in 1765. The new owner was born in England in 1728 and came to America at the age of eighteen with a commission of captaincy in the British army.

It was here that the Morris family, with their four children, spent their summers, living the domestic life typical of a British squire and family until the outbreak of the Revolution.

Colonel Morris fled to England at the beginning of hostilities, where he remained for two and one-half years.

As early in the war as August 1776, Mount Morris was taken over by the American troops and General Heath and staff were quartered there. After the disastrous Battle of Long Island, General Washington retreated to Haarlem Heights and made the place his headquarters. After Washington decided to abandon this location, the British moved in and the Morris Mansion housed General Sir Henry Clinton and his officers and, at intervals, the Hessians, during the seven years the British occupied New York.

During the following quarter of a century it was sold and resold several times and witnessed many changes in its varied career. Renamed Calumet Hall, it served for a time as a Tavern and was a stopping place for the stage coaches en route to Albany. It was the home of an unknown farmer when President Washington paid a visit to his old headquarters and entertained at dinner, among others, his cabinet members, John Adams, Alexander Hamilton, Henry Knox, and their wives.

The locality was one that Stephen Jumel with his sprightly and ambitious wife delighted driving out to on a summer's day from their home on Whitehall Street. Mme. Jumel became entranced with the nearby old Morris Mansion and persuaded her husband to purchase it for their home in 1810, for the sum of $10,000 which included 35 acres of land still remaining of the original tract.

The old house was fast falling into decay when Mme. Jumel energetically went about renovating and refurnishing it, and when completed, it was one of the most beautiful homes in the country. The Jumels restored the mansion in the style of the early nineteenth century, when the Federal influence was in fashion.

Mme. Jumel first married, some say by trickery, the rich Frenchman, Stephen Jumel. He had at one time owned a large plantation in Santo Domingo from whence he was obliged to flee at the time of the insurrection. Arriving in the United States, a comparatively poor man, he soon amassed a new fortune as a wine merchant, and at his death in 1832, his wife became one of the richest women in America. A year later she married Aaron Burr, former vice president of the United States. This second marriage, however, was of short duration and ended in divorce. Mme. Jumel died at the age of 93 in 1865.

The Morris-Jumel Mansion is of the mid-Georgian period of architecture. The front facade has four columns, two stories in height, with a pediment at the top.

The exterior is painted white. One of the post-Colonial features added by the Jumels is the imposing front entrance doorway, with flanking sidelights and elliptical fanlight.

In the interior, the wide central hall with arches is furnished with late eighteenth and early nineteenth century pieces. At the left of the entrance is the small parlor or tearoom where the marriage ceremony of the Widow Jumel and Aaron Burr was performed in 1833 when the bride was fifty-eight and the groom twenty years her senior.

Across the hall is the stately Georgian dining room where many persons of fame assembled for elaborate dinner parties.

At the rear of the hall is the large octagonal drawing room.

The broad stairway leads to the spacious hall on the upper floor, which is furnished with personal belongings of the Jumels. There is a group portrait of Mme. Jumel and the young son and daughter of her adopted daughter, Mary Eliza, who married Nelson Chase.

The northwest bedroom contains furniture owned by the Jumels, including a carved four-poster bed.

In the old days the rooms on the third floor were probably used as extra guest chambers since the servants' quarters were then located in the basement with the kitchen.

On January 19, 1964, a small group of people assembled in Betsy Jumel's old sitting room upstairs. Present were a few members of the New York Historical Society and the Daughters of the American Revolution, *Journal-American* writer Nat Adams, and a late-comer, Harry Altschuler of the *World-Telegram*. I was accompanied by Ethel Meyers, who had not been told where we were going that winter afternoon, and Jessyca Russell Gaver, who was serving as my secretary and doing a magazine article on our work at the same time.

We had barely arrived when Ethel went in and out of the Jumel bedroom as if someone were forcing her to do so. As she approached the room across the hall, her shoulder sagged and one arm hung loose as if her side had been injured!

"I feel funny on my left side," Ethel finally said, and her voice had already taken on some of the coloring of someone else's voice.

We went back to the bedroom, which is normally closed to the public. One side is occupied by a huge carved four-poster, once the property of Napoleon I, and there are small chairs of the period in various spots throughout the room. In one corner, there is a large mirror.

"The issue is confused," Ethel said, and sounded confused herself. "There is more than one disturbed person here. I almost feel as though three people were involved. There has been sickness and a change of heart. Someone got a raw deal."

Suddenly, Ethel turned to one of the men who had sat down on Napoleon's bed. "Someone wants you to get up from that bed," she said, and evinced difficulty in speaking. As if bitten by a tarantula, the young man shot up from the bed. No ghost was going to goose *him*.

Ethel again struggled to her feet, despite my restraining touch on her arm. "I've got to go back to that other room again," she mumbled, and off she went, with me trailing after her. She walked almost as if she were being taken over by an outside force. In front of the picture of Mme. Jumel, she suddenly fell to her knees.

"I never can go forward here . . . I fall whenever I'm near there." She pointed at the large picture above her, and almost shouted, "My name isn't on that picture. I want my name there!"

Mrs. Campbell, the curator, took me aside in agitation. "That's very strange she should say that," she remarked. "You see, her name really used to be on that picture a long time ago. But that picture wasn't in this spot when Betsy Jumel was alive."

I thanked her and led Ethel Meyers back to her chair in the other room.

"Henry . . . and a Johann . . . around her . . . ," she mumbled as she started to go into a deep trance. Hoarse sounds emanated from her lips. At first they were unintelligible. Gradually I was able to make them out. Halfway into a trance, she moved over to the bed and lay down on it. I placed my chair next to her head. The others strained to hear. There was an eerie silence about the room, interrupted only by the soft words of the entranced medium.

"You think me dead . . . " a harsh, male voice now said.

"No, I've come to talk to you, to help you," I replied.

"Go away," the ghostly voice said. "Go away!"

"Are you a man or a woman?" I asked.

A bitter laugh was the reply.

"Man . . . ha!" the voice finally said.

"What is your name?"

"Everybody knows who I am."

"I don't. What is your name?" I repeated.

"Let me sleep."

"Is anything troubling you?"

There was a moment of silence, then the voice was a bit softer. "Who are *you*?"

"I'm a friend come to help you."

"Nobody talks to me. They think I'm dead."

"What exactly happened to you?"

"They took me away," the voice said in plaintive tones. "I am not dead yet. Why did they take me away?"

Now the body of the medium shook as if in great agitation, while I spoke soothing words to calm the atmosphere. Suddenly, the ghost speaking through the medium was gone, and in his place was the crisp, matter-of-fact voice of Albert, Ethel's control. I asked Albert to tell us through the entranced medium who the ghost was.

"I don't hear a name, but I see a sturdy body and round face. He complains he was pronounced dead when he in fact wasn't. I believe he is the owner of the house and it bears his name. There are many jealousies in this house. There is an artist who is also under suspicion."

"Is there a woman here?"

"One thwarted of what she desired and who wants to throw herself out the window."

"Why?" I asked.

"Thwarted in love and under suspicion."

Later, I asked Mrs. Campbell about this. She thought for a moment, then confirmed the following facts: A young servant girl involved with one of the family tried to commit suicide by jumping out the window.

I questioned Albert further. "Is there a restless woman in this house?"

"That is right. The one in the picture. Her conscience disturbs her."

"About what?"

The medium now grabbed her side, as if in pain. "I am being threatened," Albert said now, "I feel the revelation would disturb."

"But how can I release her unless I know what is holding her here?"

"It has to do with the death of her husband. That he was strangled in his coffin."

I tried to question him further, but he cut us short. The medium had to be released now.

Soon, Ethel Meyers was back to her own self. She remembered very little of the trance, but her impressions of a clairvoyant nature continued for a while. I queried her about the person on the bed.

"I get the initial J," she replied and rubbed her side.

I turned to Mrs. Campbell. "What about the story of Mme. Jumel's guilty conscience?"

"Well," the curator replied, "after her husband's death, she refused to live in this house for some time. She always felt guilty about it."

We were standing in a corner where the medium could not hear us. "Stephen Jumel bled to death from a wound he had gotten in a carriage accident. Mme. Jumel allegedly tore off his bandage and let him die. That much we know."

Mrs. Campbell naturally is a specialist on Betsy Jumel and her life, and she knows many intimate details unknown to the general public or even to researchers.

It was five-thirty in the afternoon when we left the house, which must be closed for the night after that hour.

* * *

The next morning two newspaper accounts appeared: One, fairly accurate, in the *Journal,* and a silly one in the *Telegram,* by a man who stood outside the room of the investigation and heard very little, if anything.

Several weeks went by and my ghost-hunting activities took me all over the country. Then I received a telephone call from Mrs. Campbell.

"Did you know that May twenty-second is the anniversary of Stephen Jumel's death?" I didn't and I wagered her nobody else did, except herself and the late Mr. Jumel. She allowed as to that and suggested we have another go at the case on that date. I have always felt that anniversaries are good times to solve murder cases so I readily agreed.

This time, the *Journal* and *Telegram* reporters weren't invited, but the *New York Times,* in the person of reporter Grace Glueck, was, and I am indebted to her for the notes she took of the proceedings that warm May afternoon.

Present also were the general manager of King Features, Frank McLearn; Clark Kinnaird, literary critic of the *Journal;* John Allen and Bob O'Brien of *Reader's Digest;* Emeline Paige, the editor of *The Villager;* writers Elizabeth Byrd and Beverly Balin; Ed Joyce of CBS; and several members of the New York Historical Society, presumably there as observers ready to rewrite history as needed since the famous Aaron Burr might be involved.

Ethel Meyers was told nothing about the significance of the date, nor had I discussed with her the results of the first seance.

Again we assembled in the upstairs bedroom and Ed Joyce set up his tape recorder in front of Napoleon's bed, while Ethel sat on the bed itself and I next to her on a chair. To my left, the young lady from the *Times* took her seat. All in all there must have been twenty-five anxious people in the room, straining to hear all that was said and keeping a respectful silence when asked to. Within a few minutes, Ethel was in a deep trance, and a male voice spoke through her vocal chords.

"Who are you?" I asked as I usually do when an unknown person comes through a medium.

"*Je suis Stephen,*" the voice said.

"Do you speak English?"

In answer the medium clutched at her body and groaned, "Doctor! Doctor! Where is the doctor?"

"What is hurting you?" I asked.

The voice was firm and defiant now. "I'm alive, I'm alive . . . don't take me away."

"Did you have an accident? What happened to you?"

"She tricked me."

"Who tricked you?"

"I can't breathe . . . where is she? She tricked me. Look at her!"

"Don't worry about her," I said. "She's dead."

"But I'm alive!" the entranced voice continued.

"In a sense, you are. But you have also passed over."

"No — they put me in the grave when I was not yet dead."

"How did you get hurt?" I wanted to know.

The ghost gave a bitter snort. "What matter — I'm dead. You said so."

"I didn't say you were dead." I replied.

The voice became furious again. "She took it, she took it — that woman. She took my life. Go away."

"I'm your friend."

"I haven't any friends . . . that Aaron . . . "

"Aaron? Was he involved in your death?"

"That strumpet . . . hold him! They buried me alive, I tell you."

"When did this happen?"

"It was cold. She made me a fool, a fool!"

"How did she do that?"

"All the time I loved her, she tricked me."

"I want to help you."

"I'm bleeding."

"How did this happen?"

"Pitchfork . . . wagon . . . hay . . . "

"Was it an accident, yes or no?"

"I fell on it."

"You fell on the pitchfork?"

"Look at the blood bath . . . on Napoleon's bed."

"What about that pitchfork?" I insisted.

"There was a boy in the hay, and he pushed me off."

"Did you know this boy?"

"Yes . . . give me *her*. She wanted to be a lady. I saw it. I wasn't so foolish I didn't see it."

"What happened when you got home?"

"She told me I was going to die."

"Did you have a doctor?"

"Yes."

"Wasn't the wound bandaged?"

"They took me out alive. I was a live man he put in the grave. I want to be free from that grave!"

"Do you want me to set you free?"

"God bless you!"

"It is your hatred that keeps you here. You must forgive."

"She did it to me."

I then pleaded with the ghost to join his own family and let go of his memories. "Do you realize how much time has gone on since? A hundred years!"

"Hundred years!"

The medium, still entranced, buried her head in her hands: "I'm mad!"

"Go from this house and don't return."

"Mary, Mary!"

Mary was the name of Jumel's daughter, a fact not known to the medium at the time.

"Go and join Mary!" I commanded, and asked that Albert, the control, help the unhappy one find the way.

Just as soon as Jumel's ghost had left us, someone else slipped into the medium's body, or so it seemed, for she sat up and peered at us with a suspicious expression: "Who are you?"

"I'm a friend, come to help," I replied.

"I didn't ask for you."

"My name is Holzer, and I have come to seek you out. If you have a name worth mentioning, please tell us."

"Get out or I'll call the police! This is my house."

There was real anger now on the medium's entranced face.

I kept asking for identification. Finally, the disdainful lips opened and in cold tones, the voice said, "I am the wife of the vice president of the United States! Leave my house!"

I checked with Mrs. Campbell and found that Betsy Jumel did so identify herself frequently. On one occasion, driving through crowded New York streets long after her divorce from Aaron Burr, she shouted, "Make way for the wife of the vice president of the United States!"

"Didn't you marry someone else before that?" I asked. "How did your husband die?"

"Bastard!"

"You've been dead a hundred years, Madam," I said pleasantly.

"You are made like the billow in the captain's cabin," she replied, somewhat cryptically. Later I checked this out. A sea captain was one of her favorite lovers while married to Jumel.

"Did you murder your husband?" I inquired and drew back a little just in case.

"You belong in the scullery with my maids," she replied disdainfully, but I repeated the accusation, adding that her husband had claimed she had killed him.

"I will call for help," she countered.

"There is no help. The police are on your trail!" I suggested.

"I am the wife of the vice president of the United States!"

"I will help you if you tell me what you did. Did you cause his death?"

"The rats that crawl . . . they bit me. Where am I?"

"You're between two worlds. Do you wish to be helped?"

"Where is Joseph?"

"You must leave this house. Your husband has forgiven you."

"I adored him!"

"Go away, and you will see Stephen Jumel again."

"Only the crest on the carriage! That's all I did. He was a great man."

I had the feeling she wasn't at all keen on Monsieur Jumel. But that happens, even to ghosts.

I finally gave up trying to get her to go and join Jumel and tried another way.

"Go and join the vice president of the United States. He awaits you." To my surprise, this didn't work either.

"He is evil, evil," she said.

Perplexed, I asked, "Whom do you wish to join?"

"Mary."

"Then call out her name, and she'll join you and take you with her."

"No crime, no crime."

"You've been forgiven. Mary will take you away from here."

I asked Albert, the control, to come and help us get things moving, but evidently Madame had a change of heart: "This is my house. I'll stay here."

"This is no longer your house. You must go!"

The struggle continued. She called for Christopher, but wouldn't tell me who Christopher was.

"He's the only one I ever trusted," she volunteered, finally.

"It's not too late," I repeated. "You can join your loved ones."

"Good-bye."

I called for Albert, who quickly took control. "She's no longer in the right mind," he said, as soon as he had firm control of the medium's vocal chords. "You may have to talk with her again."

"Is she guilty of Jumel's death?"

"Yes. It was arranged."

"Who was the boy who pushed him?"

"A trusty in the house. She told him to."

"What about Stephen Jumel?"

"He is in a better frame of mind."

"Is there anything else we did not bring out? Who is this Christopher she mentioned?"

"A sea captain. She buried him in Providence."

Mrs. Campbell later confirmed the important role the sea captain played in Betsy's life. There was also another man named Brown.

"Did Aaron Burr help bury Jumel?"

"That is true. Burr believed Mme. Jumel had more finances than she actually had."

"What about the doctor who buried him alive? Is his name known?"

"Couldn't stop the bleeding."

"Was Aaron Burr in on the crime?"

"He is very much aware that he is guilty. He still possesses his full mental faculties."

I then asked the control to help keep the peace in the house and to bring the medium back to her own body.

A few minutes later, Ethel Meyers was herself again, remembering nothing of the ordeal she had gone through the past hour, and none the worse for it.

Jumel died in 1832 and, as far as I could find, the first ghostly reports date back to 1865. The question was: Could his remains disclose any clues as to the manner in which he died? If he suffocated in his coffin, would not the position of his bones so indicate?

I queried two physicians who disagreed in the matter. One thought that nothing would be left by now; the other thought it was worth looking into.

I thought so, too. However, my application to reopen the grave of Stephen Jumel, down in the old Catholic cemetery on Mott Street, got the official run-around. The District Attorney's office sent me to Dr. Halpern, the chief medical examiner, who told me it would be of no use to check. When I insisted, I was referred to the church offices of old St. Patrick's, which has nominal jurisdiction over the plot.

Have you ever tried to reopen a grave in the City of New York? It's easier to dig a new one, believe me!

As the years passed, I often returned to the mansion. I made several television documentaries there with the helpful support of the curator, who now is the affable and knowledgeable Patrick Broom. The famous blue gown is no longer on display, alas, having disintegrated shortly after I first published the story. But the legend persists, and the footfalls are still heard on lonely nights when the security guard locks up. Whether the Jumels, the remorseful Betsy and the victimized Stephen, have since made up on the Other Side, is a moot question, and I doubt that Aaron Burr will want anything further to do with the, ah, lady, either.